Magic Kingdoms

A History of the Disney Theme Parks

Stephanie Barczewski, Ph.D.

Theme Park Press
www.ThemeParkPress.com

Theme Park Press is not associated with the Walt Disney Company.

The views expressed in this book are those of the author and do not necessarily reflect the views of Theme Park Press.

Theme Park Press publishes its books in a variety of print and electronic formats. Some content that appears in one format may not appear in another.

Editor: Bob McLain
Layout: Artisanal Text

ISBN 978-1-68390-013-9
Printed in the United States of America

Theme Park Press | **www.ThemeParkPress.com**
Address queries to bob@themeparkpress.com

Contents

Introduction

All Disney histories should begin with a disclosure: what does the author consider to be his or her "home" park? Born in Wilmington, Delaware, and raised in Atlanta, I am very much an East Coast Disney person. My parents first took me to Walt Disney World in the summer of 1972, when I was four and when the Magic Kingdom had been open for less than a year. I do not remember a thing, but the trip must have imprinted something deeply upon me, because ever since then the Disney theme parks have been special places for me. I visited Disney World twice more as a child and once when I graduated from high school in 1986. Every time brought a sense of excitement and fun that no other destination could duplicate.

Fourteen years elapsed before I went back as an adult in the year 2000. My husband was attending an academic conference at Disney's Coronado Springs Resort, and I jumped at the chance to go with him. There were two entire parks, Disney MGM-Studios and Disney's Animal Kingdom, that I had never set foot in, and the Magic Kingdom and Epcot were much changed from my previous visits. It was a short trip, but I vividly remember going to the Magic Kingdom by myself while my husband was at the conference and being acutely conscious of how much I loved it. Even so, however, I did not return for seven more years, as I believed that visiting too frequently would somehow ruin the magic. But on that trip, I had a revelation: Disney theme parks get better the more you visit them. Frequent visits lead to increased knowledge, comfort. and a sense of belonging, perhaps even possession, that, for me, makes each trip more enjoyable than the last. I now go to Disney World multiple times each year, most often with my husband, but sometimes with friends and other family members. Christmas is my favorite time to visit, though I escape before the massive crowds arrive. My Walt Disney World annual pass ranks among my most prized possessions.

I could not possibly say which Orlando park is my favorite. The Magic Kingdom will always have a special place in my heart as the first Disney park that I ever visited, and the grandeur and bustle of its Main Street, U.S.A. leading to that magnificent castle is, and always will be, my favorite Disney vista. Epcot is perhaps the oddest combination of elements in any theme park in the world, but somehow it works, and works splendidly. There is no more relaxing Disney space in which to stroll than World Showcase. Animal Kingdom contains some of the richest detail in any Disney park: Harambe village in Africa and Anandapur in Asia are two of the Imagineers' most impressive, and immersive, environments. Thanks to the unpredictably of the animals who are its stars, Animal Kingdom rewards a leisurely pace and repeated visits; it does not demand a frantic dash from attraction to attraction like the Magic Kingdom. And even Hollywood Studios has its charms, such as the neon signage on Hollywood Boulevard at night. I look forward, however, to the arrival of Toy Story and Star Wars Lands, which should elevate the park to the level of its Florida siblings, and (fingers crossed) even beyond.

No true Disney theme park fan can limit their enjoyment to one resort. And certainly he or she cannot ignore Disneyland, the oldest and most historically significant park. I first went to Anaheim when I was in my thirties, and now visit at least once a year. I envy southern Californians who grow up with Disneyland; they have a sense of familiarity and ownership that no East Coast Disney fan can hope to emulate. Disneyland is their park, in their city. And what a park it is, as it ages gracefully and elegantly. No other Disney park packs as much into its space, or can be peeled back to reveal so many layers of Disney history. Disneyland is, of course, much changed since 1955, but enough of the original remains to give guests a glimpse of how it all began. And what Disney fan, as he or she leaves the park for the night, does not take one last look at the light in the window over the fire station, where Walt's apartment is still preserved? Since 2001, Anaheim has had a second park, California Adventure, which initially disappointed many guests but has now become a worthy sibling to Disneyland. The change was largely due to the addition of Cars Land, perhaps the best immersive environment the Imagineers have yet created.

Of the international parks, Tokyo Disneyland most closely resembles Disneyland as a park predominantly for local urbanites. I went there in December 2013, and was struck by the contrast between Tokyo Disneyland, a closer copy of the original Disneyland than either the Magic Kingdom or Disneyland Paris, and Tokyo DisneySea, a unique park of dazzling creativity in which the Imagineers were clearly given the resources to let their imaginations run riot. The Tokyo Disneyland Resort is in every way as delightful and magical as its American counterparts, and one of the most enjoyable aspects of visiting it is watching how Japanese people make something so quintessentially American very much their own.

In August 2015, I visited Disneyland Paris for the first time. Unfairly maligned, usually by people who have never been there, the park has nothing to apologize for, and much to be proud of. Built to a more lavish standard than any other Disney park, it interacts with its predecessors in

Anaheim and Orlando in fascinating ways. Of the Disneyland-type, classic hub-and-spoke parks, it is by some measure the most distinctive, and the most beautiful. Of its sister park, Walt Disney Studios, there is not much to be said, except to express a hope that in the future it will add more original rides, like the delightful Crush's Coaster, and more richly themed areas, like the section surrounding the new trackless 3D attraction Ratatouille: L'Aventure Totalement Toquée Rémy. Full disclosure requires me to confess to never having been to Hong Kong Disneyland, and the writing of this book was complete before Shanghai Disneyland opened. I will almost certainly visit both in the near future. For now, ten of twelve is not bad.

I hope that this book makes it clear that I have never met a Disney resort that I didn't love. That does not mean I am not occasionally, and I hope gently, critical: one cannot be a true Disney theme park fan without from time to time feeling that something could be better, or that management has made a poor decision. Changes in things we love can be difficult to accept, even if most of them eventually work out for the best. But even if I must confess to rare moments of disappointment or frustration, I will always look up and smile as the monorail whooshes by overhead outside the entrance to the Magic Kingdom, and I will always recite the Ghost Host's monologue along with him in the stretching room of the Haunted Mansion. The last time I did the latter, a gentleman standing nearby laughed and said, "You have obviously done this WAY too many times." I laughed, too, and told him that, for me, such a thing could never be true.

Writing the acknowledgements for a book is always bittersweet: it provides an opportunity to express gratitude to all the people who've helped see it into print, but it also means that it's time to let go of a project into which much blood, sweat, and tears has been poured. This book elicits different emotions from me than my previous ones, because it is less academic and more personal. So it is only appropriate that I thank the people who have been a part of my trips to Disney theme parks in recent years: Patsy Barczewski, Caroline Dunn, Charlotte Clark, Joanna Grisinger, Elijah Moore, Marcos Moore, Rachel Moore, Megan Shockley, Scott Shockley, and Criss Smith. Anne Dabb deserves special praise for spending an incredibly hot day at Disneyland taking photos of park details, and for her ear-splitting screams on Space Mountain. One of the best things about being a Disney-theme park expert is that you get to share your knowledge and experience the parks through the eyes of others, and all of these people have increased my enjoyment of them immeasurably. Bob McLain has been a patient, wise, and encouraging steward to this project. But the biggest thanks must go to my husband, Michael Silvestri, who humors and even enjoys my Disney obsession. No one could ask more of a spouse than to have what makes you happy make him happy.

ONE
Walt Disney and Los Angeles

Understanding what the Disney theme parks are requires understanding where they are. So we will begin with a basic question: why is Disneyland in Los Angeles? For the first Disney theme park—in contrast to the second one in Orlando—the issue of location is a simple one. Disneyland is in Los Angeles because that's where the Walt Disney Company was (and is) based, and because Walt Disney lived there for forty-one of his sixty-five years. Since 1939, Disney's corporate headquarters and film studio has been located in a 51-acre complex in Burbank, northwest of downtown Los Angeles. To get from there to Disneyland in Anaheim is a straight shot south on Interstate 5; Google Maps optimistically estimates the journey at forty minutes, though it is more likely to take two hours or more on what is one of Los Angeles' most congested freeways. Even so, only forty miles separates the studio and Disneyland, and their geographical proximity mirrors their close relationship in the Disney universe. Because the studio was in Los Angeles, so was Disney's first theme park.

But how did the studio get there? The story was in some ways a common one: its founder Walt Disney was one of millions of migrants who came to California in the 1920s from other parts of America. Born in the Hermosa neighborhood of northwest Chicago in 1901, Walter Elias Disney was the fourth of five children, with three older brothers—Herbert, Raymond, and Roy—and a sister, Ruth, who was two years younger. The son of Irish immigrants, Walt's father Elias was a jack-of-all trades who worked at everything from railroad construction to fiddle playing. In the late 1880s, after a peripatetic youth that included stops in Kansas, Colorado, and possibly California, he moved to Florida to try his luck at farming. He purchased 150 acres of land not far from Kissimmee, very close to where Walt Disney World is now located. After the farm failed, Elias worked as a rural letter carrier, with the Kissimmee post office as his base. In 1889, his wife Flora used her savings to purchase a nearby citrus grove, but that winter a severe frost destroyed local orange crops, and Elias decided to move to Chicago. He found work as a carpenter for the World's Columbian

Exposition, a celebration of the four-hundredth anniversary of Christopher Columbus' voyage to the Americas, which opened in 1893. Elias parlayed this experience into a modestly successful stint as a home-builder, but as more immigrants flowed into Chicago in the first decade of the twentieth century, he became increasingly concerned about crime. After two boys from the neighborhood in which the Disneys lived were arrested for killing a policeman during a robbery, Elias decided that it was time to leave.

Image 1.1: The Hermosa neighborhood in northwest Chicago today. Walt Disney was born here in 1901; he was baptized in the church in the center of the image.

In 1906, the family moved to Marceline, Missouri, about 120 miles northeast of Kansas City, where Elias's brother Robert already owned 500 acres. Elias purchased a modest farm that had previously been the property of Civil War veteran William Crane. There, Walt enjoyed what became in his memory an idyllic existence; he recalled his time in Marceline so fondly that he later built an exact replica of the farm's barn in the backyard of his house in Los Angeles. It was in Marceline that two of the seeds for Disneyland were sown. First, it was here that Walt formed his romanticized view of small-town life, which would later be manifested by Main Street, U.S.A. (Though, as we will see, it was not an exact replica of Marceline, as is so often assumed.)

Image 1.2: (*Opposite, top*) Marceline, Missouri, around 1915, four years after the Disney family moved back to Chicago. Though it was not a direct model for Disneyland's Main Street, U.S.A., Marceline played a key role in creating Walt Disney's romanticized view of small-town life as well as his love of railroads.

And second, it was in Marceline that Walt first developed his love of trains. The railroad tracks of the Atchison, Topeka and Santa Fe, the same railway that would later sponsor the railroad at Disneyland, ran near the farm, and Walt and his older brother Roy would often put their ears to the tracks to see if they could feel the vibrations that heralded an approaching train. Their uncle Mike Martin, who was married to Flora's sister, was an engineer on the line, and he would wave and blow the horn to the boys from the cab. Other indications of Walt's future avocation also first appeared in Marceline: it was here that he first began to draw, and here that he first began to stage amateur theatrical productions, using animals dressed in human clothing as his actors. As Walt himself later stated, "More things of importance happened to me in Marceline than have happened since—or are likely to in the future."

But the Marceline idyll did not last long. In 1908, Elias Disney contracted either diphtheria or typhoid fever, possibly from contaminated well water. He slowly recovered, but he was no longer capable of performing the strenuous labor that farming demanded, and the farm had to be sold. After a brief stay in a rented house in town so that the younger Disney children could finish the school year, the family moved to Kansas City in 1911. Elias purchased a newspaper delivery route and put two of his sons, nine-year-old Walt and seventeen-year-old Roy, to work. It was an exhausting job that required Walt to awaken at 3:30am seven days a week and, in Kansas City's frigid winters, to tramp through snowdrifts that sometimes came up to his neck. Not surprisingly, Walt was a mediocre student in both grammar and high school, but his artistic talent was beginning to emerge: his classmates recalled that he drew constantly.

Image 1.3: The house at 3028 Bellefontaine Avenue on the east side of Kansas City that the Disney family moved into in 1911, after Elias's illness forced them to sell the farm in Marceline.

In 1917, Elias, Flora, and Ruth moved back to Chicago, but Walt remained behind in Kansas City with Herbert and Roy. He found a summer job as a news butcher, or vendor of snacks, drinks, and tobacco, on board trains. This increased his love of railroads, but not his income, as he ate so much candy and drank so much pop that his profits were minimal. That fall, he joined his father, mother, and sister in Chicago and began his senior year at McKinley High School, where he obtained a post as junior art editor of the school magazine, *The Voice*. Now thinking of a career as a newspaper cartoonist, he enrolled in night classes at the Chicago Academy of Fine Arts. To make money, he took a number of part-time jobs, as a handyman and janitor at the O-Zell jelly and soda factory in which his father had invested and as a guard and gate man on Chicago's elevated railway. The following spring, he went to work sorting and delivering mail for the post office. A few months later, he was nearly killed when an anarchist's bomb exploded in the lobby of the Federal Building on West Adams Street, where Walt was delivering the mail. He escaped unharmed, but four people were killed and another seventy-five injured. "I missed that darn thing by about three minutes," Walt later recalled.

The money he made from the post office job paid for his first movie camera, which he purchased in 1918 for $70. His first film was of himself imitating Charlie Chaplin. But at this point, events far from Kansas City interrupted Walt's fledgling efforts as a cartoonist and filmmaker. In April 1917, the United States entered World War I. Walt's brother Raymond immediately joined the army, and Roy, to whom Walt was very close, volunteered for the navy in June. At sixteen, Walt was too young for the armed services, but he heard that the Red Cross, which desperately needed ambulance drivers, was less fussy about age. There was only one problem: to go to Europe he needed a passport, and to obtain one he needed both to be seventeen and to obtain his parents' signatures on the relevant form. He used his artistic talents to change the "1" of his birth year on his birth certificate to a "0," and then attempted to convince his parents to sign. Elias refused, but Flora, fearing that Walt would run away if she did not relent, reluctantly agreed to sign both for herself and for her husband.

After surviving a bout with the Spanish flu, which killed as many as 100 million people worldwide in 1918 and 1919, Walt was sent to France. He landed at Le Havre on December 4, 1918, three weeks after the end of the war. In between ferrying supplies and chauffeuring dignitaries, Walt partnered in a side business in which a volunteer from Georgia, nicknamed the Cracker, scavenged German helmets from the battlefields and had Walt paint them in camouflage colors. The Cracker sold these "sniper helmets" at a premium price to demobilized troops looking for souvenirs to take home. After being released by the Red Cross, Walt returned to Chicago. His father tried to convince him to take a job at the O-Zell factory, but Walt was determined to pursue a career as an artist. He returned to Kansas City, where he moved back in with Herbert and Roy and found work with the Gray Advertising Company making drawings for catalogs and advertisements. Although it lasted for only six weeks during the busy Christmas season, this was Walt's first paying job as an artist.

Even though his time at Gray Advertising had been brief, Walt felt that he had gained sufficient experience to go into business for himself. He convinced Ubbe Iwerks, who had worked with him at Gray, to partner in what he called "a little commercial art shop," which they called Iwerks-Disney. (They thought that Disney-Iwerks sounded too much like an optician's office.) Working out of an unused bathroom in the offices of their first client, the National Restaurant Association, they enjoyed some initial success, earning $125 in their first month, more than their combined pay at Gray. But the second month was much slower, and in early 1920 Walt decided to take a job with the Kansas City Slide Company (later the Kansas City Film Ad Company), making $35 a week for drawing one-minute animated advertisements that appeared before films.[1]

---

1   Ubbe Iwerks initially attempted to keep Iwerks-Disney afloat, but he soon went to work for the Slide Company as well.

This was a moment of huge significance in Disney history, as it marked Walt's transition from artist to animator. Animation, or the creation of motion by rapidly displaying a series of drawings that differed slightly from each other, was in its infancy in the early twentieth century. Fascinated by the new form, Walt spent his free time learning about and experimenting with it. He read every book he could get from the local library, and borrowed an old camera from the Film Ad Company, with which he began making animated films in the garage of his family's house. Roy remembered that he would "come home long after everyone else was in bed and be out there still puttering away, working, experimenting, trying this and that." In 1921, his experiments led him to produce a series of short cartoons that he initially called Local Happenings but subsequently renamed Laugh-O-Grams, which made light of civic issues such as the need for street repairs, slow streetcar service, and police corruption. He was able to sell them to Frank Newman, the owner of a chain of local theaters, for exhibition before feature films.

Walt decided that the opportunities in animation were promising enough for him to open an independent studio in partnership with his friend Fred Harman, though both young men kept their day jobs at Film Ad. Calling the new venture Kaycee Studios, they paid the bills by supplying newsreel footage of local events to Pathé and other news agencies, while they continued to experiment with both live-action and animated film. Their most ambitious project was a series of animated retellings of fairytales, the first two of which were *Little Red Riding Hood* and *The Four Musicians of Bremen*, but they also produced short films featuring simple sight gags called Lafflets. None of these efforts was profitable, but even so Walt decided in the spring of 1922 that it was time to leave Film Ad and strike out on his own. He launched an independent studio called Laugh-O-Gram Films, which continued to produce the fairy-tale films, with *Jack and the Beanstalk* as its first effort. With three films now complete, Walt dispatched his sales manager, Leslie Mace, to New York to find a distributor for his "modernized fairy tales." Mace struck out with the major distributors, but he persuaded the Pictorial Club of Tennessee, which showed films in schools, churches, and other non-theatrical venues, to buy six films for $11,000. The terms of the contract, however, called for the Pictorial Club to put down only $100 up front, with the rest of the money to be paid fifteen months later, after the films were delivered. This left Laugh-O-Gram, in the words of animator Rudy Ising, "worse than broke," because they had to meet the expenses of producing the films without any payment. And to make matters worse, soon after signing the contract, the Pictorial Club went bankrupt.

Image 1.4: In May 1922, Walt Disney rented space in which to produce his Laugh-O-Grams on the second floor of the McConaughey Building at 1127 East 31st Street in Kansas City. A year later, the studio went bankrupt, and Walt left for California. Once slated for demolition, the building has been saved by preservationists seeking to transform it into a museum or digital animation facility.

Other projects were slow to trickle in, though a local dentist, Thomas McCrum, paid $500 for an animated educational film on dental hygiene called *Tommy Tucker's Tooth*. The bills continued to pile up; most of Laugh-O-Gram's employees had not been paid in months, and Walt, who survived by eating ten-cent cans of beans, later recalled this as "probably the blackest time of my life." Evicted from his apartment, he slept on a couch at the studio and went to Union Station once a week for a bath. He was not only broke but also lonely, as his two brothers had left Kansas City. Herbert, who worked for the post office, had been transferred to Portland, Oregon, while Roy had been diagnosed with tuberculosis and sent by the Veterans Administration to a sanatorium in Santa Fe, New Mexico.

Desperate to attract new investors, Walt came up with an idea to combine animation with live action in a series of films in which a real little girl named Alice, played by four-year-old Virginia Davis, would be inserted into a cartoon world. (This was a reversal of Max Fleischer's popular *Out of the Inkwell* series of cartoons, which featured an animated main character in a live-action world.) Walt began shooting the first "Alice comedy," titled *Alice's Wonderland*, but ran out of money before he could finish it. Hounded by creditors at every turn, Walt, as he so often did, turned to his older brother for advice. Roy told him "to call it quits." In 1923, Walt declared bankruptcy and closed Laugh-O-Gram Films.

After the collapse of Laugh-O-Gram, Walt decided that it was time to leave Kansas City. He considered going to New York, where the fledgling animation industry was based, but instead he decided to head for Los Angeles. "The pull toward Hollywood became strong," Walt recalled. "Animation was big there, and if I couldn't be successful at that, I wanted to be a director or a writer." In Los Angeles, he could take advantage of a family connection to help establish himself. Following the death of his wife in 1920, Walt's uncle Robert Disney, formerly a successful real-estate investor in Missouri, had moved to a bungalow at 4406 Kingswell Avenue in the Los Feliz neighborhood. Walt had never been especially fond of Robert, whom he described as "kind of pompous," but his uncle did provide him with a place to stay, in return for $5 a week in rent. Also pulling Walt west was Roy, who after leaving the sanatorium in Santa Fe had been working as a door-to-door salesman in Glendale, California, when he suffered a relapse of tuberculosis and was admitted to a veterans' hospital in Sawtelle in west Los Angeles.

After he arrived in Los Angeles in July 1923, Walt made the rounds of the motion-picture studios. In the 1890s, the New-Jersey-based Edison Company had developed the technology to make motion pictures. In 1908, Edison and the other major producers formed the Motion Pictures Patent Company, which quickly became known as "the Trust," in order to regulate the production and distribution of motion pictures. In an effort to get out from under the Trust's watchful eye, some smaller producers headed to California, where it was more difficult to monitor their activities and where they could easily flee across the Mexican border to avoid process servers bearing subpoenas and lawsuits. With its sunny weather, varied scenery, cheap labor, and plenty of open land for filming, Los Angeles quickly became the capital of the American film industry. The earliest studios opened in 1908, but the crucial decade was 1914 to 1924, when Universal, United Artists, and Metro-Goldwyn-Meyer were all established. By 1930, the city's fifty-two studios employed 15,000 people and grossed $1.5 billion annually, making film the fifth-largest industry in America. Los Feliz, where Walt lived, was located just to the west of Hollywood and was an emerging hub of the film business. Vitagraph, one of the oldest and largest film studios, was only a block from Robert Disney's house.

Walt was unsuccessful, however, in convincing a film studio to give him a job. "For two months," he remembered, "I tramped from one studio to another, trying to sell myself as a writer, a director, a day laborer—anything to get through those magic gates of big-time show business. But nobody bought." As a result, he decided to "give cartooning another whirl" and began searching for a distributor for *Alice's Wonderland*. He contacted Margaret Winkler in New York, who had previously shown interest in the film. His timing was perfect: Winkler's contracts to distribute the popular *Felix the Cat* and *Out of the Inkwell* series were about to expire, and she was seeking a new cartoon franchise. She offered Walt advantageous terms: $1500 each for six Alice films, with an option for six more. (She later expanded the offer to twenty-four films; Walt ultimately produced a total of fifty-six Alice comedies.) In a panic over how he was actually going to make and deliver the films, Walt went that night to the Veterans Hospital to see Roy. Roy agreed to go into business with Walt; in the morning, Roy checked himself out of the hospital and never returned. Feeling that he was on the cusp of success, Walt wrote to his father, "I'll make the name Disney famous around the world."

Walt and Roy initially rented space behind the Holly-Vermont Realty Company's office at 4651 Kingswell Avenue for $10 a month, but in February 1924 they moved next door to larger quarters.[2] This became the first true Disney studio, called Disney Brothers. One of their first employees was twenty-five-year-old Lillian Bounds, who had arrived in Los Angeles from Idaho in late 1923 and who worked as a secretary and animation cel painter. Money was so tight that Walt sometimes had to ask her to delay cashing her $15-a-week paycheck, but even so, she was flattered when the boss began flirting with her, and soon a romantic relationship kindled. Lillian described the young Walt Disney as "a wonderful man in every way—kind, gentle, brilliant, lots of energy and humility." Walt and Lillian were married in 1925; when he proposed, he told her that he only had $75, so he could either buy a car or a wedding ring. She chose the ring. They lived in a string of apartments, until in 1927 the modest success of the Alice comedies allowed Walt and Roy, who had married his high-school sweetheart Edna Francis, to purchase a lot on Lyric Avenue in Silver Lake, on the edge of Los Feliz. They built adjacent prefabricated "Ready-Cut" houses made by the Pacific Corporation. The lot and houses cost a total of $16,000, which Walt thought "exorbitant."

The income from the Alice comedies also allowed Walt and Roy to put down a $400 deposit on a sixty-by-forty-foot lot at 2719 Hyperion Avenue, also in Silver Lake, on which they built a new studio. The animators moved into the 1600-square-foot building in February 1926. The move came with a name change, the origin of which remains a point of debate in Disney

2   In his book *Walt Before Mickey: Disney's Early Years, 1919-1928*, Timothy S. Susanin records the name of the real-estate company as McRae & Abernathy.

history. The most common version claims that it was Roy who suggested that, since Walt was the "creative member of the team," the studio should bear his name, and so it became first the "Walt Disney Studios" and then, three years later, "Walt Disney Productions." Others, however, recalled that the change was made at Walt's request and only after a heated argument between the two brothers, or that Roy was hurt by the suggestion and only reluctantly agreed. The studio remained in the Hyperion Avenue location for a decade, but by the late 1930s, Disney had outgrown the space, as a large number of animators was required for the feature films that the studio was now producing. The massive profits from *Snow White and the Seven Dwarfs* allowed Walt to build a lavish new complex in Burbank. Disney moved there in 1939, and the company remains there today.

What sort of place was the Los Angeles in which Walt Disney arrived in the 1920s? Los Angeles is distinct from other American cities. There is no reason for it to be where it is: it has no fertile soil, no natural harbor, no navigable rivers, and no natural resources. Despite this, Los Angeles experienced massive growth from 1850 to 1930, transforming it from a small agricultural settlement of 1500 people into a metropolis of 2.3 million, the largest city on the West Coast and the fourth-largest city in the United States. No region in America has ever experienced such a rapid pace of growth as southern California did in the early twentieth century.

Mass immigration to California began after gold was discovered in 1848, the same year that the United States acquired the territory from Mexico. In 1840, there were only about 8000 Mexican and American Californians; by 1850, the non-indigenous population had soared to 200,000. And as California grew, Los Angeles grew along with it. The city's population increased from 4400 in 1865 to 20,000 in 1885. A key factor in this growth was the completion of the Southern Pacific's transcontinental railroad in 1869 and the extension of the line from San Francisco to Los Angeles seven years later. In the 1880s, the Santa Fe's line from Topeka to Los Angeles was completed, and the two railroad companies became locked in a rate war that dropped the cross-country fare to as little as a dollar. Aggressively promoting southern California as an ideal place in which to live, the railroads organized special "excursion parties" on which passengers were royally entertained as they traveled across the country and, once they reached the West Coast, were taken to see various scenic spots.

The people who chose to settle in California often relied on the land to support themselves, but they were not self-sufficient subsistence farmers. Instead, they depended on middle men to transport and sell their produce and on local manufacturers to provide many of the things that they needed. In addition, they sought opportunities for social interaction, communal religious worship, and cultural pursuits. They were thus very different from an earlier generation of pioneers in the American West who had struck out across the plains in their Conestoga wagons. For these immigrants, California was not an extension of the frontier, but rather its end. They saw the natural environment not as an untamed wilderness, but rather as an orderly and civilized landscape. California was thus from the beginning a utopian destination in which the achievement of the good life was based upon comfort and civil society, not upon back-breaking labor in a harsh and isolated environment.[3] As the late-nineteenth-century California writer Charles Fletcher Lummis wrote, the flow of people to California represented "the least heroic migration in history, but the most judicious; the least impulsive but the most reasonable... In fact they were ... by far the most comfortable immigrants, financially, in history... Instead of by Shank's Mare, or prairie schooner, or reeking steerage, they came on palatial trains; instead of cabins, they put up beautiful homes."

The influx of immigrants meant that Los Angeles evolved rapidly from a Spanish colonial village to an American city. Or more accurately, an agglomeration of American towns, as its metropolitan area was comprised of the numerous individual suburban nodes that were established throughout the region by eager developers. Between 1884 and 1888 alone, over a hundred new towns were laid out. These towns were later swallowed up by Los Angeles. Hollywood, for example, was first developed by the real-estate magnate Horace Whitley in the 1880s and was incorporated into the city in 1910. Most significantly, the 260-square-mile San Fernando Valley was annexed in 1915, increasing the city's geographical area fivefold.

Attempting to lure both tourists and permanent residents, boosters aggressively promoted Los Angeles, which became the best-advertised city in the nation. This was a time when many Americans were looking to leave farming and take up residence and employment in cities. They were no longer willing to perform strenuous labor in the hope of acquiring great wealth, but rather wanted to live in comfort and enjoy more leisure time. They did not, however, want to live in traditional urban settings, which they associated with crime, grime, and corruption. Los Angeles offered them exactly what they sought. Between 1890 and 1930 migrants poured into the city, increasing the population from 50,000 to 1.2 million, with a million more in Los Angeles County. By 1930, Los Angeles had surpassed Boston as fourth-largest city in America. Developers feverishly converted farm and wasteland into suburban neighborhoods to accommodate the influx. Whereas before people had preceded the infrastructure, now developers

3   Kevin Starr, *Inventing the Dream: California through the Progressive Era* (New York and Oxford: Oxford University Press, 1985), p. 46.

built train lines and streets and installed utilities in order to entice new arrivals to choose their subdivisions. These improvements were often far in advance of needs, but the risk generally paid off. Constant expansion, rather than manufacturing or other conventional commercial activities, became Los Angeles's main industry. It was the real-estate developers who made the decisions about where, when, and how land was subdivided; they, not the municipal authorities, determined the city's future and ensured that the metropolis was dispersed over a wide area instead of being concentrated in an urban downtown.

Los Angeles' increasing sprawl was not only because most infrastructure development was put in the hands of private companies that had an incentive to keep expanding. It was also due to the nature of the city's population. Most people moved to Los Angeles by choice, not because of economic necessity. They were relatively affluent, and their conception of the good life included a big single-family house on a large lot in a location that was isolated from commerce, industry, and urban dangers. They saw city life as immoral and corrupt, and felt that the suburbs were more conducive to the ideal family life. As a result of these factors, Los Angeles had significantly fewer people than Chicago or Philadelphia but covered many more square miles.

One of 1.3 million people who moved to Los Angeles between 1920 and 1930, Walt Disney was part of the largest internal migration in American history. He was one of many Americans lured to southern California by promises of an affluent lifestyle and an ideal climate. Though Disney fans usually think of Walt as exceptional, he was in reality a very typical migrant. Most of the new arrivals were, like him, from urban or suburban backgrounds, in contrast to the hardy farmers who had come west a few decades earlier. Although he was interested in bettering himself financially, he was motivated more by the opportunity that California offered to develop his creative talents. This again was typical: migrants to California expected to use their intellectual and creative abilities to earn a living, not their muscles. Walt came from Missouri, which was the state with the second-largest contingent—numbering 50,000—in Los Angeles in 1930, trailing only Illinois. He became part of the four-fifths of the city's population in the 1920s who had not been born in California, and part of the 90 percent of migrants who stayed there once they arrived. Walt's status as a typical Californian is a key factor in explaining how his vision of Disneyland came to be a beloved and entrenched part of Los Angeles' urban fabric. In Los Angeles, Disneyland did not reflect unreality and fantasy, but rather the reality of a city that had always been envisioned as the idealized embodiment of the dreams of the millions of people who had come there in the first half of the twentieth century.

TWO
The Origins of Disneyland

Like many things Disney, the origins of Disneyland are shrouded in myth, some of which was created by Walt Disney himself. When he was asked in 1963 by the Canadian Broadcasting Company where the idea for Disneyland had come from, Walt talked about how Saturday was "daddy's day" with his two daughters Diane and Sharon. One of their favorite destinations was Griffith Park, which contained a popular merry-go-round. As Walt sat on a bench watching the two girls ride, he thought that "there should be something built where the parents and the children could have fun together."

Image 2.1: Now on display in the Disney Gallery at the train-station end of Main Street, U.S.A. in Disneyland, this bench from Griffith Park is supposedly the one that Walt sat on as he watched his daughters ride the merry-go-round and first began to think of building an amusement park that children and adults could enjoy together. The Walt Disney Family Museum in San Francisco possesses another bench from Griffith Park that it claims is actually the one Walt used. It is possible that both claims are true, as Walt took his daughters to the merry-go-round multiple times and probably sat on multiple benches.

This is the most commonly cited tale of Disneyland's birth, with supporting evidence provided by the bench on which Walt sat, which is preserved today in the Opera House on Main Street, U.S.A. in Disneyland. But in reality, the origin of Disneyland was far more complex than this nostalgic tale suggests, and there were multiple strands in Walt Disney's life that led him to the idea. As a child, Walt loved amusement parks. After his family moved to Kansas City when he was ten years old, the Disneys lived only fifteen blocks from Electric Park, which advertised itself as "Kansas City's Coney Island." Walt was a frequent visitor, though he sometimes had to sneak in because he could not afford the admission. As an adult, he continued to enjoy going to Electric Park, and he told one of his employees at his first animation studio in Kansas City that "one of these days I'm going to build an amusement park." Already thinking of ways to improve on existing models, he added, "And it's going to be clean!"

Another source of inspiration for Disneyland was the motion-picture industry. When Walt first arrived in Hollywood, he visited several movie studios in search of a job. He was particularly fascinated by Universal City, the home of Universal Studios, which had opened to the public in 1915. Even after Universal turned him down, Walt used the press card he had obtained for his work on newsreels in Kansas City to obtain a pass so that he could return to the studio lot again and again. He loved how on the backlot he could go from the Old West to ancient Rome to the African jungle in minutes. He was also impressed by how Universal put up grandstands and charged people twenty-five cents to watch the production of a silent film and five cents for a box lunch.

Only five years later, Walt Disney was himself the owner of a studio that people wanted to visit. By early 1927, Charles Mintz, who had taken over the distribution of the Alice comedies after he married Margaret Winkler in 1924, was pushing Walt to develop a new cartoon series, as, after fifty-six shorts, profits from the Alice cartoons were dwindling. After Mintz told him that "there are too many cats on the market," Walt gathered his animators together and had them draw rabbits. Walt sent the best of the sketches to Mintz, who showed them to Universal. Universal executives liked the character, which they named Oswald the Lucky Rabbit. In March 1927, Walt signed a new contract in which he agreed to provide twenty-six Oswald shorts in return for a $2250 advance on each one. Universal was dissatisfied with the first Oswald short, *Poor Papa*, and refused to release it, but the second, *Trolley Troubles*, was a hit, as were subsequent installments. For the first time, the Walt Disney Studio was solidly profitable.

But, behind the scenes, all was not well. Sensing an opportunity to produce the Oswald cartoons more cheaply, Mintz began plotting to hire away Walt's best animators. In February 1928, Walt traveled to New York to ask for a raise to $2500 per film; if Mintz balked, he was prepared to seek another distributor. Mintz countered with $1750 per short plus 50 percent of the profits. When Walt refused, Mintz lowered the price even further, to $1400 per short, making it impossible for the studio to make a profit. Mintz told Walt that "either you come at my price, or I'll take your organization from you." Walt, having struck out in his attempts to find another distributor and recognizing that he was in a power struggle that he could not win, walked away from Mintz, and from Oswald. Mintz then set up his own studio and hired away most of Walt's animators to continue drawing Oswald.

Oscillating between anger and despondence, Walt boarded a train back to Los Angeles. He was, according to his wife Lillian, like a "raging lion." According to Disney legend, on the three-day journey Walt conceived a new character to replace Oswald. He chose a mouse, because mice were "cute characters, and they hadn't been overdone in the picture field." Walt originally called the mouse Mortimer, but Lillian thought it was a terrible name. After he thought about it for a while, Walt suggested naming the mouse Mickey instead. Lillian grudgingly conceded that at least it was better than Mortimer, and so Mickey Mouse was born. This story is the best-known version of Mickey Mouse's origin, but its truth remains a matter of debate. The man who became Mickey's primary artist, Ub Iwerks, referred to the train story as "highly exaggerated publicity material."[1] Iwerks claimed that the idea for Mickey actually came from the magazines that he, Walt, and Roy flipped through as they desperately sought a spark of inspiration for a character to replace Oswald. They saw some drawings by Clifton Meek, a cartoon artist whose work appeared frequently in contemporary humor magazines. One of Meek's mice led Iwerks to draw a mouse of his own with a "pear-shaped body, ball on top, couple of thin legs."

Whatever the truth of Mickey Mouse's origin, the character proved the making of Disney, both the man and the studio. Walt and Iwerks set about creating *Plane Crazy*, the first animated short starring Mickey Mouse. But when it was finished, Walt could not convince a distributor to buy it. Walt knew that he needed something novel to help sell Mickey. In 1927, *The Jazz Singer*, the first "talking" motion picture (meaning that the images were synchronized to spoken words) had been released by Warner Brothers. Now, Walt had the idea to do the same thing with animation. The second Mickey Mouse short, *The Gallopin' Gaucho*, was already in production, but Walt was eager to move on to the third, which would be the first to feature synchronized sound. The biggest technical challenge was to find a way to time the recording of the soundtrack to match the film. Walt solved this problem by printing a ball on both the soundtrack and the film that went up and down in time to the beat, accompanied by a faintly audible "click." It worked perfectly. The third Mickey Mouse cartoon, *Steamboat*

---

1   Prior to moving to California in 1924, Iwerks usually spelled his name "Ubbe," but after that point he favored "Ub," and so I have used this spelling here.

Willie (1928), became the most famous animated cartoon in history and a motion-picture landmark.[2]

Mickey Mouse swiftly became a popular sensation and the biggest movie star in Hollywood. His merchandise was everywhere, he received tens of thousands of fan letters each week, and millions of people around the world saw his cartoons, a new one of which was released every month. At the same time, Walt continued to introduce technical innovations to animation. In 1932, *Flowers and Trees*, part of the more experimental *Silly Symphonies* series, became the first animated film to use Technicolor, which had recently evolved to allow full-color films to be produced. It, too, proved very popular, and in 1935 Mickey made his Technicolor debut in *The Band Concert*.

After Mickey became a huge star, Walt Disney was bombarded by letters from children (and some adults) asking to come to the studio and meet the famous character. He regretted that all they would see was "a bunch of guys bending over drawings," and that he had to lie to those children who did visit that Mickey had gone out to buy cheese and would not be back for hours. In an effort to satisfy visitors hoping to meet his famous characters, Walt purchased two 1931 Austin roadsters, one for Mickey and one for Minnie, and parked them in a small garage on the studio lot. Recognizing that the public wanted to have a way to interact with Disney's animated stars in real life, he began to envision a studio tour that would incorporate some amusement-park elements, such as a train that would encircle the grounds and pass through a model village. Disney never did offer a studio tour—it still does not today except in special circumstances—but Disneyland eventually took its place.

In 1937, *Snow White and the Seven Dwarfs* became another Disney animation landmark. The first full-length cel-animated feature film, it entailed enormous risk. It took over three years to produce and cost $1.5 million, an immense sum for the time. But the risk paid off: *Snow White* took in almost $8 million at the box office. Adjusted for inflation, it remains one of the top ten most profitable films of all time. At the film's premiere at the Carthay Circle Theater in Los Angeles, there were signs that Walt was thinking in ways that were leading him closer to Disneyland. Costumed characters of Mickey Mouse, Minnie Mouse, and Donald Duck were on hand; there was also Dwarfland, which had been specially commissioned by Walt himself at a cost of $10,000. NBC radio broadcaster Don Wilson described it as a:

---

2   *Steamboat Willie* was not actually the first animated film to feature synchronized sound, as the series *Song Car-Tunes*, produced by Max and Dave Fleischer between 1924 and 1927, had made limited use of it. But it was the first animated film to feature a *fully* synchronized soundtrack.

... replica of the dwarf cottage that appeared in the film. The cottage is only ten feet high and not quite so wide, but every kid in this town has been through it. Outside are mushrooms three feet tall painted yellow and blue and pink. Weird looking trees with eyes that light up and long arms that reach out and grab at you just like the way they grab at Snow White in the film.

There's a little Dwarfs' mill wheel and a diamond mine sparkling in the spotlights that illuminate the entire scene. The Dwarfs' garden stretches for about two blocks. It's filled with all sorts of strange-looking statuary and stumps and toadstools and flowers by the hundreds and hundreds. A stream flows from the garden that turns the mill wheel. The crowds stand around watching the antics of the seven little dwarfs. Actual dwarfs dressed in quaint medieval costumes who work the diamond mine, rake the garden, run in and out of the house, putting on a great show.

On the night of the premiere, Walt told animator Wilfred Jackson that he was intending to build an amusement park full of similar attractions.

Walt's first attempt to bring his animated characters to life, Dwarfland remained on display for *Snow White's* entire four-month run at the Carthay Circle, though the live dwarfs were replaced by concrete replicas. And there were other indications in the late 1930s that Walt was beginning to think about ways to translate his cinematic vision into three-dimensional form. In 1938, he became a major investor in the Hollywood Sports Garden, which included an indoor arena for high-school and college basketball games, an ice-skating rink, a bowling alley, an indoor skiing facility, a gymnasium, and a private, members-only club. The project had first been proposed by Zack Farmer, the builder of the Los Angeles Coliseum and the driving force behind the 1932 Los Angeles Olympics. Farmer's idea was to build a West Coast version of New York's Madison Square Garden on a 34-acre parcel of land in Hancock Park, in the section of Los Angeles known as Gilmore Island. Flush with cash after *Snow White's* success, Walt was looking for investment opportunities, and using his celebrity contacts, he took on the primary responsibility for raising the $1.5 million the project required. The initial response was promising, but the proponents of the Sports Garden neglected to obtain the support of the local community, who feared that the project would bring traffic and crime to their neighborhood. Sympathetic to the residents' concerns, the Los Angeles County Board of Supporters denied the request to rezone the property for commercial use. Farmer and Walt briefly considered moving the project to a new site in Crenshaw, about five miles from the original location, but in September 1939 the Second World War broke out. Cut off from their overseas markets, Hollywood's film studios saw a sharp decline in profits, and it suddenly became impossible to find investors.[3]

Though it seems a long way from Disneyland, Walt's interest in the Hollywood Sports Garden demonstrated that his primary interest was shifting from animated films to the development of physical space as his preferred means of bringing his creative ideas to life. Always looking for something new, Walt felt that he had achieved almost everything he could in animation with *Snow White*. Now, he began to think of moving from the two-dimensional world of animation to the three-dimensional world of an amusement park. Though some of his friends and employees were mystified by his new direction, for him it was all part of the same creative path. His current mode of thinking was demonstrated during the production of *Snow White's* successor *Pinocchio* (1940), for which animation modeler Bob Jones built a maquette, or scale model, of Geppetto's village. Summoned to Walt's office one day, Jones was surprised to see the maquette sitting on his desk. Walt wanted to know how much it would cost to build a full-size version.

Another influence on Walt's thinking in the late 1930s came from the numerous international exhibitions of the time. Most prominent among them was the 1939 New York World's Fair, which was notable for being the first exhibition of its kind to take the future as its theme. According to the program, "The eyes of the Fair are on the future — not in the sense of peering toward the unknown nor attempting to foretell the events of tomorrow and the shape of things to come, but in the sense of presenting a new and clearer view of today in preparation for tomorrow; a view of the forces and ideas that prevail as well as the machines." The Fair was divided into zones, such as the Transportation Zone, the Communications and Business Systems Zone, the Food Zone, and the Government Zone, each of which was housed in an innovative and often experimental building. The centerpiece of the Fair was the Theme Center, which consisted of the 700-foot-tall spike-like Trylon and the ball-shaped Perisphere. The latter housed an exhibit sponsored by General Motors that featured a model of the City of Tomorrow, which visitors viewed from seats mounted on a moving conveyer belt.

---

3   This information about the Hollywood Sports Garden comes from the six-part series "Walt's First Park" by Todd James Pierce on the Disney History Institute website. The first part of the series can be found at: http://disneyhistoryinstitute.com/2013/12/walts-first-park-part-1.html. This was not the last time that Walt invested in a sports-entertainment facility. In 1960, he convinced his friend Art Linkletter and other Hollywood celebrities to participate in a venture called the Celebrity Sports Center in Denver. It contained a bowling alley, an Olympic-sized swimming pool and an arcade, but it was never profitable, and Walt had the studio buy out the shares of his unhappy partners after only two years. Disney later used the Celebrity Sports Center as a training center for Disneyland management.

Although Disney contributed a new Mickey Mouse cartoon called *Mickey's Surprise Party* to the pavilion that was sponsored by Nabisco, there is no firm evidence that Walt Disney himself attended the 1939 World's Fair.[4] But its influence on Disneyland's Tomorrowland, and later on Epcot, was obvious, suggesting that Walt or some members of his design team were familiar with it. Walt definitely visited two other contemporary international exhibitions, the 1933 A Century of Progress International Exposition in Chicago and the 1939 Golden Gate International Exposition in San Francisco. The former planted at least three seeds for the future. An exhibit featuring the evolution of a typical room in a Chicago house over the previous four decades helped to inspire the Carousel of Progress, which Disney developed for another international exhibition, the 1964 New York World's Fair, and later transplanted to Disneyland. The House of Tomorrow, which formed part of a display of twelve model homes that was intended to show that affordable housing could be mass-produced from pre-manufactured parts, much like cars on an assembly line, presaged Disneyland's Monsanto House of the Future.

Image 2.2: The interior of the second floor of the House of Tomorrow from the 1933 Century of Progress Exposition in Chicago. Walt Disney attended the exposition, and may have later used the house as one of the inspirations for the Monsanto-sponsored House of the Future that stood in Disneyland's Tomorrowland from 1957 to 1967.

---

4   Even though Walt hated commercials, the cartoon was essentially an advertisement for Nabisco products. When Disney first released it on VHS as part of the compilation *The Spirit of Mickey* in 1998, the Nabisco references were removed. Subsequent DVD releases, however, have preserved the original.

And finally, the ethnic and historical section, with its recreations of "villages" from various European countries and its Streets of Paris exhibit, served as an early prototype for Epcot's World Showcase.

The West Coast branch of the World's Fair, the Golden Gate International Exposition offered an eclectic mix of Spanish and Art Deco architecture and displays featuring contemporary tract homes. The most popular exhibit, however, was the doll-house-like Thorne Room Miniatures, thirty-two shadowboxes furnished in European and American styles ranging from the medieval to the contemporary. The models were conceived by Narcissa Niblack Thorne of Chicago, the wife of James Ward Thorne, an heir to the Montgomery Ward department-store fortune. Walt was clearly enthralled by the Thorne Rooms, which can be seen today in the Art Institute of Chicago, because after he returned from San Francisco, he began to collect miniatures and combine them into different scenes. In 1951, he wrote

to a friend that his hobby was a "life saver": "When I work with these small objects, I become so absorbed that the cares of the studio fade away ... at least for a time." By allowing Walt to build a world that he could control in every detail, these miniatures had a significant impact on the development of his ideas for Disneyland, as we will see below.

Image 2.3: Walt Disney at the Golden Gate International Exposition in 1939. The animated short *Mickey's Surprise Party*, an advertisement for Nabisco products, had originally been produced for the World's Fair in New York City.

The success of *Snow White and the Seven Dwarfs* allowed Disney to build a lavish new studio in Burbank. In some ways, the studio was Walt Disney's first attempt to create a full-sized world in three dimensions rather than two, and was thus another important step along the road to Disneyland. It was designed, as Disneyland would be, by an in-house team rather than by a professional architect, because Walt felt that only his own employees would truly understand the needs of the animation business. The animation studios had a large number of north-facing windows in order to ensure the maximum amount of natural light, and General Electric was hired to install a special air-conditioning system that would keep dust to a minimum, in order to protect freshly painted celluloid sheets.

The studio functioned as a precursor to Disneyland in another way, as its expanded size allowed Walt to consider the possibility of building a small amusement park on its grounds. He first cast his eye on a two-and-a-half-acre site on the backlot, but quickly came to focus on a sixteen-acre plot that Disney owned across Riverside Drive. In 1941, he discussed the idea with Bob Jones and another animation modeler named Bill Jones, telling them that he wanted to create a park that was clean, safe, and beautiful. Over the next six weeks, the two Joneses were dispatched to visit amusement parks in the Los Angeles area. The ideas that they presented to Walt included many of the early components of Disneyland: they suggested a combination of standard amusement-park rides, such as a merry-go-round, and new attractions based on Disney films. The latter included an early version of a Snow White dark ride that included a descent into the Seven Dwarfs' mine, with figures that would be made to move through the use of cables. Guests would enter the park through a Bavarian-style village resembling the one in *Pinocchio*, and a train would encircle the park, just inside the high fence and shrubbery barrier that would block views of the outside world.

For the foreseeable future, however, the studio's financial position did not allow Walt to proceed further with his plans for the park. The new studio had cost $3 million, which overstretched even *Snow White's* massive profits and forced Disney to take out a loan from the Reconstruction Finance Corporation, a federal Depression-relief program. At the same time, the animators were struggling to follow up on *Snow White*, as the films that were released between 1940 and 1942—*Pinocchio*, *Fantasia*, *Dumbo*, and *Bambi*—were unable to duplicate its box-office success. *Pinocchio*, which had cost almost twice as much to make as Snow White, lost $1 million, while the high cost of the special Fantasound sound system that had been designed for *Fantasia* caused it to lose even more. Only the more cheaply made *Dumbo* made a substantial profit.

Disney's box-office problems were largely due to the outbreak of World War II in September 1939, which took away lucrative overseas markets. Two million dollars of *Snow White's* profits had come from Europe, but only $200,000 of *Pinocchio's* did, and none of *Fantasia's*. In this difficult period, the studio regularly posted annual losses, requiring it to take out more loans. The bankers exerted an increasing amount of control over Disney's activities, and even ordered the studio to stop producing feature films until the debt was reduced. After the bombing of Pearl Harbor brought the United States into World War II in December 1941, government contracts for propaganda work brought in little revenue, as Disney recouped only its costs.

The government's requirements, meanwhile, diminished Walt's creative control, as did the arrival of the Army Signal Corps, who commandeered the studio grounds in order to protect the nearby Lockheed aircraft factory. In 1942, *Coronet* magazine reported:

> Donald Duck and Dopey have enlisted. Goofy and Pluto are in for the duration. Mickey Mouse is now in khaki, doing his bit for Uncle Sam. Their home has become a fortress, its gates guarded constantly; troops are quartered in the buildings, which formerly housed artists and animators. An entire wing ... has been taken over by the Navy Department and not even Walt Disney may enter its mysterious precincts without a pass.

Image 2.4: A new PT-9 boat being tested in June 1940. Cheap to build, fast, and highly maneuverable, PT boats were nicknamed the "mosquito fleet." Disney designed the logo on the side of the boat, which depicted a mosquito riding atop a torpedo; this was one of approximately 1200 insignias that Disney artists designed during World War II, not only for American combat units, but also for units from Great Britain, France, Poland, Canada, New Zealand, South Africa, and China.

The mounting financial pressure forced the studio to cut salaries and bonuses and even to lay off employees, which generated discontent among the animators, at a time when labor unions were on the rise in the motion-picture industry. Art Babbitt, one of Disney's most prominent animators, tried to convince his colleagues to join the Screen Cartoonists Guild. Vehemently anti-union, Walt refused to meet the guild's salary demands and fired Babbitt, whom he called a "Bolshevik," in May 1941. The next day, a significant percentage—the precise number is debated—of Disney's animators went on strike. The strike lasted for five weeks before it was settled through the intervention of a federal mediator; the union prevailed on nearly every point, and Disney has been a union shop ever since. The studio was clearly no longer the "happy family" it had been in the early days: some of Disney's best animators left as a result of the labor dispute, while those who remained did not have the same cozy relationship with their employer. For his part, Walt no longer felt the same degree of trust toward his workforce. He was so upset by the strike that he agreed to take an extended trip to South America as part of a government effort to diminish Nazi influence there. "I think the strike changed everybody," animator Marc Davis recalled. "I think that Walt became resigned that he had to operate in a more hard-nosed way, like a lot of other people who have something forced on them that they don't like. ... I'm sure that he had to feel that it was a thing against him personally, and I guess in some areas it certainly was."

Even after the end of the war, things did not improve quickly for Disney, which was $4.5 million in debt. Roy Disney later recalled the 1940s as "a bad decade for us. We really got into a tight bind around here." The Disney studio was not the entertainment juggernaut in the 1940s and early 1950s that it is today. Disney released no more than two feature films per year, usually only one, and sometimes none. By comparison, a big studio such as MGM released around fifty films annually. Walt recognized that to get bigger, Disney would have to diversify and expand into new areas. As most theaters now showed double bills of two feature-length films, the market for short cartoons had all but disappeared. The studio had not been able to work on feature films during the war, and so the first projects that were released afterwards, including *Make Mine Music* (1946), *Fun and Fancy Free* (1947), *Melody Time* (1948), and *The Adventures of Ichabod and Mr. Toad* (1949), were "package" films comprised of several short segments that were loosely stitched together. Seeking to break into new markets, Walt considered making promotional films, educational films, nature films—anything that would help to bring in additional revenue.

The most obvious space for expansion was live-action films. After several experiments with hybrid films that combined live action and animation, such as *The Reluctant Dragon* (1941), *The Three Caballeros* (1945), and *Song of the South* (1946), Disney began producing fully live-action films in the early 1950s. In part, this development was motivated by the policies of the cash-strapped postwar British government, which refused to allow the profits of American films to be taken out of the country. Disney thus began investing those profits in filming in Britain; its first effort, *Treasure Island* (1949), was made in Cornwall in southwestern England. It was followed by *Robin Hood and His Merry Men* (1952), *The Sword and the Rose* (1953), and *Rob Roy, the Highland Rogue* (1954). For Walt, this was sound business, but he was not personally committed to live-action films in the way that he had been to the first animated features. He told the actor Douglas Fairbanks, Jr. that Disney's foray into live action was "purely a move of economy."

With film no longer providing the creative outlet that it once had, Walt began to focus more and more on the idea of building an amusement park. He wanted to find a new arena that offered him complete control of the world that he sought to depict. He had previously used animation for this purpose, but the box-office failures of *Pinocchio*, *Fantasia*, and *Bambi* had dented his confidence in that medium. Now, he saw an amusement park as the best means of bringing his creative ideas to life. He also, however, thought of it as a business venture. In most Disney histories, Walt is depicted as the dreamer, while his older brother Roy is the pragmatist who kept his eye on the bottom line. But these stereotypes are too simple. It is true that Walt wanted a new outlet for his creativity, but he also sought a new project for the studio that would both be profitable in its own right and would allow profits to be reinvested in order to reduce the company's tax burden. Even if he thought of the potential financial benefits primarily as a means to fund his creative ideas in the future, it is inaccurate to say that he did not care about the revenues that the park would bring in. Walt knew that if it proved a success it would provide a steady annual revenue stream, in contrast to the more unpredictable performance of Disney's films.

In August 1948, Walt sent a memo to production designer Dick Kelsey that contained the first detailed account of his ideas for what at this point was called Mickey Mouse Park or Mickey Mouse Village. Guests entered through the Main Village, which had a railroad station at one end and a town hall at the other. Built around a "village green or informal park," the village also contained an opera house and a movie theater; the latter would be used for "little kids' plays," as well as for motion pictures and radio and television broadcasts. "Little stores" would sell Disney toys, while a horse car would carry guests to the end of the street, where they could "continue on to the Western village" or "loop around and come back by way of the Carnival section." The Western village included a stage coach that passed a farm, an Indian village and an old mill, as well as a donkey pack train. There would also be "typical Midway stuff," such as a merry-go-round.

But at this point, Walt's idea was just a dream. "I couldn't get anybody to go with me because we were going through this financial depression," Walt recalled. "Whenever I'd go down and talk to my brother about it, why he'd always suddenly get busy with some figures. I didn't dare bring it up." Roy thought that Walt's fixation would pass. "Walt does a lot of talking about an amusement park," he wrote in a letter from the early 1950s, "but really, I don't know how deep his interest really is. I think he's more interested in ideas that would be good in an amusement park than in actually running one himself." Telling Walt that the studio simply could not afford any additional expenses, Roy refused to invest more than $10,000 of the studio's money in the amusement park, which had an estimated budget of $1.5 million. Walt tried to shame Roy into changing his stance by having the studio's nurse, Hazel George, who was a close friend of Walt's, organize a collection fund among Disney employees, who chipped in contributions of $10 or $20 each toward the construction of the amusement park. But still Roy refused to budge. "When [Walt] started Disneyland," remembered animator Frank Thomas, "he didn't have a friend in the world."

But Walt was determined. His biographers often depict him in this era as restless and unfocused. Bored with film and with nothing left to achieve in animation, he turned to hobbies and travel. But these were not mere distractions; instead, Walt was gathering ideas for his amusement park. As a means of experimenting with three-dimensional space, he continued to pursue his miniature-collecting hobby. While on a trip to Europe in 1949, he spent hundreds of dollars in a Paris shop that specialized in miniature furniture.[5] He put animator Ken Anderson on his personal payroll and told him to work on a series of drawings of "an old western town." Walt intended for Anderson's drawings to serve as the models for twenty-four miniature rooms. He began with a replica of Granny Kincaid's cabin from the Disney film *So Dear to My Heart* (1948), which he loved for its nostalgic depiction of midwestern America. The idea for a miniature town evolved into a project called Disneylandia, in which the model buildings would be taken around the country in three Pullman railroad cars that people could walk through. Walt tested Disneylandia for the first time at the Festival of California Living, which was held in Los Angeles' Pan-Pacific Auditorium in 1952. Built almost entirely by hand by Walt Disney himself, the meticulously

---

5   Walt later visited Madurodam, an attraction that featured miniature versions of Europe's architectural and historical treasures, which opened in the Netherlands in 1952.

detailed Granny Kincaid's Cabin was displayed with taped narration by Beulah Bondi, the actress who had played Granny Kincaid in *So Dear to My Heart*. The cost of sending Disneylandia around the country by rail proved exorbitant, but Walt's love of miniatures continued to influence his ideas.

By the late 1940s, Walt's miniatures hobby was forced to compete with a revival of his long-standing interest in trains. In August of 1948, he visited the Chicago Railroad Fair. Organized by thirty-eight major American rail carriers, the Railroad Fair celebrated the centennial of the first steam train in Chicago. Walt had a great time riding in the cabs and blowing the whistles of the trains on display; he even donned a Victorian costume so that he could participate in the pageant of railroad history that was performed twice daily. But Walt was not just playing with trains; he was gathering ideas. He noticed that a train circled the grounds of the fair, and that the railway companies had set up a number of "lands," including replicas of the French Quarter of New Orleans and the American West, in order to show visitors the destinations to which the railroad could bring them. These lands included costumed workers and restaurants serving themed food.

Image 2.5: A sign directing guests to two of the attractions at the Chicago Railroad Fair in 1948. Dixieland was a section representing the antebellum South; its central feature was the Show Boat Theater, a theater designed to look like a Mississippi riverboat. Walt Disney attended the fair with animator Ward Kimball; its themed areas influenced his early thinking about Disneyland.

Before he returned home, Walt took a side trip to the Henry Ford Museum and adjacent Greenfield Village in Detroit. He had previously visited Greenfield Village eight years earlier, and its use of historical buildings arranged in a village setting influenced Walt's thinking about the Main Street that he wanted to serve as the entrance to his amusement park.

Walt's companion on the trip had been animator Ward Kimball. In the late 1930s, Kimball had acquired a vintage Baldwin steam locomotive and the last surviving passenger coach from the Carson and Colorado Railroad. They became the first components of what Kimball called the Grizzly Flats Railroad, a collection of old steam locomotives and rolling stock that he ran on a short stretch of narrow-gauge track in his backyard. Envious of Kimball's creation, Walt wanted to build his own railroad, but he wanted it to run farther, which meant that it had to be more akin to the one-twelfth-scale La Cañada Valley Railroad, another backyard set-up that had been built by Disney animator Ollie Johnston. In 1949, soon after he moved into Carolwood, his new house in the exclusive Holmby Hills section of Los Angeles, Walt began constructing a one-eighth-scale railroad that covered five acres of his backyard. The 2200-foot-long track included a fully functioning signaling system, a forty-six-foot-long trestle, and a ninety-foot-long tunnel, the latter necessary because Walt's wife Lillian would not let him lay track through her flower beds. Walt also built an earthen berm so that the track would be screened from the neighbors. Fabricated by engineer Roger Broggie in the Disney machine shop and named the *Lilly Belle* in honor of Lillian, the working steam locomotive was based on a real Central Pacific model. Even though the train was only one-eighth scale, it was still powerful enough for Walt to ride on the tender for the engine and for other adults and children to ride on the cars and caboose. Walt used the railroad, which he named the Carolwood Pacific, to entertain his friends; neighborhood children, including Candice Bergen and Nancy Sinatra; and celebrities such as Red Skelton, Mary Pickford, and Salvador Dali.[6] A reporter from *The New York Times*, Bosley Crowther, visited Walt's Carolwood estate in the early 1950s and recalled that Walt "seemed totally disinterested in movies, and wholly, almost weirdly concerned with the

---

6   In 1956, Walt invited the actor Kirk Douglas, who had starred in the Disney film *20,000 Leagues Under the Sea* (1954) and his two young sons Joel and Michael (later a famous actor in his own right) to Carolwood. He filmed them riding the train, and later used the footage in an episode of the *Disneyland* television show. Douglas was furious, and wrote a letter to Walt complaining. Walt immediately sent Douglas an apology, but when the episode was rerun a few months later, the footage was still included. A furious Douglas filed a lawsuit claiming that his privacy had been invaded and that he should have been compensated for the appearance. Disney's lawyers countered that Douglas was contracted to perform publicity duties for *20,000 Leagues*. Telling the press, "You can't sue God," Douglas eventually dropped the suit.

building of a miniature railroad engine and a string of cars in the work-shops of the studio." But Crowther missed the point: Walt was not thinking about the movies, he was thinking about his amusement park, and the Carolwood Pacific, a small-scale version of the kind of attractions he was envisioning, offered a way for him to do that.

Around this time, Walt thought of little else besides the amusement park. Animator Milt Kahl said that "every time you had a meeting with Walt on something else, why, the park would come up." One of the story researchers at Disney was Bernice Bradley, whose husband David owned Beverly Park, a small amusement park that stood on the site of what is now the Beverly Center shopping mall. Walt quizzed Bradley about ride operations, food consumption, and queue lengths.[7] He also visited some of the most famous amusement parks in the world, ranging from local favor-ites like Knott's Berry Farm and Fairyland in Oakland to Tivoli Gardens in Belgium. His good friend Art Linkletter, who accompanied Walt to Tivoli, recalled that Walt took copious notes throughout his visit. He was par-ticularly impressed by how Tivoli was clean, alcohol-free, and as popular with adults as it was with children.

Before Walt could get serious about building an amusement park, how-ever, something had to happen to relieve the financial pressure on the studio. The studio's first postwar animated feature (as opposed to a pack-age film) was clearly going to be crucial in this respect. The subject matter that was selected to carry this massive burden was Charles Perrault's late-seventeenth-century folk tale *Cinderella*. To hold down costs, the vast majority of the scenes were filmed in live action, so that the ani-mators could use the footage as the basis of their drawings. Even so, the film cost $3 million, making it a massive risk for the heavily indebted studio, which may well have been forced to close had the film flopped. Fortunately, it did not. Released in 1950, Cinderella made $34 million and became Disney's biggest hit since *Snow White and the Seven Dwarfs*. It was a narrow escape. The other animated feature that the studio was working on in the early 1950s was an adaptation of Lewis Carroll's nine-teenth-century novels *Alice's Adventures in Wonderland* and *Through the Looking Glass*. Walt was initially thinking of finishing *Alice in Wonderland* first, but the animators made more rapid progress on *Cinderella*. Released in 1951, *Alice in Wonderland* proved a box-office disappointment, earning

---

7 Bradley later became a paid consultant for Disneyland, and his advice influenced its development in several important ways. Believing that "an appealing ride must tie together participation of the customer, make the customer feel comfortable and still be an adventure," he stressed the importance of cleanliness and respectability. Bradley also suggested that the buildings on Main Street should be built in 7/8th scale so that they would not overwhelm the guests.

only $2.4 million, which did not even recoup its cost. Today, the prominent presence of Alice in Wonderland in Disney theme parks is ironic, given the fact that, if it had been released before *Cinderella*, there almost certainly would have been no Disneyland, and the entire Disney studio might well have gone out of business.

With the studio out of danger and cash flowing once again, Walt could begin to focus more seriously on his amusement park. In the early 1950s, Walt's animators frequently spotted him pacing off distances on the empty lot across from the studio, or crouching down so that he could see things from a child's perspective. He also discussed the possibility of building an eight-mile-long railroad that would link the studio directly to the merry-go-round in Griffith Park. While he was on a trip to London in 1951, Walt decided to visit a store called Basset-Lowke, which sold model trains. There, he encountered Harper Goff, a fellow American who was an art director in Hollywood. Walt invited Goff to come to the Disney studio, and he was soon employed in making sketches of Walt's amusement park. The attractions included a roller coaster, a boat ride through a miniaturized Lilliputian Land, and a haunted house. Walt then hired a young architect named John Cowles to make architectural drawings from Goff's sketches. It was also around this time that Walt decided to give the amusement park a new name: Disneyland. There is no record of when it was first used, but writer Bill Cottrell recalled that "the name was suddenly said by Walt, and it sounded good, and that was it."[8]

By the spring of 1952, Walt was ready to announce his plans for the Riverside Drive site in Burbank to the public. On the 27th of March, the *Burbank Daily Review* announced that Walt Disney was planning to build Disneyland, a "spectacular world of make-believe" that would cost $1.5 million and would include "various scenes of Americana, rides in a 'Space Ship' and submarine, a zoo of miniature animals and exhibit halls." Walt made a presentation about the park to the Burbank Parks and Recreation Board, as the municipal authorities would have to approve his plans. The board granted preliminary approval, but the city council proved less amenable. When Walt presented his ideas to them, they were skeptical that an amusement park, which they saw as tawdry and tacky despite Walt's protestations that his would be clean and wholesome. In the fall of 1952, the city council rejected Walt's proposal; one councilor explained that they did not want a "carny atmosphere" to take over the town.

---

8   This was not the first time that the term "Disneyland" had been used. A memo survives from this period in which the non-theatrical release of an old *Snow White* promotional film was referred to as *A Trip through Disneyland*, and a series of miniatures that Walt had built as part of a scheme to display them in railroad cars that would travel around the country had been called Disneylandia.

Walt was initially angry; Harper Goff, who had accompanied him to the fateful meeting, recalled that Walt felt like the councilors had "sneered" at his ideas. But his disappointment soon dissipated. He had learned that the state of California was going to build the Ventura Freeway right next to the Riverside Drive site, and in any event, the scale of his ideas had expanded far beyond its capacity. Now envisioning that he needed around a hundred acres to bring his vision to life, he could begin to search for the right site.

THREE
Anaheim

After his proposal to build a small amusement park across from the Disney studio was rejected by the Burbank City Council in the fall of 1952, the question for Walt Disney became: where in the vicinity of Los Angeles could he acquire a large amount of land at a cheap price, in a location that people could access easily? To understand why Disneyland ended up where it did, we have to look at two histories: the history of southern California's agriculture and the history of the California freeway system. It was the intersection of those two histories in the 1950s that led to Disneyland being located in Anaheim.

In the late eighteenth century, the Spanish colonial government began making use of southern California's fertile soil to support their missions, using indigenous people as a cheap source of labor. At the same time, the Spanish made land grants to veteran army officers. Among them was Manuel Nieto, an officer assigned to the Presidio, or fortified military base, at Monterey. Presidio soldiers earned additional income by raising cattle, and by the early 1780s Nieto had more stock than his land could support. In 1784, he was granted additional grazing rights to 300,000 acres of land between the San Gabriel and Santa Ana Rivers, covering most of what is now western Orange County. Other soldiers followed, marking the beginning of Orange County's transition to agricultural production on large landholdings called ranchos.

After Mexican independence in 1821, California was opened to foreign merchants, and soon the ranchos were engaged in a thriving trade in hides and tallow with American ships that landed along the coast. In 1848, victory in the Mexican-American War led to the American takeover of California; two years later, California became the thirty-first state. The following decades saw a steady transfer of land from Spanish and Mexican to American hands. The scale and variety of southern California's agriculture was transformed by the Gold Rush of the late 1840s and the arrival of tens of thousands of miners. To meet the demand, production rapidly shifted from hides and tallow to food. The state's produce was sold almost exclusively locally, however, as California was too remote from the rest of the United States for food exports to be practical. Two things changed that: the arrival of the transcontinental railroad in 1869 and the large-scale planting of wheat, which was sufficiently non-perishable to be shipped long distances. At the same time, an aggressive campaign to encourage immigration to California lured more farmers to the state from the eastern United States and Europe. By 1880, agriculture had supplanted mining as California's most important industry.

But what really made it possible for California to become the source of so much of America's food was the invention of the refrigerated railway car, or reefer, in the late 1870s, which made the shipment of perishable produce to the East Coast and even to Europe possible. The sector of agriculture that benefitted the most from refrigeration was fruit production. By 1906, over 80,000 reefers of fruit were being shipped east from California each year. They carried a wide variety of fruit—apples, pears, apricots, cherries, and plums—but there was one crop in particular that came not only to achieve paramount economic importance but also to symbolize California's identity as a sun-soaked paradise: the orange.

First brought to America by the Spanish, oranges were being grown in California by Franciscan missionaries by the middle of the eighteenth century. By the 1830s, a handful of orange groves had been planted, but the true commercial production of oranges in California began in 1873, when Eliza Tibbets, the wife of Riverside farmer Luther Tibbets, sought advice from her friend, the United States Department of Agriculture's superintendent of gardens and grounds William Saunders. Eliza wanted to know what crops would grow well in southern California. Saunders had recently imported the seedless Bahia orange from Brazil. Hoping that the variety, which he renamed the Washington navel, would do well in California, he sent two cuttings budded to rootstocks to the Tibbets. When the trees reached maturity, they began producing delicious oranges that regularly won prizes at local agricultural fairs. The trees became so famous that people traveled from all over southern California to see them, and Seedless Orange Tibbets, as Luther came to be known, had to surround them with a padlocked fence and barbed wire to prevent thieves from stripping their buds. Soon, growers were rushing to rip out other types of fruit trees and plant Washington navels in their place.

Washington navels did not, however, do as well in southern California's more humid coastal zones. Instead, it was another variety that flourished there. In 1830, a fur trapper named William Wolfskill arrived in southern California from New Mexico. Wolfskill acquired a parcel of land near what is now downtown Los Angeles, on which he planted vineyards that rapidly made him one of the largest producers of grapes and wine in California.

He also branched into other crops, including oranges and lemons, which he began producing when he discovered that Gold Rush miners would pay a dollar for a crate of citrus fruit. With his fruit in high demand, Wolfskill began experimenting with hybridization in order to produce varieties that would do well in the specific climatic conditions of his groves. His efforts led to the creation of the Valencia orange, named after Valencia, Spain, which was famous for its sweet oranges. The Valencia is a seeded variety that would later be used predominantly for orange juice. It is harvested in the summer rather than in the winter like the Washington navel, which meant that California oranges were now available year-round. In the 1860s, Wolfskill sold his hybrid orange to the Irvine Ranch, which had been buying up old Mexican land grants in southern California and which would come to own over 120,000 acres of land. The Irvine Ranch had previously focused on the grazing of sheep, but in the mid-1880s a severe drought forced a change in strategy. The ranch's owner, James Irvine, Jr., introduced a new scheme of irrigation, and his tenant farmers shifted to the production of fruits and vegetables. Over half the ranch's land was soon devoted to Valencia orange groves.

The first southern California oranges were shipped east in 1877; only ten years later, enough of the fruit was being produced to fill 2000 railcars annually. But on the East Coast, oranges were still an exotic luxury, and many growers struggled to earn a profit. It was not until the 1890s, when the growers formed cooperatives that could share the expenses and risks of citrus cultivation, that the money began to roll in. In 1893, the formation of the California Fruit Growers Exchange marked a key step forward for the citrus industry. In 1908, the exchange coined the name Sunkist for use in its advertising campaigns, and it quickly became the most famous brand of fruit in the world. Thanks to such savvy marketing, Americans came to associate oranges with good health. Prior to the late nineteenth century, few Americans had ever seen, let alone tasted, an orange, but by the first decades of the twentieth, they consumed an average of forty a year. By this point, twelve million crates of fruit were being shipped east annually from an "Orange Empire" that surrounded Los Angeles on all sides. Worth $60 million annually, California's orange crop was surpassed only by oil as the state's largest revenue-producer.

Image 3.1: A display in the late 1930s at the Orange Ball, the highlight of California Orange Week, an annual celebration of the orange's importance to California's economy.

Anaheim lay squarely in the middle of the Valencia orange belt to the south of Los Angeles, though the city predated the citrus boom. In 1850, a German violinist named Charles Kohler emigrated first to New York and then to San Francisco, where he helped to found the Germania Concert Society. One of the members was a flautist and fellow German named John Frohling. According to legend, Kohler and Frohling were so impressed when they sampled some California wine at a picnic in 1854 that they decided to become vintners themselves. Although they knew nothing about the wine business, they raised $12,000 in capital, which they used to purchase a vineyard near what is now the intersection of Seventh Street and Central Avenue in Los Angeles. At first, Kohler and Frohling produced only a few hundred gallons of wine each year, which they sold to their friends and contacts in San Francisco. By the late 1850s, however, they owned 20,000 acres of land, and their output had expanded to 100,000 gallons annually, much of which was shipped east to New York and Boston.

Seeking to expand production even further, in 1857 Kohler and Frohling decided to establish a colony of fellow German immigrants on land they had acquired to the south of Los Angeles. The colony took the first part of its name from the nearby Santa Ana River and the second from the German word *heim*, meaning "home," making it Anaheim.

Image 3.2: The Mother Colony house in Anaheim. Dating from 1857, the house was occupied by George Hansen, the agricultural colony's first superintendent.

For the next three decades, dozens of wineries operated in or near the town, making Anaheim the center of American wine production. But in the 1880s, a mysterious blight, now known to be Pierce's disease, wiped out virtually all of Anaheim's vines. Desperate to find a new crop, local farmers had some success with walnuts and chili peppers, but it was citrus production that proved their salvation. Dead grape vines were replaced by orange trees, 20,000 of which had been planted by 1915. By the 1930s, one-sixth of the nation's Valencia oranges were being produced near Anaheim. Citrus production peaked around 1940, when five million orange trees covered 70,000 acres of the county's land.

The arrival of the Southern Pacific Railway in 1875, followed by the Santa Fe a decade later, brought an influx of new settlers to the area. This population surge fostered a desire for greater independence from Los Angeles, and local leaders began to press the state government for permission to secede from Los Angeles County. In 1889, they succeeded. Boosters chose the name of the new county not because of the importance of citrus production, which was still in its infancy at the time, but because they wanted it to have a semi-tropical flavor that would attract new settlers. It worked: at the time it was founded, Orange County contained a mere three incorporated cities—Anaheim, Santa Ana, and Orange—and a population of 15,000 people. By 1930, Orange County had thirteen incorporated towns and 120,000 inhabitants. But impressive as this rate of growth was, Orange County's population was tiny in comparison to the 2.2 million people who lived in Los Angeles County at the time. Throughout the first half of the twentieth century, it remained a sleepy agricultural backwater.

The rise of southern California's agriculture took half a century; its fall would occur much more swiftly. After World War II, the region's population growth accelerated dramatically, as returning GIs were lured by the warm climate, low housing prices, and employment opportunities in the aerospace and defense-contracting industries. By 1960, Orange County's population had surged to 700,000. These new arrivals wanted the same thing from California that their forebears had: the good life, which in this context entailed a detached suburban house. The price of land thus began to rise sharply. Increased values meant higher taxes, at a time when many orange growers had to bear the expense of ripping out their groves and replanting, as the productive lifespan of an orange tree was around fifty years. To make matters worse for Orange County's farmers, the increased competition for the region's scant water supply further drove up costs, while the blight tristeza, or Quick Decline, destroyed 50,000 acres of trees. First smaller growers and then larger ones sold out to speculators. The growers moved to the Central Valley, which had been irrigated in the 1930s by the federal and state government. There, land was plentiful and cheap. Nor was there a need to plant expensive, slow-maturing orange trees: the Central Valley supported a range of crops, including grapes, cotton, nuts, and vegetables. (Today, it is the most productive agricultural region in the United States.) As the farmers left in the 1950s and early 1960s, millions of Orange County's citrus trees were bulldozed to make room for homes.

In 1955, the year that Disneyland opened, a record 27,675 lots were subdivided to create spaces for new homes. "Pretty soon it will be Orange County no longer," wrote a reporter for the *Long Beach Independent-Press-Telegram*. "It will be 'Tract County'."

Image 3.3: Tract homes along Gilbert Avenue in Anaheim in 1957.

The second history that we need to trace in order to understand why Disneyland is in Anaheim is that of the California freeways. As the population of Los Angeles' suburbs grew, they became able to support their own commercial enterprises, which then moved out of downtown. The resulting sprawl created a need for public transportation to link the disparate communities together. Beginning in the 1880s, Los Angeles built the nation's largest inter-urban streetcar network, with over 1200 miles of track linking fifty communities scattered across Los Angeles, Orange, Riverside, and San Bernardino counties. The streetcar lines, however, were intended to make specific real-estate developments more accessible rather than to create a true urban transportation system, which led to overbuilding and redundancy. By the 1920s, Los Angeles' electric railways were caught in a vicious cycle of increasing costs and declining revenues that prevented them from making improvements. One possible solution was for the municipal authorities to take over mass transit, but although a number of studies endorsed this idea, it was never acted upon. By the late 1920s and 1930s, Los Angeles' electric streetcar network was being dismantled, and by the 1960s, what had been one of the best mass-transit systems in the country had been completely destroyed.

As their mass-transit system crumbled, the people of Los Angeles increasingly resorted to the automobile. By the 1930s, cars accounted for 80 percent of the passenger miles traveled in the city. This led to massive traffic congestion, but as quickly as roads were expanded, they became choked with cars once again. To alleviate the problem, the city's traffic engineers advocated the creation of roads that were reserved exclusively for cars, in imitation of the parkways that already existed in northeastern and midwestern cities. In 1937, the Automobile Club of Los Angeles endorsed this idea in its landmark *Traffic Survey*, which called for the construction of "motorways" that would be accessed via on- and off-ramps and cloverleaf interchanges. In rural and suburban areas, they would have wide rights-of-way, while in urban areas they would be elevated above existing roads.

As early as 1924, voters approved a "stop-free express highway" to connect downtown Los Angeles to the San Fernando Valley; this was the earliest conception of what would become the famous Hollywood Freeway. The "freeway" method was first pioneered, however, on a four-mile stretch of Ramona Boulevard, dubbed the Air Line Route, which opened in 1935 and linked downtown Los Angeles to the southern San Gabriel Valley. Other freeways soon followed. In 1940, the first segment of what became the Hollywood Freeway opened when a two-mile stretch of the narrow, twisting road between Hollywood and the San Fernando Valley was replaced by the six-lane-wide Cahuenga Pass Freeway. But the first

true California freeway, and indeed the first true freeway in the western
United States, was the seven-mile-long Arroyo Seco Parkway, which also
opened in 1940 to link Los Angeles and Pasadena.

New Deal projects that were intended to help the local economy during
the Depression, these early California freeways were largely funded by
federal dollars. Limited in distance, they were supposed to be part of
a multi-modal transportation system that incorporated mass transit.
By the early 1940s, however, federal funds were being diverted to fight
the Second World War, and California's state government was forced to
find the funds to pay for the continued expansion of the freeway system.
In 1947, the legislature passed the Collier-Burns Highway Act, which
increased the statewide fuel tax from 1 to 1.5 percent and doubled motor
vehicle registration fees in order to pay for new freeway construction. This
influx of cash led to a burst of new freeways. Los Angeles County, which
contributed almost half of the state's highway taxes, got the lion's share
of the allocation, and its freeway mileage increased by a factor of five. The
next decade saw the construction of significant portions of the Hollywood,
Harbor, Santa Ana, San Bernardino, and Santa Monica Freeways as the
basis of an integrated system of freeways in southern California.

As in the rest of the Los Angeles area, Orange County's residential development initially followed the lines of the electric-railway network. The Pacific
Electric's Long Beach Line, which ran for fifteen miles along the coast, was
completed in 1902, and the Santa Ana Line, which ran from Watts to Santa
Ana, followed three years later. But as was the case elsewhere in southern
California, by the 1920s Orange County's electric railways were struggling
as people shifted toward the automobile as their preferred mode of transportation. A freeway linking Orange County to downtown Los Angeles
had been planned since 1939; its construction began in 1947 and was
completed eleven years later. What was then called the Santa Ana Parkway,
now Interstate 5 or the Santa Ana Freeway, opened to traffic in 1954.

The Santa Ana Freeway proved a key factor in bringing Disneyland to
Anaheim. After the Burbank City Council rejected his plans to build an
amusement park across the street from the Disney studio in 1952, Walt
Disney began searching for a new site. He considered a number of possibili-
ties, including parcels in La Cañada Flintridge to the east of downtown Los
Angeles; Chatsworth and Sepulveda (now North Hills) in the San Fernando
Valley to the north of the city; Calabasas, also in the San Fernando Valley
but slightly farther south; and Palos Verdes to the southwest of downtown.[1]

---

1   In 1953, Disney actually purchased forty acres of land in Calabasas due to fears that another
buyer would pre-empt him.

None of these sites was anywhere near Anaheim, but Walt did dispatch his employees Dick Irvine and Nat Winecoff to look at possible locations along the planned route of the Santa Ana Freeway in Orange County.

Walt knew how important it was to choose the right site, so although he preferred to do things in-house, he knew that in this case Disney did not possess the required expertise. The Stanford Research Institute (SRI), established in 1946 by Stanford University to support economic development in California, had already done work for Disney to find a site where they could store the studio's large props. Now, Walt decided to pay SRI $25,000 to conduct a location study for Disneyland. He explained his requirements to SRI's Harrison "Buzz" Price: at least one hundred acres of undeveloped land that would cost no more than $4500 an acre. It also needed to be as close to flat as possible and with a single owner or at least a small number of owners to make negotiating the purchase easier. The site had to be within a rough triangle bounded by Chatsworth and Pomona to the north and Tustin and Balboa to the south, and it could not be near the coast because Walt did not want to attract the "barefoot beach crowd."

After assessing Walt's list of demands, Price told him that he would need a minimum of 150 acres; Walt initially resisted increasing the amount of land because of the added expense, but ultimately came to agree with Price. To find the right spot, Price divided the triangle into ten districts and eliminated those that were already fully developed, had oil underneath them, were not topographically suitable, or were under undesirable forms of government regulation. This eliminated eight of the ten districts; the remaining two were both along the Santa Ana Freeway corridor, one on the southern edge of Los Angeles County in the Whittier-Norwalk area and the other farther south in Orange County. Price believed that over the next decades the freeway corridor was going to experience the most rapid growth in the Los Angeles area. This was confirmed when Nat Winecoff asked his neighbor, who worked as a civil engineer for the city of Los Angeles, about plans for future freeway development. The man told him that the Santa Ana Freeway was going to be the "biggest" and that "everything was going to move in that direction." Real-estate speculators, in fact, were already beginning to buy up land near the freeway corridor.

Image 3.4: The Santa Ana Freeway passing through Orange County in the late 1950s.

In the two districts that remained in contention, Price considered forty-three sites, but he quickly narrowed the list to three. Two sites on the boundary of Los Angeles and Orange Counties were accessible from the Santa Ana Freeway's Valley View Avenue exit: a 170-acre parcel along the Southern Pacific Railway's right-of-way and the McNally Ranch in La Mirada, where 750 acres were available from the Shaw Construction Company. The only site that was fully in Orange County was that of the Willowick Country Club near Santa Ana, but it did not have direct freeway access. It was not until just before he was about to submit his report to Walt in August of 1953 that Price learned of a 139-acre parcel in Anaheim, near the intersection of Harbor Boulevard and Ball Road. Planted with 4000 orange trees, the site was owned by seventeen different people, but they had already been contemplating selling their land for a residential subdivision and thus could be basically treated as a single owner. The price—$4800 an acre—was higher than Walt's limit, but the site, which quickly became known as the Ball Road subdivision, was otherwise perfect: it was flat and had excellent access not only to the Santa Ana Freeway but to two other highways, plus property taxes were lower in Anaheim than in nearby communities. Price quickly came to prefer this site, and when Walt heard his presentation, he decided to visit it for himself and was impressed by what he saw. Adding to the site's attractiveness, Anaheim's municipal officials were eager to have Disneyland located in their city. In the early 1950s, as residential subdivisions replaced orange groves, Anaheim's leaders knew that they needed a replacement for agriculture's contribution to the local economy. Wanting to know more about their willingness to annex land into the city and to provide utility services, Walt dispatched Nat Winecoff to get a feel for their likely level of cooperation. Impressed by the attitude he encountered, Winecoff gave Walt a favorable report.

Walt authorized SRI to get in touch with the property owners. The negotiations began with a key piece of land, known as the Bauer property, that was leased to the Viking Trailer Manufacturing Company. Walt agreed to pay $100,000, or $5300 an acre, for the land, but almost immediately someone bought twenty acres of property next door, in the hopes that the purchaser of the Bauer property would be forced to pay a premium for it in order to complete whatever development was being planned. Rather than pay the increased price, Walt walked away from the $10,000 deposit he had put down. At this point, it looked like Walt might have to look elsewhere, but a search for other sites along the Santa Ana Freeway corridor quickly revealed that they would be considerably more expensive. So Disney returned to Anaheim. City manager Keith Murdoch and Earne Moeller, the executive secretary of the Anaheim Chamber of Commerce, came up with two possibilities. One was too close to a decrepit cemetery, and Walt rejected it out of hand. The other, on La Palma Avenue, looked more promising, but on the way back to Burbank, Walt and the Disney team stopped for lunch at Knott's Berry Farm, the Old West-themed amusement park in Buena Park, about six miles from Anaheim. A local realtor overheard him discussing his plans, and the price of the land suddenly shot up. Knowing what a massive boost Disneyland would be for Anaheim's economy, however, Murdoch and Moeller kept looking. As Moeller stared at a map of the town, he had a revelation: if the original Ball Road site was shifted one block further south, so that it now crossed Cerritos Avenue, there was sufficient land.[2]

But even after the site had been identified, there were still complications. Cerritos Avenue, which ran through the center of the property, would have to be closed, which could only occur if all of the adjacent landowners and county officials agreed. They did, allowing the deal to proceed. Another problem was that only part of the site was located in the city of Anaheim; much of it was in unincorporated Orange County, where property taxes were higher. Walt insisted that all of the land be incorporated into the city, which duly initiated the process of annexing the land. The annexation was held up, however, by a joint lawsuit filed by Moore Built Homes, which was building a subdivision nearby; William and Dyke Lansdale, who owned the

---

2   Disney eventually purchased the Bauer property in 1957 and used it as a backstage area.

rights to supply water to the property; and the Walnut Company, which provided other services to the site. The first plaintiff feared that the presence of a large theme park would decrease property values, while the latter two thought that it would hurt their businesses. The city convinced the plaintiffs to drop the lawsuit by granting the Lansdales and the Walnut Company the right to provide independent services to the site, rather than using the normal municipal ones. Finally, the annexation had to be approved by both the landowners and the residents of Anaheim; the former voted overwhelmingly in favor by a margin of 56 to 2, while the latter approved it more narrowly by a 56 percent margin.

Image 3.5: Walt Disney discusses his plans for Disneyland with Orange County officials in December 1954. The image was taken at the Disney studio in Burbank.

Now, Walt could get serious about purchasing the land. He acquired a total of 160 acres, paying his limit of $4000 an acre for most of the property, though one owner held out for $5000, and others received extra sums for buildings and other improvements that were on their land.[3] Walt

---

3   To put this price in perspective, in 1998 Disney purchased an additional 52.5 acres from the Fujishige family, who for over four decades had refused to sell their strawberry farm, the largest undeveloped tract of land near the park. Though the price was not disclosed, real-estate experts estimated that the land cost Disney between $65 million and $78 million, or between $1.2 million and $1.5 million per acre. Even accounting for inflation, this means that the land increased in value by between thirty-four and forty-three times between 1955 and 1998.

was so eager to complete the purchase that he agreed to a variety of bizarre conditions. The Dominguez family demanded that a Canary Island date palm tree that had been a wedding present to their parents in 1896 be preserved.[4] The Claussen family required that their daughters be permitted to keep living in their farmhouse, which was located on land was slated to become Disneyland's parking lot.[5] In order to keep the price from escalating, the purchase was made by local realtors, and the identity of the purchaser was kept secret. In a preview of the far more elaborate methods that Disney would later use to conceal its land acquisitions in central Florida, Stanford Research's C.V. Wood crafted a misdirection campaign by leaking stories to the press that Disney was planning to build an amusement park in the San Fernando Valley. While the purchases were ongoing, Walt brought his good friend Art Linkletter down to Anaheim to see the site. In all directions, Linkletter could see little but orange trees and dirt. "I remember thinking to myself," he recalled, "these people are crazy... Who's going to come way out here?"

---

4   The Dominguez's young son Ron went on to work for Disneyland for almost forty years, rising from ticket-taker to executive vice-president. After he retired in 1994, he was honored with a window over the Market House on Main Street, U.S.A., which is titled Orange Grove Property Mgt. in reference to his family history. The palm tree, which was in a location designated to be covered by the Disneyland parking lot, was transplanted to Adventureland. It is still there, near the FastPass entrance to the Indiana Jones Adventure. In 1994, when the Jungle Cruise queue building was rebuilt, the palm was carefully protected. The new structure was built as close to the tree as possible without risking damage to it.

5   The Claussen house caught fire and burned to the ground in the summer of 1955. In his book *Three Years in Wonderland*, Todd James Pierce implies that C.V. Wood, who had been hired away from Stanford Research to become Disneyland's first general manager, encouraged one of his employees to commit arson in order to get rid of it. Today, only one farmhouse remains that predates the park, and it has been moved twice. The house was for many years the residence of Owen and Dolly Pope, who managed Disneyland's pony farm. In 1951, when he was just beginning to think seriously about building an amusement park, Walt installed the Popes in a trailer on the grounds of the studio in Burbank. Once the construction of Disneyland got underway, they were given a choice of the houses that were being removed from the Anaheim property. The one they selected was moved to the site of the pony farm, later renamed the Circle D Corral. The Popes lived in the house until early 1971, when they moved to Orlando to supervise the building of the Tri-Circle-D Ranch there. In 2016, the Pope House had to be moved for a second time to make way for Star Wars Land. The house is now located in the visitor parking lot of the Team Disney building.

FOUR
Building Disneyland

In the fall of 1953, Disneyland's opening day was less than two years away. Ground had not yet been broken on the 160 acres that Walt Disney had purchased in Anaheim, but the process of designing the park had begun. The first question had been who would design it. In January 1952, when the park was still going to be in Burbank, Walt paid Los Angeles architects Roy Pereira and Charles Luckman $3000 to create a master plan, but neither he nor they were happy with the work, in part because the site was too small to contain all of Walt's ideas and in part because, as the Stanford Research Institute's Buzz Price recalled, Walt had "a hard time articulating his ideas in architectural terms so he could have a dialogue with guys like that."[1] Walt turned to another architect, his friend Welton Becket, who advised him, "No one can design Disneyland for you. You have to do it yourself."

If he was going to build Disneyland himself, Walt needed a team of designers and engineers that was completely under his control. Because Roy would not allow him to use the studio's resources, in December 1952 he established a new company called Walt Disney Enterprises and appointed himself president. But Roy was concerned that Disney stockholders would be confused by the similarity of the name to Walt Disney Productions. Walt agreed to change the new company's name to Walt Disney, Incorporated, but Roy still feared that there would be confusion, and so he asked Walt to eliminate the name Disney altogether. So Walt changed the name for a second time, to WED (for Walter Elias Disney) Enterprises. Walt owned a third of WED himself, while the other two-thirds were owned by his daughters Diane and Sharon.[2] Walt Disney Productions then agreed to

---

1   Pereira and Luckman did contribute one key idea to Disneyland. They told Walt that his amusement park should have only one entrance, because that way he could better control the way that guests experienced it.

2   Although the idea to protect Walt's name had come from Roy, Walt's brother was not entirely happy about the direction in which Walt took WED. He felt that Walt had used it as an opportunity to benefit his own family at the expense of Roy's, and that Walt was attempting to separate himself from the studio.

license Walt's name for forty years and to employ Walt on a personal services contract.

Walt quickly recruited a team of animators, artists, and other creative types, both from within the studio and outside of it, and installed them in a ramshackle bungalow on the studio grounds. Initially, it was unclear what WED's primary focus would be. The television networks had long been pursuing Walt to produce a weekly series, and he saw this as an opportunity to generate revenue that could be used to fund Disneyland. Walt had acquired the rights to Johnston McCulley's *Zorro* stories about a dashing Spanish nobleman turned outlaw, and he assigned a team of writers to develop scripts for individual episodes. But when the networks proved to be far more interested in obtaining the rights to Disney's animation library, Walt abandoned the idea. *Zorro*, in any event, had always been a temporary expedient; what Walt really wanted WED to do was design his amusement park. One day in 1953, Walt came in and told the WED team, "Let's put *Zorro* on hold and get started on the park."

WED employees began traveling the country, visiting amusement parks, museums, and historical attractions. They brought the ideas they gleaned back to the bungalow, where they wrote them down on squares of paper that were tacked onto a board, much like storyboarding a film. Walt was engaged in every aspect of the planning process, much as he had been engaged in every aspect of producing the studio's early animated shorts and *Snow White*. He saw WED as much more than a business arrangement. For him, it represented an opportunity to return to the old days when the studio had been smaller and more fun and creative. He referred to WED as "my backyard laboratory, my workshop away from work."

Now that Disneyland had expanded beyond the small Burbank site, Harper Goff's drawings from 1951, which featured only a Main Street, a Western town, and a few midway rides, were clearly inadequate. In March 1953, Walt Disney hired Marvin Davis, an art director from 20th Century Fox, to produce a new series of drawings. At this point, however, Walt had not yet purchased the Anaheim property, and so Davis's initial drawings were not based on that site. It was not until August 1953, a month before the land purchase was finalized, that Davis began to assume that the park would be built in Anaheim. Only then did the drawings of Disneyland begin to assume the distinctive heart shape that we know so well today.

There was one big problem, however: Walt did not have the money that he needed to build the park. He had already spent $1 million purchasing the land, and he estimated that he would require $5 million more to build the park. There was no way that the studio could provide this amount of money: in 1953, its net annual profit was only $500,000. To raise millions of dollars, Walt needed Roy's help. Fortunately, Roy's attitude toward the idea of an amusement park had finally softened. When he learned that Walt had cashed in a $250,000 life-insurance policy and taken out several personal loans in order to come up with $100,000 to get the plans for Disneyland off the ground, he realized how important the park was to his brother. In the spring of 1953, Walt was discussing his frustrations with the Burbank City Council over their failure to approve the Riverside Drive site. Roy put an arm around Walt's shoulders, told him that the site was too small anyway, and said that if they were going to build an amusement park, they should "do it in a bigger way."

But doing it in a bigger way required more money. Initially, Walt and Roy tried to convince local backers. In the summer of 1953, they met with representatives of Charles "Doc" Strub, the builder and owner of the Santa Anita Park horse-racing track. Strub verbally agreed to put up half the money for Disneyland, with the other half to come from the studio, but then the negotiations hit several snags. First, Strub insisted that Disneyland be built near the ocean, but Walt, who thought that the "barefoot beach crowd" would bring an unsavory atmosphere to his park, objected. "I told him that was the one place where I would not build it," Walt recalled in an interview in 1965. Second, Walt was not eager to associate Disneyland with the gambling industry. And third, Strub insisted that his team, rather than Walt's, would operate Disneyland. When Walt made it clear that there was no way that he was going to give up control of his park, Strub told him, "Well, then I guess we don't have a deal."

So the Disney brothers had to come up with a new plan. With the local possibilities exhausted, they decided that Roy would go to New York to try and find the money. So that he would have something to show to potential investors, Walt put together a detailed prospectus describing Disneyland. But at the last minute, he realized that potential investors would need more than words; they needed a detailed visual image. On September 23, two days before Roy was scheduled to depart, Walt asked artist Herbert Ryman to meet him at the studio. Ryman did not even work for Disney at this point, as he had left the studio in the late 1940s to go to work for 20th Century Fox. He was now a freelance artist who did work for Fox and MGM. When the phone rang, he was surprised to hear Walt's voice on the line, as he had always thought Walt was mad at him for leaving Disney. But Walt simply asked him to come to the studio. When Ryman protested that it was Saturday, Walt replied, "It's my studio. I can work on Saturday." He refused to give Ryman any details about what he had in mind. Curious, Ryman drove the ten miles to Burbank. When he arrived, an unshaven Walt was waiting impatiently outside. Walt explained to him about Disneyland and told him that he was going to draw it, so that Roy would have something to show potential investors when he went to New York on Monday. Ryman protested that he could not produce something so quickly, but Walt, his eyes teary, pleaded with him. "Herbie, this is my dream," he told him. "I've wanted this for years, and I need your help. You're the only one who can do it." Working almost continuously for thirty-six hours, Ryman produced the first detailed rendering of Disneyland. It was completed late Sunday night, only a few hours before Roy was scheduled to leave.

Image 4.1: The first detailed rendering of Disneyland, drawn by Herb Ryman in September 1953 for the prospectus that Roy Disney took to New York to show potential backers.

The text of the prospectus described Disneyland as "something of a fair, an exhibition, a playground, a community center, a museum of living facts and a showplace of beauty and magic… Like Alice stepping through the Looking Glass, to step through the portals of Disneyland will be like entering another world." Main Street, with its "nostalgic quality that makes it everybody's hometown," led to a central hub, behind which was a castle, with medieval-style turreted walls partially surrounding "Fantasy Land," which contained rides based on *Snow White and the Seven Dwarfs*, *Alice in Wonderland*, and *Peter Pan*. In "True-Life Adventureland" (the name derived from the True-Life nature documentaries that Disney had begun producing in the late 1940s), the main attraction was a Jungle-Cruise-like "Explorer's Boat with a native guide for a cruise down the River of Romance," which had "birds and animals living in their natural habitat" along its banks. To the right of the hub was the "Land of Tomorrow," though it was unclear what it would contain beyond "fascinating exhibits of the miracles of science and industry," to which guests would be "effortlessly" carried on a moving sidewalk.

These parts of the park bore some resemblance to what was ultimately built. Other areas, however, never made it off the drawing board. The first spoke to the left off of the hub was "Holiday Land," which was "a showcase of attractions that would change with the seasons." Behind Frontier Land was Treasure Island, a schizophrenic area that included a "pirate cove and buried treasure" along with broadcast facilities for *The Mickey Mouse Club* television show. Between Fantasy Land and the Land of Tomorrow was Lilliputian Land, "a miniature Americana village inhabited by mechanical people nine inches high," where guests would be able to snack on "miniature ice cream cones" and "the world's smallest hot dog on a tiny bun." Finally, a large section of the park was given over to Recreation Land, which contained picnic facilities that could be rented by school and community groups.

It was with this document in hand that Roy Disney headed to New York. There was little chance that banks would lend the money for such a risky venture, especially at a time when the studio was still over $3 million in debt, but Walt had another idea that might pay for the park: television, which is why his first assignment to the WED team had been to develop the *Zorro* series. In signing the original distribution contracts for his animated shorts in the 1930s, Walt had the foresight to retain the television rights to them, which meant that he had a rich library of material available for Disney-related programming. In 1950, he commissioned a report from the consulting firm C. J. LaRoche on the possibilities that television offered for the studio. Its optimistic conclusions convinced him to put together Disney's first television production, a Coca-Cola-sponsored special called *One Hour in Wonderland*, which, hosted by Walt himself, was broadcast on NBC on Christmas Day 1950. Intended primarily to promote the release of Disney's next animated feature, *Alice in Wonderland*, the show was extremely popular: over half of all households that owned televisions watched it. The following year, Disney broadcast a second Christmas special, *The Walt Disney Christmas Show*, on CBS, which enjoyed equally high ratings. The success of these two specials convinced Walt that television could be a source of major profits.

Roy's job was to convince one of the three major television networks to buy Walt's idea for a weekly series. He met first with the two most prestigious networks, CBS and NBC; the latter was interested, but the negotiations stalled because its president, David Sarnoff, was unwilling to purchase the 25 percent share in Disneyland that Roy required to be part of any deal. That left ABC, only two years old and with a mere fourteen stations, as compared to NBC's sixty-three and CBS's thirty. ABC was something of a joke; the comedian Milton Berle, the star of a popular show on NBC, cracked, "In case they drop the big bomb, go to ABC. They've never had a hit." To increase its stature, ABC was eager to form alliances with prominent Hollywood producers, and its owner Leonard Goldenson had been courting Walt Disney for years. Walt had previously resisted ABC's entreaties, but now he was desperate to find the money to build Disneyland. After several months of negotiations, Disney and ABC signed a contract on April 2, 1954. The deal shocked many people in Hollywood. In the early 1950s, film studios saw television as an enemy that was going to steal their audiences, and theater chains threatened to boycott studios that produced content for it. But Walt saw television as symbiotic rather than parasitic to the film industry, and in any event he was desperate. ABC agreed to contribute $500,000 to the building of Disneyland and to guarantee additional loans of $4.5 million, which would allow Roy to borrow the rest of the cash that Walt needed.[3] In return, Disney would provide twenty-one annual episodes of a weekly television program called *Disneyland* for a period of three years, for which ABC would pay $50,000 each in the first year, $60,000 in the second, and $70,000 in the third. ABC had the option to renew the contract for an additional seven years, with the price per episode to be negotiated. There was also a mutual option for two more television shows, which turned out to be *The Mickey Mouse Club*, which ran from 1955 to 1959, and *Zorro*, which ran from 1957 to 1959. This was a major jolt to the studio, which would now have to produce more content in a week than it had been producing in a year, at the same time as many of its employees would be cannibalized by WED to design and build Disneyland. In return for its investment, ABC would own 34.485 percent of Disneyland, and it would receive all of the profits from the park's food concessions for its first ten years of operation.[4] Walt Disney Productions, which had contributed $500,000 to the park's cost, owned 34.48 percent of the park. Walt, who had managed to scrape together $250,000 by selling his house in Palm Springs, owned 16.55 percent. Finally, Western Publishing, the publisher of Disney books, contributed $200,000 and owned 13.8 percent.

Even after signing the contract with ABC, however, Walt did not have all of the money that he needed. Disneyland's construction costs rapidly ballooned from the original estimate of $5 million to $15 million. (They would finally top out at $17 million.) Disneyland's vice-president and

---

3   Even with ABC guaranteeing the loans, no bank in New York or Los Angeles would back Disneyland. Goldensen turned to a Texas banker and theater-owner named Karl Hoblitzelle, who owed him a favor. Hoblitzelle extended Disneyland, Inc., a $4.5 million line of credit.

4   From today's perspective, the deal appears to have been very much in ABC's favor. Goldenson remembered Roy as "a very good businessman" who "bargained for the last cent." Crucially, Roy negotiated an option for Disney to purchase ABC's shares within seven years, which it exercised for $7.5 million after Disneyland proved immensely profitable. The studio also acquired Walt and Western Publishing's shares, and by 1960 the park was entirely owned by Walt Disney Productions.

general manager, Commodore Vanderbilt "C.V." Wood, whom Walt had hired away from Stanford Research, identified two ways to attract additional funding.[5] First, large corporations were targeted as sponsors for particular attractions. Second, food, beverage, and retail companies were offered opportunities to lease concession space in the park. Walt did not like the idea of allowing outside vendors into Disneyland, but he had to get more money from somewhere. In early July, he sent letters to companies that already had a relationship with Disney or whose presidents he knew personally. In his letter to Joyce Hall, the president of Hallmark Greeting Cards, Walt wrote that Disneyland was "going to be one Hell of a show!... I definitely feel you will want a spot somewhere in the setup."

The initial response to Walt's solicitations was underwhelming: not a single company signed up. So Walt put Wood in charge of making the pitches, and the results improved dramatically. The original attraction sponsors were the Atchison, Topeka and Santa Fe Railway (which paid $50,000 annually to sponsor the Santa Fe & Disneyland Railway); Richfield Oil ($45,000 for Autopia); TWA ($45,000 for Rocket to the Moon); Kaiser Aluminum ($37,500 for the Hall of Aluminum); Monsanto ($30,000 for the Hall of Chemistry); and the National Lead Company ($9000 for the Dutch Boy Paints Color Gallery). Swift Meats, the first food company to sign on, paid $110,000 a year to lease a restaurant on Main Street. Other food concessionaires included Maxwell House Coffee, Carnation, Aunt Jemima Pancakes, Chicken of the Sea Tuna, Frito-Lay, and both Coca-Cola and Pepsi. Retail vendors included Eastman Kodak, Bluebird Children's Shoes, Upjohn Pharmacies, Sunnyview Farms Jams and Jellies, Gibson Greeting Cards, and Wurlitzer Organs; they generally paid $20 per square foot for their leased space, with payment for the first and fifth years due upon signing. They also had to pay Disney to design the interiors of their shops. There was even the Hollywood Maxwell Intimate Apparel Shop, which not only sold ladies' lingerie but also featured a show hosted by the Wonderful Wizard of Bras, an androgynous mannequin on a revolving stage who explained the history of underwear via a tape-recorded voice.[6]

Through these sponsorships and concessions, Walt was able to accumulate another $2.3 million. But this still left him with only around half of the total amount of money that he needed to finish Disneyland. Where was the remainder going to come from? The studio was an obvious source, as it

---

5   Some sources claim that Wood's first name was Cornelius. Wood did not like his given names and always insisted on being referred to as C.V. or Woody.

6   The Hollywood Maxwell shop lasted only until December 1956; as Pete Clark from the Disneyland merchandising department observed, "Nobody comes to Disneyland to look at corsets."

was now back on a firm financial footing. Released in 1953, the animated feature *Peter Pan* was an enormous hit, racking up box-office receipts in excess of $40 million. A big chunk of these profits, however, was plowed back into *20,000 Leagues Under the Sea*, Disney's most expensive live-action film to date. Production, which began in the spring of 1954, took place on specially built soundstages at the Disney studio and on location in Jamaica and the Bahamas. *20,000 Leagues* contained action sequences so complex that they required a crew of over 400 people. The most famous scene, in which a giant squid attacks the *Nautilus* submarine, was originally filmed in daylight and in a calm sea, which meant that the cables used to move the squid were clearly visible. After Walt complained that it looked like a scene from a Keystone Cops movie, it was reshot at night and in a storm, a change that cost $250,000. The decision to film *20,000 Leagues* in the new CinemaScope widescreen format drove up costs even further; the film ended up costing a whopping $4.2 million. The studio was forced to borrow $2 million on top of its other debts to finish the film and the animated feature that was currently in production, *Lady and the Tramp*. Although both films ultimately became huge hits, while they were being made their high costs were very worrying to the Disney studio.

With the studio reluctant to incur another major financial risk, Walt was not going to get the additional cash he needed from it. Once again, television came to the rescue, though this time it was more luck than planning that did the trick. In the 1940s, when wartime patriotism was running high, Walt had conceived an animated anthology about American heroes, among whom would be featured the frontiersman Davy Crockett. Now, as the writers of the *Disneyland* television show scrambled for material to fill twenty hours of annual programming, they returned to the Crockett idea as the basis for three of the "Frontierland" episodes. A lanky, unknown actor named Fess Parker was hired to play Crockett, and the episodes were shot on location in Tennessee. When the producers returned to the studio and began editing the footage, however, they discovered that they were a few minutes short of the hour that each episode needed to fill. Walt, who had not liked the original storyboards for the show, suggested that a song would help to liven it up. Studio composer George Burns was quickly summoned to write a theme song, "The Ballad of Davy Crockett," which Parker sang himself.

The first of the three episodes, "Davy Crockett: Indian Fighter." was broadcast on December 15, 1954, with two more—"Davy Crockett Goes to Congress" and "Davy Crockett at the Alamo"—following in January and February 1955. They were massively popular, attracting audiences of forty million people, or a quarter of the American population at the time. The episodes themselves did not generate any profits for Disney; in fact, they lost money, as Disney received only $50,000 per broadcast from ABC for the show, whereas the Davy Crockett episodes cost around $250,000 each. But the studio reaped enormous profits from merchandising. Over $300 million worth of Crockett-related items, including ten million replicas of the coonskin cap that Parker wore on the show, were sold before the craze petered out in late 1955. Many of the items were not licensed by Disney, but many of them were, and Disney made as much as $30 million on Crockett merchandise. To be sure, much of that money did not flow in until after Disneyland was finished, but in the final months of construction Walt could be more confident that he was not going to bankrupt the studio.

By mid-1954, the planning for Disneyland had ratcheted up significantly. Bringing in more artists and animators from the studio, Walt had gradually expanded the WED team in both size and professional diversity. They designed attractions as if they were making films, outlining them on storyboards first. Walt was involved in every detail; just as he had done with Disney's early cartoons and animated features, he would act out what he wanted. Not everything at Disneyland would be built by WED, however. Walt knew that he had to find an amusement-ride company that could build some of the components of Disneyland's attractions. Most such companies built cheap and tacky attractions for small-scale carnivals and fairs, but WED's Dick Irvine was impressed by a steamboat that had been built by Arrow Development,

Image 4.2: One of the most unusual manifestations of the Davy Crockett craze of the mid-1950s were the M-28 and M-29 Davy Crockett tactical nuclear recoilless gun. Built to fire an M-388 nuclear projectile, it was developed for use against Soviet or North Korean troops in the event of war in Europe or on the Korean peninsula. Production began in 1956, and it remained in service until 1968.

which was based in San Francisco. When Walt flew up to meet with Arrow's management, a Model-T-type car caught his eye. The car was similar to the ride vehicles that he had envisioned for a dark ride based on the "Mr. Toad" half of the 1949 animated film *The Adventures of Ichabod and Mr. Toad*. He asked the Arrow designers if they could improve on the car, and they agreed to build a prototype for what would become Mr. Toad's Wild Ride. Walt was very pleased with the work, and Arrow was then commissioned to build a circus train based on the one from the film *Dumbo*. In total, Arrow would design key parts of six of Disneyland's opening-day attractions, and the company would continue to design and develop ride systems for Disney into the early 1970s.

At the same time, Walt and the WED team tried to learn everything they could about the amusement-park business. Walt commissioned Stanford Research to carry out a study of amusement-park operations. Buzz Price and C.V. Wood visited ten parks around the country (and made a trip to Walt's beloved Tivoli Gardens in Copenhagen). They concluded that the management of such enterprises was a delicate business. The operator had to have enough attractions so that lines were not so long that guests got fed up and left, but not so many that there were no lines, as people would perceive an attraction that had no line as unpopular and would not buy tickets for it. After SRI had completed its report, Walt invited seven prominent amusement-park operators to Burbank so that he could present his plans for Disneyland to them. They were uniformly unenthusiastic: they told him that he was spending too much on things like the castle and attractive landscaping that would not bring in any money.

Ground was broken for Disneyland on July 12, 1954. With opening day only a year away, construction had to proceed swiftly. The builders were forced to lay out foundations and frame buildings before the architects had finished designing all of their details. Toward the end of 1954, Walt hired the former rear admiral Joseph Fowler to serve as Disneyland's construction manager. After retiring from the navy, Fowler had been engaged in building tract houses in the Bay Area near San Francisco. He was dismayed when he realized the true state of things: of the twenty attractions planned for opening day, only six were likely to be finished in time, while eleven were doubtful and three were hopelessly behind schedule. The designs for Main Street and Fantasyland were mostly complete, but those for the rest of the park were little more than rough sketches of empty buildings.

Image 4.3: (*Opposite, top*) Taken on June 4, 1955, only six weeks before the opening of Disneyland, this image shows Harbor Boulevard in Anaheim. The still-under-construction park can be seen on the right; the barren bank adjacent to the road has recently been planted with young trees.

Problems continued to pop up. The first attempt to fill the Rivers of America failed when the water seeped away in the sandy soil, and so a mixture of clay and cement was used to seal the ground. But it could not be fully tested until right before opening, and so it was unclear if the solution would work. The Orange County plant that had contracted to supply the asphalt went on strike, and so the asphalt had to be hauled in from San Diego instead. When the track and sets for Mr. Toad's Wild Ride were transferred from WED headquarters in Burbank to Disneyland, they did not fit in the show building, and so the building had to be expanded to accommodate them. When a color-blind bulldozer operator failed to realize that different-colored tags had been tied to the existing trees, indicating which ones should be kept and which ones removed, he removed all of them.[7] Increasingly frustrated, Walt kept asking his WED team if the site would ever look like "something other than a hole in the ground." He had been visiting the construction site nearly every Saturday, but now he stepped up the frequency of appearances to many weekdays as well. Fearing that his critics would be proven right and his Disneyland would turn out to be a colossal failure, he oscillated between irritation and despair. One day, he and Harper Goff climbed up to the top of rickety observation tower that overlooked the site. As he gazed out at the bare dirt, he told Goff despondently, "I have half the money spent, and nothing to show for it."

But Walt's team kept working to get Disneyland built. Given only a modest budget, head landscaper Bill Evans resorted to a variety of creative strategies. He was so desperate for mature trees that he would drive up to Pasadena, which was famous for its tree-lined streets, and offer homeowners up to $200 for a specimen. He also obtained trees for $25 each from CalTrans, which was clearing the rights-of-way for the numerous freeways that were being built in and around Los Angeles at the time.

---

7   This last story might have been exaggerated over time, but it does appear that an overzealous construction worker removed at the very least a significant portion of the trees that were supposed to be retained for the Jungle Cruise's landscaping.

He found a perfect banyan tree in Beverly Hills and was delighted to find out that the homeowner was thinking of chopping it down anyway. He transported the banyan to Adventureland, where it was installed at the back of the hippo pool for the Jungle Cruise.[8] Also on the Jungle Cruise, Evans left some of Anaheim's orange trees in place and covered them with vines, while other orange trees turned upside-down in the water so that their roots resembled mangroves.[9] Elsewhere in the park, areas filled with weeds were heavily watered in the weeks prior to opening in order to ensure that at least the bare dirt was covered. The landscapers then put Latin signs on the weeds to fool guests into thinking they were exotic plantings. If all else failed, Evans simply spray-painted the brown dirt green. The Fantasyland attraction called the Canal Boats of the World had originally been supposed to float past miniature landmarks from around the world, but Walt changed his mind at the last minute. So for the first two months of Disneyland's operation, the canal boats had no theme, and no landscaping, at all; the WED team nicknamed it the Mud Bank Ride because of the barren slopes that the boats floated past.

Right up to the last minute, plans continued to change. Because construction had fallen so far behind schedule, in late 1954 Walt had agreed to delay the opening of Tomorrowland, which would now be treated as an "expansion area" that would not welcome its first guests until 1956. But in January of 1955, only six months before the park was scheduled to open, he suddenly changed his mind. A construction crew was rushed in and paid overtime on a weekend to begin preparing the land, as the WED team frantically tried to come up with ideas for attractions that could be built quickly. Some had to be discarded as unfeasible, such as a display of dinosaurs on a rotating turntable and a dark ride in which guests would visit Mars while riding in vehicles designed to make them feel like they were wearing space helmets.

The final stages of construction were beset by labor conflicts. The Inland Boatmans' Union declared that the cast members who piloted the *Mark Twain* riverboat had to be members, and the American Guild of Variety Artists made the same claim about the guides for the Jungle Cruise, whom they asserted were performers rather than mere ride operators. When the studio's artists painted the Casey Jr. Circus Train before dispatching it to Anaheim, Disneyland's union painters stripped the paint off and repainted it. Right before opening day, the plumbers went on strike, forcing Walt to

---

8   It's still there today; in fact, most of the bigger trees in Adventureland are originals planted by Evans.

9   In the early years, the park's horticultural team had to go out in the morning and pick oranges off the trees to prevent guests from realizing what they were.

make a choice between enough water fountains for his guests and bathrooms. (Observing that "people can buy Pepsi-Cola, but they can't pee in the street," he chose the latter, and hired a non-union company to install temporary bathrooms.)

There was a huge rush to get everything done in time for the July opening, or at least enough things to prevent a complete embarrassment. "It was frantic, frantic work," recalled Herb Ryman. As late as early June, Sleeping Beauty Castle was not finished, and many of the mechanical animals had not been installed in the Jungle Cruise. The worst problems were in Tomorrowland, where plans were in flux until the last possible minute: a moving sidewalk remained in the plans until early June, a mere six weeks before opening day. Walt was forced to pay hundreds of construction workers massive amounts of overtime; many of them made over $1000 a week in the final month, at a time when the average American worker earned less than $100 per week. Disney owed so many local businesses so much money that some began demanding payment in cash, and both Walt and Wood secured last-minute personal loans to pay for the park's completion. Things were so desperate that Wood wanted to delay the opening from July until September, but Fowler knew that the loss of revenue from the busy summer season could be catastrophic, and so they continued to work toward the original date.

Walt oversaw every aspect of Disneyland's construction. Nearly every day, he walked the park, notepad in hand, scribbling ideas for improvements. He ordered the buildings on Main Street to be repainted and embellished with additional gingerbread trim. He demanded that smaller rocks, more appropriate to the five-eighths scale of the trains, be used for the track ballast of the railroad. When the bandstand, which had been a central feature of Main Street, U.S.A. from its earliest conceptions, was installed in front of the train station, Walt decided that there was something "damned wrong" about its placement, because it blocked the view of the station from the castle. So in May 1955, two months before opening, it was moved to the other end of Main Street. And all the while, Walt continued to worry. Harper Goff recalled that, a few months before opening day, Walt cried as he complained that "there isn't one thing you'd call terrific out there right now." Animator Frank Thomas sensed that Walt was less-than-confident that Disneyland would be a success, though he tried to conceal it. "I don't think that he was that sure of himself on a lot of his decisions at that point," Thomas claimed. But as the park got closer to completion, he was the happiest that he had been since the studio was working on Snow White in the mid-1930s. When a new attraction was completed, he'd be the first to ride it, "just like a little kid," recalled Marvin Davis.

On July 13, four days before Disneyland was scheduled to open, Walt hosted a party at the park for friends, relatives, and celebrities to celebrate both the park's completion and his thirtieth wedding anniversary. The guests, who included Cary Grant, Spencer Tracy, and Gary Cooper, rode the train and the *Mark Twain* riverboat prior to attending a party in the Golden Horseshoe Saloon. Slightly tipsy, Walt climbed down from an opera box and fired imaginary pistols from the stage. His daughter Diane recalled that as she drove him home, an ecstatically happy Walt sat in the backseat "tootling" in her ear through a rolled-up map of Disneyland until he fell asleep.

But his excitement continued to do battle with anxiety. The day before opening, it was discovered that the projection system for the Rocket to the Moon was not working, which would prevent it from being ready in time. A crew was struggling to prevent a 900-pound elephant that had just been installed in the Jungle Cruise from sinking into the mud. The Fantasyland dark rides were temporarily disabled when the power cable was accidentally disconnected. Well after midnight, Walt retired for the night in his apartment above the fire station on Main Street. He was alone: he had told his wife and daughters to stay home, so afraid was he that Disneyland would be a humiliating failure.

On July 17, 1955, Disneyland opened to invited guests, with the opening for the general public to take place the following day. The day was so chaotic that Walt referred to it afterwards as Black Sunday; Imagineer Rolly Crump recalled that it was "just a friggin' nightmare." Over the preceding weeks, construction crews had been working around the clock to get things done, and it was not clear until the last minute what would be running on opening day and what would not. The Harbor Boulevard off-ramp of the Santa Ana Freeway had been completed a mere two days earlier, and only then after C.V. Wood begged the contractors to put in overtime to get it done in time, telling them that "without that off-ramp, traffic will be backed up to San Francisco!" Wood knew this because, for months, thousands of people had been driving to Anaheim on the weekends to see the Disneyland construction site, causing traffic jams on local streets. Even with the ramp open, the freeway backed up seven miles, and every surface in Anaheim was choked with cars. When Roy Disney arrived, a parking-lot attendant frantically informed him that children, desperate from being stuck in their cars for so long, were peeing in the parking lot. Roy was so happy to see a big crowd and to sense their excitement at being at Disneyland that he simply laughed and said, "God bless 'em, let 'em pee!"

Wood had distributed 15,000 tickets, Disneyland's estimated capacity at the time, but thousands more counterfeit tickets were printed. In addition, an enterprising local citizen leaned a ladder against the fence and charged $5 for people to climb over. At least 28,000 people managed to get in. This is not a large number by today's standards—current capacity is 75,000—but the small number of rides that were operating on opening day were quickly overwhelmed. Hundreds more guests crowded outside the gates, hoping to catch a glimpse of the many celebrities who were in attendance. To make matters worse, it was a very hot day—over 100 degrees Fahrenheit—and women's high heels became embedded in the sticky new asphalt, some of which had been poured early that morning. Lines both for attractions and food were enormously long; Disney employee Harry Tytle recalled that his family could not "get near any rides, nor places to eat." Impatient guests climbed fences and commandeered ride vehicles for themselves. The crowds made it extremely difficult for the presenters of ABC's live television special to get around the park; the actor and future president Ronald Reagan had to scale an eight-foot-high fence in Frontierland to make his cue. Because no one had as yet assessed the boat's maximum capacity, an overloaded *Mark Twain* got stuck on its guide rail in the Rivers of America. Guests had to remove their shoes, roll up their trousers, and disembark in two feet of water. The Jungle Cruise was the only ride that did not break down at some point in the day, but only two of its seven boats were operating. The Canal Boats of the World floated past bare slopes that had not yet been landscaped, and the cars on the Snow White Adventure kept derailing. Tomorrowland ended abruptly in a dirt field. Someone forgot to lock the doors leading to the interior of Sleeping Beauty Castle, and guests wandered in and climbed ladders up to second story, which was an unreinforced plywood floor that had been laid over the ceiling joists. "Get them out before they kill themselves!" a frantic C.V. Wood demanded.

The reviews in the press were terrible, but somehow, Disneyland survived. Even through the chaos, heat, and frustration, the sense of excitement and fun made it apparent that Disneyland was going to be a hit. In its first month of operation, the park attracted 20,000 visitors a day; 3.6 million guests passed through the turnstiles in the first year, and 4 million in the second. By the late 1950s, Disneyland was more popular than the Grand Canyon. And not only were there more guests than anticipated, but they spent more money as well. Buzz Price had estimated that the guests would spend $3 each per day, but they actually spent $5. Cash poured into Disney's accounts on a scale that the studio had not enjoyed since *Snow White*. In 1954, the studio's gross revenues had totaled $11 million, but in 1955, they more than doubled to $25 million.

Today's Disneyland would be both familiar and unfamiliar to Walt Disney, and his would be both familiar and unfamiliar to us. Just as they do today, guests entered via Main Street, U.S.A. It is commonly assumed that Main Street was based on Walt's nostalgic memories of Marceline, Missouri, where he lived between 1906 and 1911, but in reality its sources of inspiration were diverse. Harper Goff, who created the first detailed drawings of Main Street in the early 1950s, based them not on Marceline but on his hometown of Fort Collins, Colorado, which had the turn-of-the-century look that he wanted. When Marvin Davis made his drawings in 1953, he did not base Main Street on any real place, but rather used his training as an architect to give the buildings a Victorian look. Many other artists had a hand in designing Main Street as well; using examples that were located all over the country, they derived specific design elements from reference books on late nineteenth- and early twentieth-century architecture. In the end, the biggest influence on it was not a town in distant Missouri or Colorado, but rather a place that was much closer: Los Angeles. Main Street was first and foremost the idealized vision of America that southern California had long specialized in inventing.

A key feature of Main Street was the train station at the southern end. A railroad running around the perimeter of the park was a constant in all Disneyland designs. Both of the original 5/8th-scale engines of the Santa Fe & Disneyland Railroad were built from scratch in the Disney shop, at a cost of $40,000 each, while the cars and track cost an additional $160,000. In Disneyland's early years, two different trains departed from two different stations. The Main Street Station was the home of a passenger train that was pulled by an engine named the *E.P. Ripley*, named for the president of the ride's sponsor, the Atchison, Topeka and Santa Fe Railroad, from 1896 to 1920. The passenger train had four enclosed coaches: the Navajo Chief, the Rocky Mountains, the Land of Pueblos, and the Painted Desert, along with a fifth "observation car," the Grand Canyon, which had an open platform at the rear. From the Frontierland Station, a freight train was pulled by the *C.K. Holliday*, named for the founder of the Atchison, Topeka and Santa Fe in 1859. Meant to fit in with Frontierland's rustic look, it featured three cattle cars, two open gondola cars, and a caboose.

Both trains went all the way around the track without stopping at the other station, and so they were purely rides rather than modes of transportation from one part of the park to the other. There was only a single track, with sidings in the stations that made it possible for them to pass each other. The passenger train proved to be far more popular than the freight train: in Disneyland's first week of operation, 48,000 passengers rode the former, whereas only 9000 rode the latter. This was for two reasons. First, people entered the park underneath the Main Street Station, and many of them decided to get on the train right away. Second, the passenger coaches were much more comfortable than the cattle cars, which guests complained made them feel like livestock. To draw more passengers to the freight train, Walt Disney considered developing a Wild West show that guests would watch while the train was stopped on a siding, but this never happened.

Image 4.4: A cattle car and gondola of the Santa Fe & Disneyland Railroad's freight train, which departed from the Frontierland Station. Guests found both options uncomfortable, and vastly preferred to ride the passenger train, which departed from the Main Street Station. The trains ran independently until 1958, when a third train was added to the line and two new stations opened in Fantasyland and Tomorowland.

The railroad provides insight into Disneyland's complex financial arrangements in its early years. Originally, the highest level in the standard eight-ticket book was a C-ticket, which cost thirty cents. The railroad, however, was ticketed separately, and cost fifty cents for an adult and thirty-five cents for a child. This was because it was not actually owned by Disneyland, but by WED. (This was also true of the Main Street vehicles, and later of the monorail and the Viewliner.) WED paid Disneyland 20 percent of its gross receipts in return for the right of way around the park. This meant that the railroad employees were on Walt's payroll rather than Disneyland's.[10]

10   When WED was acquired by Walt Disney Productions in 1965, Walt retained ownership of some of WED's assets, including the railroad and the monorail, via a new company called Retlaw (Walter spelled backwards). It was not until 1982, when Disney purchased Retlaw for 818,000 shares of company stock, that the railroad and monorail ceased to be owned by Walt's family.

What was originally called True-Life Adventureland was supposed to be on the opposite side of the hub, where Tomorrowland is now. It was moved because landscape designer Bill Evans wanted to use the large eucalyptus trees that existed on the west side of the park for the dense vegetation required for the Jungle Cruise. (The trees had been planted by a citrus farmer in order to serve as a windbreak for his orange trees.) This section of the park was linked to the *True-Life Adventure* nature documentaries that Disney had begun producing in the late 1940s. Fourteen *True-Life Adventure* films were produced before the series ended in 1960; five of them won Academy Awards.

Until the Swiss Family Treehouse opened in 1962, the Jungle Cruise was Adventureland's only attraction. Disneyland's most popular ride in the early days, it covered three of Adventureland's four acres. Designed by Harper Goff, the Jungle Cruise was inspired not only by the *True-Life Adventure* films, but also the film *The African Queen* (1951), starring Katherine Hepburn and Humphrey Bogart. Although the basic concept remained consistent throughout the design process, many specific aspects of the ride changed. Because he thought that engines would be noisy, smelly, and prone to catching on fire, Walt originally wanted the boats to be pushed along by the current, as they are in It's a Small World and Pirates of the Caribbean. It would have taken the boats too long to complete the circuit, however, and so forty-horsepower natural-gas-powered engines were used instead. Walt also wanted the riverbanks to be filled with live animals, but this idea was scrapped when the attraction's designers realized that they would be most frequently seen sleeping. Mechanical animals were installed instead, divided into three categories: motionless figures, stationary figures that moved only one part such as a tail, and showcase figures that performed more complex movements. Although their movements seem primitive now, they represented state-of-the-art animatronics in 1955. There was one attempt to introduce live animals, in the form of a tank of live baby alligators at the entrance, but after one escaped, the display was swiftly dismantled. Originally, the Jungle Cruise had a serious and educational tone; it was not until the early 1960s that the narration took on the humorous aspect that it has today.

Next to Adventureland was Frontierland, which at twenty acres was five times larger than its neighbor. Its geographical references were equally vast: Frontierland covered the entire western United States, ranging from the paddlewheel steamers of the Mississippi to the desert landscapes of the Southwest. Walt Disney intended Frontierland to look like the conception of a Western town that Americans had gleaned from the movies, rather than a real place; in contrast to Main Street, U.S.A., no one has ever argued for a real-life antecedent for Frontierland, because there is none. The Golden

Horseshoe, for example, was copied by Harper Goff from the set designs he had previously produced for the Warner Brothers film *Calamity Jane* (1953); according to some sources, Goff even used the same blueprints.

The *Mark Twain* riverboat was a perfect example of how some parts of Disneyland, despite budgetary pressures, were built to lavish standards. Like the railroad, a paddlewheel steamer was part of the earliest Disneyland designs, dating back to the small park across the street from the Burbank studio. But even though it only plied the shallow, placid waters of the River of America along a guiderail, the *Mark Twain* was built according to the standards of the American Bureau of Shipping. Its steel hull was built by the Todd Pacific Shipyards in San Pedro, while the wooden superstructure and steam engines were built by WED in Burbank, with some details finished in the temporary mill shop in the Opera House on Main Street. Because no paddlewheel steamer had been built in the United States for over half a century, the Disney team had to carry out extensive research on how to go about it. They designed the *Mark Twain* to look as if it was from the 1870s, though it was built to only five-eighths scale because a full-sized boat would have been too large for Disneyland's limited space. Featuring a high level of detail and top-quality materials, it cost $250,000. When funds ran low, Walt Disney paid for the boat's completion out of his own pocket. In the early days, passengers could buy non-alcoholic mint juleps, listen to Dixieland jazz, and watch card sharps attempt to cheat each other.

The remainder of Frontierland was taken up by Indian Country and the Painted Desert. Located between the Golden Horseshoe and the train station, the Indian Village contained a variety of Native American dwellings, including tepees, wigwams, and lodging houses from the Pacific Northwest, as well as a trading post where guests could buy crafts. On weekends and holidays and during the busy summer season, the Indians performed ceremonial dances. Despite the somewhat exploitative nature of the attraction, Disney was sensitive to the differences among indigenous Americans, and employed Indian consultants to make sure that the different peoples were depicted accurately. The Painted Desert served as the backdrop for rides on a stagecoach, Conestoga wagon, or mule. All proved problematic to varying degrees. Pulled by miniature horses, the Rainbow Mountain Stagecoach was less than full-scale, but since the passengers were full-sized, it was prone to tipping over if the horses got excited, which happened frequently when they were spooked by the whistle of the train or riverboat. The Conestoga wagons, which were introduced in August 1955, also suffered from the unpredictable behavior of the two horses that pulled them. Both the stagecoach and the wagons had limited capacity for guests, and they were removed in 1959. The mules were more popular, but they too suffered from low capacity. The mules were roped together in a train of seven or eight with a trail boss in front, and only two teams could be on the trail at the same time. This meant that full capacity was only around fifteen guests at a time, so wait times were very long. But Walt Disney tolerated this, along with the mules' tendency to bite the guests, because he loved the element of authenticity they brought. The mules lasted until 1973.

Image 4.5: Walt Disney and his granddaughter Tammy Miller ride the pack mules at Disneyland in 1960.

Many people think of Fantasyland as the heart of Disneyland, but it was not necessarily treated as such in the planning and construction stages. With the lion's share of money and attention going to Main Street, U.S.A. and Frontierland, Fantasyland ended up being, apart from the castle, a bit of an afterthought. There was not enough money to create the fairy-tale-village or "storybook" look that Walt wanted, and so the buildings were basically industrial sheds dressed up as tents at a medieval joust. This meant that Disney's usually scrupulous attention to theming was abandoned, as the building façades did not correspond to the attractions inside. It was not until the early 1980s that Fantasyland was given a makeover that brought it into line with the original conception.

But even with its deficiencies, Fantasyland got the most spectacular entrance of any land, because the direct route to it from Main Street went through the castle. Though it was not present in the earliest plans, by late 1953 a castle at the center was a core element of Disneyland. It served two main functions. First, it was what Walt called a wienie, or a large visual icon that pulled guests toward it.[11] Second, the castle signaled a transition from the quasi-real world of Main Street to a fantasy world. It was in that sense figuratively as well as literally a gateway to Fantasyland, a magic portal at the end of Main Street that represented the culmination of the transition from the external world to the magical world of Disneyland. Because it was so important, the castle went through a number of design iterations. Models that were considered but discarded included Robin Hood's castle from the 1952 Disney live-action film starring Richard Todd and the castle from the 1950 animated feature *Cinderella*. Some elements were derived from the Chateau d'Ussé in the Loire region of northern France and from Bavaria's Castle Neuschwanstein, but Disneyland's castle was never intended to resemble an actual medieval building. In the end, *Sleeping Beauty*, which was in production at the time, was chosen for its name, though the physical resemblance to the castle in the film is only slight.

Fantasyland's attractions were a blend of outdoor amusement-park rides and indoor dark rides. Among the former was the King Arthur Carrousel.[12] Walt loved the carousel in Griffith Park that he had watched his daughters play on because it contained only horses, all in the most prized jumping position. He made inquiries to the carousel's owner, Ross Davis, about the possibility of finding a duplicate, but he was told that it was a one-of-a-kind piece. So Walt hired Davis to find a substitute. He located a carousel that had been built in 1922 by William Dentzel of Philadelphia. It was of the right vintage, but it was menagerie style, meaning that it had a variety of animals and chariots in which to ride. So Davis had to find enough jumpers to replace them with. He located some in a storage facility underneath the pier at Coney Island and more closer to home in Playland in San Mateo, California. Squeezed in beside the King Arthur Carousel was the Mad Tea Party spinning teacup ride, which took its theme from the "Unbirthday Party" scene in the 1951 Disney animated film *Alice in Wonderland*. The

---

11   He came up with the name "wienie" because when he came home late at night from the studio, he would often grab a hot dog out of the refrigerator. This would cause his beloved poodle, Lady, to follow him around.

12   For the carousels in Disneyland, the Magic Kingdom, Tokyo Disneyland, and Disneyland Paris, Disney chooses to use the original French spelling of the word "carrousel," with two R's. The carousels at California Adventure, Disney Springs, Tokyo DisneySea, and Hong Kong Disneyland spell their names with only one R.

closest thing that Disney had to a thrill ride on opening day, the Mad Tea Party was a variation on a classic amusement-park tilt-a-whirl.[13] Originally, there were no governors on the cups, and so guests could spin them as fast as they wished.

Also among the original Fantasyland rides were three dark rides, or indoor attractions in which guests ride in vehicles through a series of scenes. Originally invented in the late nineteenth century, dark rides were very old-fashioned by the 1950s, but Walt liked them because they could be used to tell a story. Disneyland's early dark rides cast the guest in the role of the lead character in the story, which caused confusion, as many guests did not understand why they did not see the character for whom the ride was named. Two of the three original dark rides at Disneyland, Snow White Adventures and Peter Pan Flight, were based on films that were well known.[14] The other, Mr. Toad's Wild Ride, was based on the more obscure *The Adventures of Ichabod and Mr. Toad* (1949), one of Disney's postwar "package" films. Originally intended to be truly "wild," it would have been the park's first roller coaster, but Walt was worried that it would scare young children and older guests, and so it was altered to a flat track along which the cars drove erratically.

Two Fantasyland rides that were supposed to operate on opening day but were not yet finished were, coincidentally, themed to the 1941 animated film *Dumbo*. The Casey Jr. Circus Train was delayed because when it was first tested, the engine threatened to tip over backwards as it pulled the cars up the 45 percent grade that the designers had included in the track layout. Lead weights were attached so that the train could run once for the *Dateline: Disneyland* opening-day live television broadcast, but then it was shut down for two weeks so that the grade could be reduced to 25 percent.

Image 4.6: (*Opposite, top*) The original Dumbo the Flying Elephant ride in Fantasyland, which was noticeably less ornate than the current version and which lacked its signature Timothy Mouse atop the central axis. Designed by Arrow Development, the ride had major operations issues resulting from problems with its hydraulic lift system, which meant that it opened a month after the rest of Disneyland. The original lift system, seen here, was replaced by the end of 1955. In this image, the elephants still have their hinged ears, though the motors that were supposed to make them flap had been removed in order to reduce the weight.

---

13   Featuring freely spinning cars on a spinning platform, tilt-a-whirls were invented in the 1920s. They rely on epicycles, or the movement of a small circle inside the circumference of a larger one, to generate centrifugal force.

14   These were the original names of the attractions. Snow White Adventures became Snow White's Scary Adventures when it was remodeled in 1983, and Peter Pan Flight became Peter Pan's Flight in 1982.

The second Fantasyland ride that proved problematic was Dumbo the Flying Elephant. *Dateline: Disneyland* shows the elephants parked at staggered elevations to make it appear as if the ride was working, but in reality it was not. There was a problem with the lift system, which had been designed by Arrow Development, the firm responsible for six of Disneyland's opening-day rides. Taking advice from a NASA engineer, Arrow had used a combination of oil and nitrogen to give extra power to the hydraulic system, but the jerky movements of the ride's arms produced a shaving-cream-like foam, rendering the lift mechanism inoperative. The foam had to be removed by an Arrow technician, a job that was jokingly referred to as "milking Dumbo." A second problem was with the elephants in which guests rode. Designed by the WED team, they were extremely detailed, right down to individual motors that made each ear flap separately. But this meant that they weighed 800 pounds each even before the guests boarded, too heavy for the lift arms. So in order to make the ride work, the elephants had to be made lighter, which was accomplished, sadly, by removing the ear motors. A new lift system was installed by the end of 1955.

Tomorrowland had been green-lighted only six months prior to opening. Walt was so desperate to fill the space that only two weeks before opening day, he decided to bring over some of the props from *20,000 Leagues Under the Sea* and put them on display. The highlight of the exhibit was the giant squid that had attacked the *Nautilus* submarine, but it needed to be repaired and repainted. The WED team stayed up all night before opening day to put a fresh coat of paint on it, and when Walt stopped by to see how the work was progressing he even pitched in and did some of the background painting himself. Much of the rest of Tomorrowland was turned over to corporate sponsors such as Kaiser Aluminum, Monsanto, Dutch Boy Paints, and Richfield Oil. Because Tomorrowland was built in a hurry, its attractions were more ephemeral than those of other lands. The Phantom Boats, which opened in August 1955, achieved the dubious distinction of being the first ride to be removed from Disneyland. Although their Batmobile-style tailfins were undeniably stylish, the boats were painfully slow and prone to overheating as frustrated guests pushed them to go faster. The Phantom Boats lasted less than a year.

Image 4.7: Tomorrowland in Disneyland's first decade. On the far left is the Circarama, which made its debut one day after opening and showed the film *A Tour of the West* on multiple screens in a circular theater. In the center is the Clock of the World, which told guests the time anywhere on earth. Immediately to its right is the Space Bar, a counter-service café that sold fast-food fare typical of Disneyland's early menus. Next to it is the Moonliner, the seventy-eight-foot-high original icon, or what Walt would have called a wienie, of Tomorrowland. Designed by Imagineer John Hench, it stood in front of the Rocket to the Moon attraction. (The original Moonliner was dismantled for the 1967 makeover of Tomorrowland. The current version that stands atop the Spirit of Refreshment is a two-thirds-scale replica that was installed when Tomorrowland underwent a second major renovation in the late 1990s.) On the far right is the Monsanto Hall of Chemistry, one of a number of corporate-sponsored attractions that filled space in the hastily conceived original Tomorrowland.

But if Tomorrowland was in some ways a slapdash combination of corporate displays and poorly conceived attractions, its very haphazardness made it a reflection of trends in American popular culture at the time that it was designed, as the WED team desperately cast about for ideas. In the mid-1950s, Americans were transfixed by the space race with the Soviet Union. Embracing the trend, Disney hired the eminent aerospace engineer

Wernher von Braun to serve as the consultant for three "Tomorrowland" episodes of the *Disneyland* television show titled "Man in Space" (1955), "Man and the Moon" (1955), and "Mars and Beyond" (1957). Massively popular, they became landmarks in promoting space exploration to the American public. It is thus not surprising that several of Tomorrowland's attractions were space-related. Space Station X-1 put guests in a room that rotated around a view of the United States from ninety miles above the earth. The first photographs from space had been taken by unmanned rockets in 1946, but they were not of sufficient quality, and so artists Claude Coats and Peter Ellenshaw created a painting that was based on them instead. After Sputnik was launched in 1957, the attraction was renamed Satellite View from Space, but this did little to increase its popularity, and it was shut down in 1960. Another space-themed ride was Rocket to the Moon, which opened on July 22, 1955. The ride offered a simulated trip into lunar orbit; guests sat in a round theater with screens in the floor and ceiling, with the earth receding in the former and the moon growing larger in the latter. As it re-entered the earth's atmosphere on the return journey, the spaceship encountered a meteor shower, causing sirens to blare and warning lamps to flash, but it ultimately managed to land safely. Considerably more exciting than Space Station X-1, Rocket to the Moon lasted much longer. In 1966, it evolved into the more elaborate Flight to the Moon, and then in 1975 into Mission to Mars, which lasted until 1992.

If Space Station X-1 and Rocket to the Moon reflected the growing American interest in outer space, Autopia, the only original ride that remains in Tomorrowland today, was closely connected to something much closer to home: the California freeways. A year after Disneyland opened, President Eisenhower signed legislation that led to the creation of a nationwide system of interstate highways. Autopia represented a future of traffic-free, rapidly moving automobile travel that the highways were supposed to create. Bob Gurr, who designed the fiberglass bodies of the cars, recalled that "we wanted more than a bumper car ride. We thought of it as a ride where kids could learn to drive the freeways of the future." Just like the real California freeways, however, the Disney version turned out to be not quite as idyllic as planned. The cars constantly overheated, as the WED team had not yet learned to design things in a way that could stand up to the heavy use they received in the park. There was originally no guiderail down the center of the roadway, and the guests delighted in crashing the cars into each other, resulting in numerous trips to first aid in the early months of operation. To convince Kaiser Aluminum to become one of Disneyland's original sponsors, Wood had promised that aluminum would be used throughout the park, including on the bumpers for the Autopa cars. This proved to be a terrible choice, as the bumpers were not strong enough to withstand even minor collisions and rapidly came to be pockmarked by dents.[15] By the end of the first day, only a handful of the thirty-nine cars were still operating. Spring-loaded bumpers were quickly added to cut down on the damage, while Gurr set about redesigning the engines to make them more durable. But even with all its problems, Autopia proved immensely popular, so much so that two other versions of the ride were later added to Fantasyland, a Junior Autopia, which operated between 1956 and 1999, and a Midget Autopia for small children, which operated between 1957 and 1966.

The last section of Disneyland was also the most obscure. Holidayland was described in the 1953 prospectus as "a restoration of bygone rural America, with its farm houses, barns, fields, gardens, pastures, and live-stock." But when Disneyland opened two years later, the name was given to the area on the edge of Fantasyland (approximately where the Matterhorn is now) where the Mickey Mouse Club Circus was located. The circus was an effort to use the stars of *The Mickey Mouse Club* after filming of the television show wrapped up for the season, but it also reflected Walt's love of circuses. In two seventy-five-minute performances each day, the child stars appeared alongside acrobatic performers and trained animals.

C.V. Wood had warned Walt that people would not be interested in spending their time at Disneyland watching a circus similar to one that they could see elsewhere. He was right: attendance was lackluster, and the circus lasted for only six weeks. In 1957, the name "Holidayland" was trans-ferred to a picnic area located outside the berm, approximately where the Pirates of the Caribbean and Haunted Mansion show buildings are today. Encompassing nine acres, the new Holidayland contained playgrounds, sports facilities, and food concessions. It was the only part of Disneyland that sold alcohol, which became a problem, because inebriated guests would make their way into Disneyland via a special entrance gate. Holidayland did not prove very popular, and it was shut down in 1961. The area stood empty until it was transformed into New Orleans Square in the mid-1960s.

In the months after Disneyland opened, Walt Disney was there nearly every day, and often all night, staying in a small apartment above the fire station on Main Street, U.S.A. His wife Lillian recalled that "he practically lived there." Employees who arrived in the morning prior to opening often saw him in his bathrobe, carrying a steaming mug of coffee and strolling down Main Street, U.S.A. He frequently had lunch in the employee cafeteria so

---

15   The use of aluminum caused other problems as well. The Moonliner rocket that stood outside the Rocket to the Moon was also made out of the metal. Because it contracted in cold weather and expanded in hot, as the temperature changed throughout the day it emitted a variety of groaning and banging sounds.

that he could talk to cast members, and he sometimes donned a disguise so that he could stand in line for attractions and hear what his guests were saying first-hand. In the early days, Walt was everywhere, striding through the park, watching, riding, sometimes even pitching in to help the employees. "He knew everything that went into the park," recalled Dick Irvine, who headed the team that designed Disneyland. "He knew where every pipe was. He knew the height of every building."

By the end of the summer of 1955, Walt felt secure in the knowledge that Disneyland was a hit with the public and a financial success. But he also knew that the park was far from a finished product, and that to keep it popular he would have to fix the problems and add new attractions. The years after 1955 would see Disneyland change rapidly as it attempted to keep pace with the demands of the public and with Walt's ever-evolving vision. After releasing a film, Walt had frequently been frustrated because he could no longer fix its flaws. But Disneyland was different—an organic, ever-evolving entity that he could change and improve as often as he wanted to, or at least as often as financial considerations allowed.

FIVE
Disneyland After 1955

Soon after Disneyland opened, Walt knew that his biggest fear—that it would prove a bust—would not be realized. But now, he had to deal with other, in some ways equally challenging, issues. We might think of these issues as the two "Cs" of Disneyland's first decade of operation. The first "C" was capacity. In the first months of operation, Disneyland's attendance ran 50 percent over projections. So Walt had to figure out how to add attractions, quickly. The second "C" was competition, as Disneyland's success swiftly brought imitators. Walt had never wanted Disneyland to be just another amusement park; he wanted it to be something different, and far superior. He recognized that to stay ahead of the competition, he would have to keep introducing bigger and better things to Disneyland.

The desperate need for extra capacity required the employment of creative strategies to add attractions quickly. After the massive success of the three Davy-Crockett-themed episodes of the *Disneyland* television series, Disney realized its mistake in killing off their hero at the Alamo so soon. They quickly created two "prequel" episodes, "Davy Crockett's Keelboat Race," which aired in November 1955, and "Davy Crockett and the River Pirates," which aired the following month. These episodes featured a comic foil for Crockett named Mike Fink. Based, like Crockett, on a real historical figure, Fink was the most famous runner of keelboats, or small boats used to transport cargo, on the Ohio and Mississippi rivers in the early nineteenth century. Walt had the *Gullywhumper*, one of the two boats that had been used in the episodes, brought over to Disneyland. Dropped into the Rivers of America, it was turned into a ride called the Mike Fink Keel Boats, which opened on Christmas Day 1955.[1]

---

1   The second boat, the *Bertha Mae*, followed the *Gullywhumper* to Disneyland in May of 1956.

Image 5.1: The Mike Fink Keelboats were Walt Disney's first attempt to increase Disneyland's capacity quickly when the park proved very popular in its first months of operation. The attraction, which opened in late December 1955, was created by taking the prop boats used for two Davy-Crockett-themed episodes of the *Disneyland* television series and putting them into Frontierland's Rivers of America. The Indian Village is in the background.

There was a limit, however, to the number of attractions that could be created from television props. In January of 1956, Walt met with the Disneyland Merchants' Association in the Red Wagon Inn on Main Street, U.S.A. to tell them about his future plans. Although he was pleased with the park's initial success, he announced that he intended to spend $1 million over the next six months to make it even better. The first two new attractions were already in the works, as they could be bought "off-the-rack" rather than having to be designed and built from scratch. A spinning ride called the Roto-Jets was purchased from a German company and given a space-themed makeover. Renamed the Astro-Jets and placed in Tomorrowland, it made its debut on April 2, 1956; it holds a place in Disneyland history as the first major new ride to be added after opening day. Another new attraction also came from Europe. Walt had heard of a new gondola lift, or sky ride, that had opened in Zurich, Switzerland, in 1954, and he was eager to bring a similar attraction to Disneyland, where it could serve as both a ride and mode of transportation across the park. Walt purchased a used model from Von Roll, the same company that had built the sky ride in Zurich. The Skyway opened at Disneyland on June 23, 1956. Fantasyland got a new attraction in 1956 as well: the Mickey Mouse Club Theatre, which showed a compilation of three-dimensional animated shorts called the 3D Jamboree, the first of many 3D films to be shown in Disney theme parks.

The same meeting with the merchants' association also provides a fascinating glimpse into 1950s gender stereotypes. Walt expressed concerns that Tomorrowland was lacking in attractions that would interest female guests. "Tomorrowland has many things for the men," he said, "but very little for the women." To remedy this deficiency, Walt contracted with the Crane Plumbing Company to build the Bathroom of Tomorrow, which featured gold-plated fixtures and a posture-improving toilet seat. The following year, the House of Tomorrow, sponsored by Monsanto, was built near the entrance to Tomorrowland. Walt told the merchants' association that the House of the Future "should create a great deal of interest for [women] as the kitchen will have the most elaborate utilities and fixtures that can be imagined." Shaped like a plus-sign, the house consisted of four modules extending from a central core, with everything made out of new materials created by Monsanto's plastics division. The house was full of futuristic gadgets, including intercom, video phones, and a climate-control system that not only pumped in warm or cool air but also suffused the rooms with fragrant smells.

Image 5.2: The House of Tomorrow, the centerpiece of Walt Disney's efforts to make Tomorrowland more appealing to women. Installed in 1959, the futuristic house lasted until 1967. Made entirely of plastics manufactured by its sponsor Monsanto, the house proved so sturdy that the wrecking ball brought in to demolish it in 1967 bounced off. It took workmen two weeks to tear it apart by hand using crowbars and saws.

The next several years saw more additions. In June 1957, Disneyland got its fourth train, the Viewliner, a futuristic vehicle that looped around a figure-eight-shaped track on the edge of Tomorrowland, and the following year an Alice in Wonderland dark ride arrived in Fantasyland.[2] It was Frontierland, however, that saw the biggest changes. The WED team had fiercely debated the question of what to do with the island in the middle of the Rivers of America. One proposal was to make it Mickey Mouse Island, as Mickey's presence in the park was as yet minimal. Another was for it to contain models of famous America buildings such as Mount Vernon and West Point, or replicas of nineteenth-century river towns such as New Orleans, Natchez, and Mobile. Yet another was for it to be Treasure Island from the 1950 Disney pirate film. In the end, however, it was decided to link the island to the *Mark Twain* riverboat that sailed around it. Tom Sawyer Island opened in June 1956. It has a unique distinction in Disney history, as it was the only attraction that Walt himself designed. This was because, when Marvin Davis presented Walt with the first concept drawings, he was not satisfied. He took them home and worked on them for hours in the red barn in his backyard where he tinkered with the Carolwood Pacific Railroad. The next day, he slapped the drawings on Davis's desk, and said, "Now, that's how it should be." His plans included a treehouse, a fort, caves, and bouncy pontoon and rope bridges. Several Imagineers, including Vic Green, Herb Ryman, and Claude Coats, then set about transforming Walt's ideas into reality.

A month after Tom Sawyer Island opened, the Indian War Canoes, real canoes that were paddled by guests, joined the traffic on the Rivers of America. Also opening in July 1956 was the Rainbow Caverns Mine Train, the most elaborate of the new attractions, so much so that it required the creation of a new "D"-ticket. Built at a cost of $500,000, the train circled through the same western landscape as the pack mules, the Conestoga wagon, and the Rainbow Mountain Stagecoach, but only its passengers passed through the Rainbow Caverns, a cave in which black light illuminated multi-colored waterfalls. Two years later, Frontierland saw the arrival of the Sailing Ship *Columbia*, a replica of the first American ship to sail around the world in 1790.

---

2   The Viewliner was a small-scale replica of General Motors' streamlined Aerotrain, an experimental train that traveled at 100 miles per hour. Thanks to its Oldsmobile V-8 engine, Disney's version was able to go a third of that speed, making it "the fastest miniature train in the world." It lasted only fifteen months, closing in September 1958 to make room for the monorail.

Image 5.3: Walt Disney oversees the construction of Fort Wilderness on Tom Sawyer Island in 1956. Constructed from real hand-hewn logs, the fort was originally accessible to guests. After extensive insect and weather damage was discovered during a refurbishment in 2003, however, it was closed and, four years later, demolished. A new Fort Wilderness was built from standard milled lumber, but it is merely a set designed to be seen from the Rivers of America and is off-limits to guests.

Another addition to Disneyland in 1958 was an example of something that Walt referred to as plussing. He was always aware of the need to keep improving Disneyland, but it was not until he overheard a mother talking to her daughter that he began to think specifically about the need not only to add new attractions but also to upgrade existing ones. As he stood near the Jungle Cruise, the daughter asked her mother if they could go on the ride. The mother said no, because they had ridden it the last time they were at Disneyland. Walt realized from this conversation that, at a time when guests had to use individual tickets for each attraction, he had to offer them new things to entice them onto the same rides over and over again. He referred to this as plussing the attractions. In 1958, he decided to add a diorama depicting the Grand Canyon to the Santa Fe & Disneyland Railroad. Inspired by the Oscar-winning Disney documentary short film *Grand Canyon*, the diorama contained rocks, plants, and taxidermy animals, which were displayed in front of a 306-foot-long painted backdrop by scenic artist Delmer J. Yoakum. It cost $367,000, more than most new rides at the time.

Not all of Disneyland's capacity problems were inside the berm. In 1954, the year before Disneyland opened, Anaheim's population was a mere 14,500 people. With no obvious tourist destinations in town, there were only two motels and four small hotels, with a total of eighty-seven rooms. As soon as the park opened, it became clear that this number was woefully inadequate. Customer relations fielded as many as 800 requests a day for accommodations near Disneyland. Walt had long been aware that this was going to be a problem, but while Disneyland was under construction, he had no extra money to spend on a hotel. He tried to convince outside companies to build one, but when he approached Hilton and other major hotel chains, they all thought that Walt's venture was too risky. Walt then invited his friend Jack Wrather, a Texas oil millionaire turned television producer who had recently entered the hotel business, to come and see the Disneyland construction site in 1954. Wrather, too, was initially skeptical that the park would succeed, and he initially said no when Walt asked him to build a hotel. But Walt pleaded with him—according to some accounts with tears in his eyes—and Wrather relented. It was an indication of Walt's desperation that he offered Wrather a very advantageous deal: a ninety-nine-year lease on sixty acres of land directly across from the exit to the Disneyland parking lot, along with exclusive rights to the Disney name for any other hotels that he built in southern California. That last term of the contract is the most telling: Walt Disney was fiercely protective of his name, so his willingness to allow Wrather to use it shows how badly he wanted the hotel.

Ground was broken for the $3 million Disneyland Hotel in March 1955. It was designed by Pereira and Luckman, the same architectural firm that had done some early designs for Disneyland before Walt decided that he would have his own team build the park. Construction was slowed by labor disputes, and so the hotel did not open along with the park as intended. It was not until October 5, 1955, that it began operating, initially with only few rooms available, but soon with 104 rooms in five two-story buildings. The rooms cost between $9 and $22 a night. The following year, another ninety-six rooms were added, as well as a central building containing the lobby, a restaurant, and a shopping area. Even this was not enough: the Disneyland Hotel turned away customers nearly every night.[3]

---

3   First Walt, and then after his death the Disney company, tried repeatedly to buy the hotel from Wrather, but he refused. It was not until 1988, after both Wrather and his widow Bonita had died, that Disney was able to purchase the entire Wrather Company, including the hotel.

Image 5.4: Added in 1956, the central building of the Disneyland Hotel contained the lobby, a cocktail lounge, a restaurant, and seventeen shops. Frequented by celebrities and almost always full, the hotel was extremely luxurious by the standards of the time. Each room had its own balcony, parking space, and color television.

In addition to increasing the number of attractions and hotel rooms, Disneyland had one more problem that needed to be addressed quickly: the ticketing system. The base cost of admission was $1 for adults and fifty cents for children under twelve. Then the major attractions all had their own separate charges, ranging from ten cents to thirty-five cents each. The problem was that guests were constantly having to reach into their wallets to extract more money, which led to complaints that Disneyland was too expensive for families. Early press reports claimed that a family of four who wanted to eat and enjoy every attraction would spend over $30, a vast sum for the time. Walt was defensive about the prices, and snapped at a reporter from the Associated Press who pressed him on the subject that "we have to charge what we do because this park cost a lot to build and maintain." But he knew that something would have to be done before the idea that Disneyland was expensive took hold. On October, 11, 1955, the first ticket books were introduced. Originally, they included admission to the park and a total of eight A-, B- and C-tickets. The following year, D-tickets were introduced, and some of the more popular attractions, including the Jungle Cruise and Rocket to the Moon, were reclassified as D-ticket rides.

The second "C" that is important in understanding Disneyland's first decade is competition. Given Disneyland's immense success, it was inevitable that others would try to imitate it. One of the first attempts was located on a pier on the border of Venice and Santa Monica, to the north and east of Anaheim. Charles Strub, the owner of the racetrack at Santa Anita, had previously discussed investing in Disneyland with Walt and Roy, but the negotiations had collapsed, in part because Walt refused to build the park near the ocean. Now, Strub formed a partnership with ABC's rival CBS to build a twenty-eight-acre amusement park at a cost of $10 million. Pacific Ocean Park opened on July 28, 1958. Some of its attractions were blatant copies of Disneyland's: it featured its own House of Tomorrow and Skyway, along with a Flight to Mars and an Autopia-type ride called the Union 76 Ocean Highway. But unlike Disneyland it had thrill rides, including two roller coasters. And it also had some unique rides, including the Diving Bell, in which visitors were submerged in a tank using hydraulic pistons and then shot back to the surface when the pressure was released; and a Mystery Island Banana Train Ride, in which a train traveled through a banana plantation, experiencing a volcanic eruption and an earthquake along the way. Pacific Ocean Park outdrew Disneyland on some days in its first year, but attendance soon declined, and the CBS/Turf Club partnership sold it in 1959. It limped along for several more years, but closed its gates for good in 1967.

Image 5.5: The Ocean Sky Ride at Pacific Ocean Park, c. 1960.

Additional competition came from a source that had been crucial to the development of Disneyland. As we saw in the previous chapter, it was Disneyland's first vice president and general manager, C.V. Wood, who had convinced many of the park's early sponsors and concessionaires to sign up. He also brought in a number of employees, known as Woody's Texans, who did much of the work of actually getting the park built. But even though Wood and Walt had worked well together, they always had a somewhat tense relationship, because Wood had initially been hired by Roy without Walt's knowledge. During Disneyland's construction, Walt's lavish, ever-changing plans had repeatedly come into conflict with Wood's more pragmatic, cost-conscious approach. Walt also blamed Wood for many of the problems of opening day. And finally, Walt felt that Wood was taking too much credit for Disneyland. (One story claims that Walt was infuriated when he overheard Wood on the phone touting himself as the real force behind the park.) In January 1956, Wood was suddenly fired. Billing himself as the Master Builder of Disneyland—at least until Disney sued him and won—Wood founded a company called Marco Engineering to build amusement parks across the United States. He began with Magic Mountain in Golden, Colorado, which was conceived as a close copy of Disneyland. Construction began in 1957, but the investors soon ran into financial difficulties, and only a very scaled-down version opened in 1959. It was not a success and closed the following year. Undaunted, Wood went on to develop Pleasure Island in Wakefield, Massachusetts, which operated between 1959 and 1969 and billed itself as the Disneyland of the Northeast, and Freedomland U.S.A. in New York City, which operated between 1960 and 1964.

None of these parks ultimately proved to be serious competition for Disneyland, but in the late 1950s the picture looked very different, and Walt felt that he had to ensure that he stayed well ahead of the pack. So he planned a "second opening" for Disneyland in 1959, in which three major new rides—the Submarine Voyage, the monorail, and the Matterhorn— would be introduced, at a combined cost of $5.5 million. The three new rides opened on June 14, 1959; they required another addition to the Disneyland ticket book, and so the famous "E"-ticket was born. (Several existing rides were upgraded to "E"-tickets as well.) ABC broadcast a 90-minute special of the ceremony, which was attended by 2000 journalists, celebrities, and dignitaries, including Vice President Richard Nixon, who was from nearby Yorba Linda.

Image 5.6: A banner celebrating the "second opening" of Disneyland in 1959 stretches over Main Street, U.S.A.

The Submarine Voyage evolved from an idea conceived by WED's Dick Irvine to create a glass-bottomed boat ride to replace the short-lived Phantom Boats. Irvine's plan was to install live fish, a shipwreck, and other underwater scenes and have guests view them from above. But when Pacific Ocean Park opened in 1958, Walt was irritated by its one-upmanship of his *20,000 Leagues Under the Sea* exhibit: the new park featured a 150-foot-long model of the nuclear reactor of the U.S.S. *Nautilus*, the world's first nuclear-powered submarine. In response, Walt decided to plus the glass-bottom boat concept by creating a "real submarine ride." Originally, plans called for the submarines to be fully submerged and pulled along by cables in a mechanism similar to that used by San Francisco's cable cars. But safety concerns compelled a change: instead, the eight fifty-two-foot-long submarines rode on a rail around a concrete lagoon filled with nine million gallons of water that covered them only as far as their portholes, while sounds, air bubbles, and lighting effects were used to convince guests that they were diving deep into the ocean. Thanks in part to the $25,000 that each sub cost, the Submarine Voyage cost $2.5 million. (Previously, the most expensive new ride to be added to Disneyland was the Rainbow Caverns Mine Train, which had cost $500,000.)

Images 5.7 and 5.8: Top: the U.S.S. *Nautilus*, the navy's first nuclear-powered submarine, shortly after being launched in January 1954. Bottom: the *Skipjack*, one of eight Disney replicas of a nuclear submarine that were created for the Submarine Voyage attraction in 1959.

The Submarine Voyage was not meant to serve purely as entertainment; it was also part of a government propaganda effort. After the Second World War, the American government began using nuclear power for a variety of defense purposes, including powering submarines, but both the public and the scientific community were worried about the potential for serious accidents. To counter this opposition, the Eisenhower administration launched a public relations campaign called Atoms for Peace. They recruited Walt Disney to produce a film called *Our Friend the Atom*, which was broadcast as an episode of the *Disneyland* television series in January 1957. Made with the assistance of the navy and General Dynamics, the defense contractor who built the nuclear submarines, *Our Friend the Atom* provided a reassuring message about the safety of nuclear power. With the Submarine Voyage, Disney took the pro-nuclear campaign one step further. Bob Gurr and Roger Broggie were assigned to design ride vehicles that closely resembled the navy's nuclear submarines; each one of Disney's subs was named after one of the navy's. The ride experience, meanwhile, was supposed to duplicate what the operations manual described as "duty aboard an atomic-powered submarine." The on-board narrative, in which guests sailed under the polar ice cap, referenced the achievement of the U.S.S. *Skate* in March 1959, when it became the first submarine to surface at the North Pole. During the first few months of the attraction's operation, two naval cadets were stationed outside the entrance to interact with guests and lend an aura of authenticity. Walt was disappointed when he was denied an opportunity to insert his submarines into the real Cold War: during a visit to the United States in September 1959, Soviet premier Nikita Khrushchev wanted badly to visit Disneyland, but was denied permission for security reasons. Walt had been prepared to greet him with a reminder that Disneyland's submarine fleet was the eighth largest in the world.

The second addition to Disneyland in 1959 was the monorail. Walt had long been interested in monorails, or trains that that are either suspended from or ride on top of a single rail. The earliest designs for Tomorrowland featured a suspended monorail, but Lillian Disney worried that the swinging of the cars would make guests seasick, so Walt kept an eye out for a better design. In 1952, the German company Alweg pioneered a new monorail design that was nicknamed the "German saddle bag" because the trains straddled the beam beneath them. Six years later, Walt was on vacation in Europe when he saw a prototype of this new design on a test track near Cologne. He was impressed, and began negotiating with Alweg to build a five-eighths-scale monorail at Disneyland. Originally, it ran for only three-quarters of a mile above Tomorrowland and Fantasyland, but in 1961, a 2.3-mile extension to the Disneyland Hotel was built. In Walt's eyes, the monorail was no mere ride; it was a demonstration of the clean, quiet, and energy-efficient "rapid transit of the future."[4]

On that same trip to Europe in 1958, Walt visited Zermatt in Switzerland, where the live-action film *Third Man on the Mountain* was being filmed. The film, which starred Michael Rennie and James MacArthur, told the story of a young Swiss mountain climber's efforts to climb a fictional mountain called the Citadel, which his father had died trying to climb. As Walt observed the production, he would stare at the Matterhorn, which played the role of the Citadel in the film, for as much as an hour at a time. He was not just admiring the view—he was thinking of how he might use the mountain's distinctive shape to create Disneyland's first thrill ride. At

---

4 Walt's hopes on this score were never realized. In 1963, Alweg submitted a proposal to the city of Los Angeles to build a forty-three-mile-long monorail system at a cost of $105 million. After Standard Oil pressured city officials, however, the proposal was rejected, and Los Angeles' dependence on the automobile continued.

first, Walt had resisted the idea that his park needed thrill rides, but in the face of growing competition, he was convinced that something more exciting was required. He had previously thought of creating a toboggan ride using artificial snow, but this had been rejected as unfeasible. Now, he converted that idea to a bobsled-type roller coaster inside a mountain. He bought a postcard of the Matterhorn and mailed it to designer Vic Greene with the message, "Build This, Walt."

Image 5.9: The steel frame of the Matterhorn under construction in early 1959. The mountain's skeleton was comprised of 2175 pieces of structural steel, each one a different size. The lower slopes were covered in 500 tons of concrete, while the snow-capped top was sheathed in enough plywood to build twenty-seven houses.

And so the Matterhorn Bobsleds were born. The ride structure was a $1/100^{th}$-scale replica of the real mountain, with the world's first tubular-steel roller coaster inside it and with a hole in the top so that the Skyway could pass through. At 147 feet high, the Matterhorn was the tallest building in Orange County at the time it was built. The construction process was the most complex engineering project that Disneyland's designers had yet attempted. Inside, the roller coaster was a type known as the Wild Mouse, which uses tight, flat turns to generate lateral G-forces. (Space Mountain is the same type of roller coaster.) The tubular steel track meant that the ride, which was intended to simulate a bobsled gliding over ice, was very smooth. At the bottom, the cars landed in a pool of water to slow them down, a technique that Disneyland's construction manager Joe Fowler had seen on a ride in London. In those days, there was no computer simulation for roller-coaster design, so the track was created using marbles and a slide rule. To test it, WED's Bob Gurr was sent down in a car with three sandbags for ballast. The Matterhorn proved that there was definitely an audience for thrill rides at Disneyland, as throughout the 1960s and 1970s it boasted some of the park's longest wait times.

The Submarine Voyage, monorail, and Matterhorn all proved to be popular and long-lasting attractions, but some of the other additions to Disneyland in the late 1950s and early 1960s were less successful. As Walt continued to try and improve Tomorrowland, he suggested to WED that they develop a version of a "duck bump" ride, in which guests attempted to crash into each other while riding around a small pond on inner tubes. This idea was ultimately discarded, but around the same time the WED designers were approached by a German company that wanted to sell a single-person hovercraft boat to Disney. Bob Gurr felt that the high-speed blade beneath the hovercraft was too dangerous, but he was intrigued by the technology. He asked the engineers at Arrow Development, which had built a number of rides for Disneyland, to develop an attraction that would combine the fun of the duck bump ride with the novelty of the hovercraft.

Working together, Arrow and the WED team created a ride in which inner tubes floated on a bed of air that was forced by four large blowers through 2000 holes in the floor. (It was essentially a giant air hockey table.) The guests steered the inner tubes by leaning in the direction that they wanted to go, which released air from the opposite side of the tube and thus pushed it forward. Given an outer-space theme and named the Flying Saucers, the attraction opened in July 1961. From the beginning, however, it was plagued by technical problems, as the air pressure in the plenum, or chamber beneath the floor, was prone to dropping, which caused the saucers to drop, too. It then took a very long time to get the pressure back up. The Flying Saucers lasted only five years.[5]

Other ideas never even made it to Disneyland, but were left on the drawing board because they were infeasible or too expensive. An example was Rock Candy Mountain, which was conceived as a replacement for the Storybook Land Canal Boats in the late 1950s. Two decades earlier, when he was searching for a follow-up project to *Snow White and the Seven Dwarfs*, Walt had considered acquiring the rights to L. Frank Baum's novel *The Wonderful Wizard of Oz* (1900), but MGM had beat him to the punch and used it as the basis for the classic 1939 film. Walt retained a keen interest

---

5   In 2012, Disney tried the Flying Saucers concept again with another attraction, Luigi's Flying Tires at Disney's California Adventure, that used similar technology. It lasted for only three years.

in the Oz stories, however, and when the rights to eleven of Baum's other Oz novels became available in 1954, Disney acquired them for $60,000. Two years later, when MGM's *The Wizard of Oz* was broadcast on television for the first time, it was a ratings smash, and Walt returned to the idea of developing an Oz-related project at Disney. He began developing a feature film called *The Rainbow Road to Oz*, starring the Mouseketeers. The film was ultimately abandoned due to rising production costs, the declining popularity of the Mouseketeers, and concerns that it would not measure up to the MGM classic, but Walt still wanted to do something with the Oz story. He directed the WED team to develop a ride that would take as its theme a surprise birthday party for Dorothy, with the grand finale a giant candy mountain. But when the designers built a model using real candy, they found it revolting. "It was positively nauseating," recalled John Hench, "and, worst of all, because our building didn't have air conditioning, the whole mountain began to melt. We had to leave the door open to ventilate the place to get rid of the odor. It was like a dying candy factory." Like the Oz film, the Rock Candy Mountain attraction was abandoned.

Another idea that never came to fruition was Edison Square. Thomas Edison was one of Walt's boyhood heroes, but Walt was also interested in the idea because he hoped to get General Electric, which had begun as the Edison Electric Company, to sponsor it. In 1959, GE had become embroiled in a major price-fixing scandal, and Walt knew that the company desperately needed some good publicity. The proposal that WED put together to pitch Edison Square described it as consisting of a central plaza that would be lined with turn-of-the-century buildings from various American cities. The main attraction was a show called Harnessing the Lightning, which would feature a series of rooms showing the evolution of electrical appliances in the home over four decades, beginning in 1898 and then proceeding to 1918, 1948, and an undefined point in the future. The narrator, who was named Wilbur K.—for "Kilo"—Watt, would have been Disneyland's first audio-animatronic figure, though at the time the term was electro-mechanical. Located off the top end of Main Street where it intersected the hub, Edison Square first appeared as a coming attraction on the map of Disneyland in 1958 and remained there until 1964. But GE, despite the scandal, refused to bite. Its sponsorship of a Disney attraction had to wait until the 1964 New York World's Fair, when Harnessing the Lightning evolved into the Carousel of Progress.

A final abandoned addition to Disneyland in the late 1950s was River Town, an expansion of Frontierland that was to be located approximately where the Haunted Mansion is today. River Town was to consist mostly of shops selling things like spices, dolls, candles, and old maps that were intended to give the area an authentic mid-nineteenth-century feel. There were also some proposals that seem extremely ill-advised today, such as plans for a pet shop and a gun shop. The latter was going to be operated by the famous gun collector Hy Hunter; in a memo from 1956, Nat Winecoff wrote, "If we can get [Hunter] to come in, his exhibit of guns would be quite a show in itself." Another proposal was for a Good Hex shop selling lucky charms, amulets, crystal balls, tarot cards, and the like. The shop, which was the brainchild of local children's television presenter and magician Frank Herman, was to have featured a mechanical bulldog that barked to scare away evil spirits and an Enchanted Talking Tea Kettle that told fortunes. River Town's only attraction was to have been a Magnetic House, Disney's version of a type of roadside attraction that was popular in the 1950s in which a structure was built on a slant, which allowed the creation of optical illusions like water that appeared to flow uphill and chairs that seemed to balance on two legs. River Town appears to have been superseded by plans for a larger, New Orleans-themed expansion of Disneyland. As early as 1956, Winecoff contacted the Association of Commerce in New Orleans to inquire about "stores that manufacture or sell unusual pieces of merchandise typical of New Orleans."[6]

Two other ideas that were contemplated in the late 1950s also never made it into Disneyland, though they were recycled later for Walt Disney World. They were both intended for the small plot of land that lay behind the buildings on the eastern side of Main Street at the train station end. Early plans called for this area to be a Residential Street that would contain a church and a dilapidated haunted house on a hill, but Walt did not like the idea of a creepy old house ruining the pristine ambiance of Main Street, and so the idea was shelved. Instead, Walt decided to use the space for something that would reflect his love of travel. In late 1954, International Street began appearing in Disneyland plans. It was to contain replicas of architectural monuments from various countries, including Denmark, Germany, Spain, Japan, France, and Switzerland, all surrounding a replica of the central plaza of an Italian town. It was ultimately decided, however, that there was not enough space in that location to contain everything that Walt wanted to pack in. International Street had to wait another quarter-century, when the idea was revived for Epcot's World Showcase.

In 1956, Walt announced that Liberty Street would be opening in the space that International Street had been going to occupy. He had long wanted to incorporate more colonial American history into Disneyland, and, as an added incentive, Disney was about to release the live-action film

---

6   Much of the information in this paragraph comes from an article by Todd James Pierce for the Disney History Institute's website. http:// disneyhistoryinstitute.com/2016/01/the-frontierland-that-never-was.html.

Johnny Tremain, which was set during the American Revolution. Liberty Street would feature working craftsmen such as silversmiths and black-smiths, along with a replica of Independence Hall in Philadelphia that would contain a Hall of Presidents, featuring a show called One Nation Under God starring life-sized wax figures of all thirty-four (to that point) presidents, and a Hall of the Declaration of Independence, in which paintings and more wax figures would tell the story of 1776. Like International Street, Liberty Street did not become a reality until the development of Walt Disney World. Transformed into Liberty Square, it opened as part of the Magic Kingdom in October 1971.

Image 5.10: Concept art by Herb Ryman of Liberty Street, a never-built expansion of Disneyland.

Liberty Street was shelved in the late 1950s because Walt decided that in order to be convincing, the shows needed figures that could actually move and speak in a life-like manner. The effort to develop such figures would consume much of WED's energy for the next decade. There are two different stories as to the origin of Walt's longstanding interest in creating mechanical versions of living beings. One claims that he was in an antique shop in New Orleans in the mid-1940s when he found a nineteenth-century mechanical bird in a cage that sang and fluttered its wings when it was wound up. The bird still exists—it is currently displayed in a replica of Walt's office in the Walt Disney: One Man's Dream exhibit in Disney's Hollywood Studios in Orlando—so the story would appear to have some truth behind it. The other story, which also seems likely to be accurate because several of Walt's family members remembered it, claims that he was in Paris on a European holiday in 1949 and returned from an afternoon of shopping with two bags full of mechanical toys. He was amazed that so much movement could be generated by such simple mechanisms. This story, too, has supporting evidence: some of the toys are currently displayed in the Walt Disney Family Museum in San Francisco.

Whichever story is accurate, and perhaps they both are, it was clearly in the late 1940s that Walt began to think about the possibility of creating three-dimensional animated figures. In 1949, he contacted an attorney about obtaining a patent on figures that would have audio synchronized to their movements. This was a logical next step in Walt's conception of animation: having brought sound to animated figures in two dimensions with *Steamboat Willie*, he now wanted to do it in three. In 1951, he directed machinist Roger Broggie and sculptor Wathel Rogers to lead an experiment called Project Little Man, in which they would try to create a miniature human figure that was capable of life-like movements. Walt then hired dancer Buddy Ebsen to perform a vaudeville dance routine. The artist Charles Christadoro sculpted a nine-inch-high, jointed figure of Ebsen that Broggie and Rogers made move using a system of cables and rotating cams that were installed in a cabinet. Next, they created a more elaborate moving model featuring a barbershop quartet that sang "Down by the Old Mill Stream." These figures represented the origins of audio-animatronics, though that term for them would not be invented until the early 1960s.

Although primitive moving figures were used in the Jungle Cruise and the Submarine Voyage, the first serious advance came in 1960, when Walt decided to give the Rainbow Caverns Mine Train a major upgrade. Over 200 animals were added to the landscape through which the train traveled; to make them move, the designers used recently declassified computer technology that had been developed by NASA and the military. Because of the increased sophistication of its animated figures, the Mine Train Through Nature's Wonderland, as the attraction was now called, is considered by Disney historians to be the first true use of animatronics.

Image 5.11: The Mine Train Through Nature's Wonderland, which after it was converted from the Rainbow Caverns Mine Train in 1960 became what most Disney historians regard as the first attraction to feature animatronics, though it did not have audio synchronized to the figures' movements.

The Mine Train's figures did not have audio synchronized to their movements, however. Walt was eager to build figures that made sounds that were timed to their actions. Focusing on the pie-shaped space between Main Street and Tomorrowland previously slated for Edison Square, he conceived of a way to bring California's diversity into Disneyland by building a Chinatown in the empty space, with a Chinese restaurant as its centerpiece.[7] As the WED team continued its experiments with animatronics, they had built a head that could move its eyes and mouth. When they put a latex skin over the head to cover the mechanical elements, however, it did not fit properly around the eyes, which gave the face a stereotypically "Chinese" cast. Instead of trying to correct the mistake, the designers decided to make the head Chinese. When Walt saw it, he had an idea: to use the head in Chinatown's Chinese restaurant. And so the figure evolved into Confucius, who would seem to answer questions from the audience using his famous wisdom. (In reality, the questions would be prerecorded.) There would also be an audio-animatronic Chinese dragon, while Chinese street scenes would be projected onto the windows. Confucius later evolved into a philosopher

---

7   Another example of Walt's interest in having Disneyland reflect California's diversity was the International Christmas Parade that appeared on Main Street every holiday season in the late 1950s and early 1960s. In 1963, Disneyland had begun presenting an annual Mexican street festival.

called Chew Well and then a character named Grandfather Chung, who was created in the hopes of enticing the Chinese food company Chun King to sponsor the attraction. WED, meanwhile, kept working on the animatronic head: the team got it to blink and open and close its mouth, and were taking steps toward making it talk. "You could always tell who was working on the job," recalled Wathel Rogers, who directed the project. "They never looked at your eyes when you were talking to them, always at your mouth."

Chinatown never got off the drawing board, because Walt decided that, as there were real examples close by in Los Angeles and San Francisco, there was no need to build one in Disneyland. One element of the concept, however, was retained. The human host of the after-dinner show was to be surrounded by dozens of mechanical birds in cages. Now, the Imagineers wanted to use the birds in another way. One option was to incorporate them into the Mine Train Through Nature's Wonderland, but John Hench had a different idea. Stouffer's, which already sponsored the Plaza Pavilion on Main Street, was looking to sponsor a second restaurant. Hench thought it could feature a show with audio-animatronic tropical birds. Disneyland could then capitalize on the Tiki craze, which reached a peak in the early 1960s.

WED came up with a show called the Enchanted Tiki Room, featuring 225 birds. There was only one drawback: in tests, the guests were so fascinated by the show that they ate very slowly, so they were not done by the time the next show was ready to begin. The restaurant idea thus evolved into the Tahitian Terrace, which was sponsored by Stouffer's and which featured a show by human hula and fire dancers. The Enchanted Tiki Room, meanwhile, became a sixteen-minute show that did not involve food.[8] Walt paid for the show's development himself, and so the Enchanted Tiki Room had a separate admission charge that was not part of the ticket-book system. Because the price was a steep seventy-five cents, twenty-five cents more than an "E"-ticket, many guests initially bypassed the attraction. To draw them in, the designers created a barker bird who perched above the turnstiles and described the wonders of the show. He proved a little too effective: so many people stopped to watch him that there was a constant traffic jam in Adventureland.[9] The Enchanted Tiki Room became a hit, and a Disney theme park landmark: the first audio-animatronic attraction.

---

8   The decision to eliminate the food service came so late that some components of the restaurant survived. The fountain in the center of the room was going to serve as the coffee station, and so it still contains storage compartments for silverware in its base. The chairs that were designed for the restaurant were used as guest seating until they were replaced by benches in 2005. The Enchanted Tiki Room also has its own restrooms, another leftover from the dining concept.

9   The barker bird, Juan, was soon removed to alleviate the congestion. Some claim he was displayed in The Walt Disney Story exhibit featured in the Opera House in Disneyland's Town Square between 1973 and 2005; others claim he was recycled as one of the "side" birds in the Enchanted Tiki Room.

The Enchanted Tiki Room's success only intensified Walt's desire to create a human audio-animatronic figure. He was still keen on the Hall of Presidents idea that had been conceived for Liberty Street, and so he decided to create an audio-animatronic figure of his favorite president, Abraham Lincoln. Sculptor Blaine Gibson created the figure's head from an actual Lincoln life mask from 1860, but he had to make it bigger than life so that it could hold all of the necessary electronic components. This meant that Lincoln's body had to be bigger as well in order to be in proportion, and so the Disney Lincoln was even taller than the 6'4" inch real Lincoln. Fourteen hydraulic lines ran through the body to create different movements, while sixteen air lines in the head made fifteen different facial expressions possible. The signals that operated the figure were generated by a magnetic tape system that had been adapted from technology used on the navy's nuclear submarines; Disney paid $17,000 to acquire the patent. The signals were transmitted to a transistorized "brain" inside the Lincoln figure that activated the individual motors. Sound synchronized to the mouth movements was also fed from the tape.

In 1962, city planner Robert Moses, who had been appointed to organize the upcoming World's Fair in New York City, visited the Disney studio in search of ideas for attractions. He was so impressed by the Lincoln figure, especially when it stood up and shook his hand, that he insisted it be displayed at the Fair. But a sponsor was needed. In early 1963, the Illinois legislature passed legislation establishing a commission to create a display at the Fair with a theme called The Land of Lincoln. When Moses found out about this, he contacted the commission's chairman Fairfax Cone to tell him about the Disney Lincoln figure. Cone visited the Disney studio to see the figure for himself; he was initially skeptical but came away just as impressed as Moses. "The possibility of our using the Lincoln figure and the effect of this upon visitors to the New York World's Fair have not left my mind during any of my waking hours since I saw it," Cone wrote to Walt afterwards. There was only one problem: money. Illinois had budgeted only $1 million to build the entire pavilion, and Disney wanted $600,000 for the Lincoln figure alone.[10] Moses was so eager to have Disney's Lincoln at the Fair, however, that he convinced the World's Fair Corporation to chip in $250,000. Now all that remained was for WED to get the figure working in time. Marc Davis recalled that "it was like working on the first automobile or the first airplane or whatever and you didn't know whether it was going to fly or not." But in the end it did work, and it became one of the World's Fair's most popular attractions. Called Great Moments with Mr.

---

10   This sum did not come close to covering Disney's costs, as Lincoln probably cost around $1.5 million to develop.

Lincoln, the ten-minute show, in which the figure stood up and delivered excerpts from Lincoln's speeches, filled its 500-seat arena nearly every time.

Great Moments with Mr. Lincoln was only one aspect of Disney's involvement with the New York World's Fair. Robert Moses had set aside eight acres for a "children's village," and he hoped to convince Walt to build a miniature Disneyland there that would continue to operate after the Fair closed. Walt, however, was not interested: he knew that the state of New York would have to pony up the money to make the attraction permanent, and he did not want to deal with government bureaucracy. So Moses proposed another idea: Disney would design some of the pavilions that various corporations would be sponsoring at the Fair. He was unaware that Disney had already been in contact with several corporations about this very possibility, and in fact had already made a deal with Ford. Walt was attracted to these projects because of the money they would bring in, but he also saw them as a way to test new technology and to advertise Disneyland to an East Coast audience. In the back of his mind was the possibility of building a version of Disneyland on the East Coast. "He wanted," recalled WED's Marty Sklar, "to see if his kind of entertainment would appeal to the more sophisticated eastern audience."

Walt wanted Ford, the first company to commit to having Disney design its pavilion, to sponsor One Nation under God, the historical attraction featuring American presidents that had been conceived for Disneyland's never-built Liberty Street, but the company's executives turned that idea down. Instead, WED designed a twelve-minute attraction called the Magic Skyway, which traced the history of invention as guests rode in automated Ford cars. They created the system to drive the cars by observing an assembly line in a Ford factory in Dearborn, Michigan, which led to the idea that the cars would be pushed along by a series of wheels beneath the track. This drive system was later adapted for the PeopleMover ride in Tomorrowland, which was installed in 1967.

Next to come on board was General Electric. For years, Walt had been courting GE to sponsor Edison Square at Disneyland, and now some of the ideas for it were transferred to the company's pavilion at the World's Fair. The centerpiece of the pavilion was a show called the Carousel of Progress, which followed an audio-animatronic family as they enjoyed the comforts provided by electricity, and specifically by GE appliances, between 1900 and 1960. Instead of the audience moving through the six scenes on foot, the theater was designed so that the auditorium rotated around a stage in the center. The Carousel of Progress proved to be extremely popular, with wait times exceeding two hours.

Even with the Illinois, Ford, and GE pavilions underway, Walt still thought that Disney could contribute more to the World's Fair. In early

1963, he received a phone call from Pepsi-Cola, which had contracted with the United Nations International Children's Fund (UNICEF) to build a pavilion. The opening of the World's Fair was only a year away, and Pepsi had a budget of only $650,000. Walt was convinced that WED could come up with something, and he quickly conceived an idea for a "little boat ride" in which guests would float through various countries that would be populated by animated dolls. The initial plan was for the dolls to sing their individual national anthems, but it soon became apparent that this would produce a cacophony of sound. The brothers Robert and Richard Sherman, who were famous for their work on *Mary Poppins* (1964) and a host of other Disney films, were called in to write a song that could be sung in different languages. That song, of course, became "It's a Small World," which in turn gave the attraction its name.

Image 5.12: The Pepsi Pavilion from the 1964 New York World's Fair, which contained the It's a Small World attraction. The structure on the right is the Temple of the Four Winds. Walt Disney had it commissioned for the exterior of this building because he thought it was too austere and needed a visual icon to attract people. A "kinetic sculpture" with over a hundred moving parts, the 120-foot-high Tower was designed by Imagineer Rolly Crump at a cost $200,000. After the Fair ended in October 1965, Disney debated what to do with the Tower and considered moving it to Disneyland along with It's a Small World, but its weight of over a hundred tons proved prohibitive, and so it was dismantled and scrapped.

Not every idea that Walt pitched for the World's Fair came to fruition. He tried to convince Moses to install a monorail that would then become part of New York City's mass-transit network, but his plans were rejected due to the cost. He also approached both the U.S. Department of Commerce and Coca-Cola about sponsoring One Nation under God, which Ford had already turned down, but neither would bite. He then tried to talk Coca-Cola into an expanded version of the Enchanted Tiki Room called Legends of the Enchanted Island, which would be shown in a theater with a capacity of over 30,000 people. But this was 1963, only a year before the opening of the World's Fair, and Coke was already committed to a pavilion called The World of Refreshment. The company's executives informed Walt that it was not possible for them to change course at such a late date.

The four exhibits that Disney did build at the World's Fair proved extremely popular, and three of them later found a permanent home at Disneyland. In July 1965, an updated version of Great Moments with Mr. Lincoln was installed in the Opera House in Town Square. It's a Small World arrived in May 1966, followed by the Carousel of Progress in July 1967. Only the Magic Skyway never made it to Anaheim; it took up too much space, and Walt was not satisfied with the quality of the animatronics.[11]

The success of Great Moments with Mr. Lincoln and the Carousel of Progress made the development of audio-animatronics-based attractions WED's primary focus in the mid-1960s. It is at this point that we can begin referring to WED employees as Imagineers, because it was now that Disney started to use the term.[12] Walt was initially most interested in using audio-animatronics for patriotically-themed attractions that would recreate important moments from American history, such as the winter at Valley Forge, the signing of the Constitution, and the Louisiana Purchase. But the Imagineers had other ideas in the works as well, ideas that had long been in gestation but could now become reality thanks to the new technology. These ideas included plans for a haunted house and for a pirate-based attraction.

Walt's vision, however, would not be realized until the development of Walt Disney World in Florida, and the Imagineers had to wait as well,

---

11   The dinosaurs from the prehistoric scene were recycled for the Primeval World display that was added to the Santa Fe & Disneyland Railroad in 1966, and one of the mammoths was converted to an elephant for the Jungle Cruise.

12   Although today the term Imagineer is exclusively associated with Disney, it was not invented by the company. Instead, it dates to the 1940s, when the Alcoa Corporation began using it to describe an ideal employee, who combined imagination and engineering. In 1957, an article entitled "Brainstorming Is IMAGINation engINEERing" appeared in a Union Carbide in-house magazine. The term was probably brought to Disney by two former Union Carbide employees, Richard Conway and Gilbert Decker. Disney first began using the term Imagineering in the early 1960s, and it was trademarked by Disney in 1967.

until the New Orleans-themed area that would serve as the home of both the haunted house and the pirate attraction was built. Walt, who enjoyed visiting New Orleans, had long thought of a French Quarter-themed area as a natural addition to Disneyland, which already had a Mississippi riverboat. Seeing Mardi Gras as a source of ideas, he tried to persuade parade-float designer Blaine Kern to come to work for Disneyland. Kern refused, but New Orleans made its way into Disneyland nonetheless. From the beginning, there was a short New Orleans Street in Frontierland, while the Plantation House Restaurant featured a New Orleans-style façade on one side. Jazz musicians frequently played in the Frontierland's bandstand, and in 1960, the first Dixieland at Disneyland special event, which included a floating Mardi Gras parade on the Rivers of America and performances by several jazz bands, was held. The event continued for eleven years, and featured prominent jazz musicians such as Louis Armstrong, Al Hirt, and the Dukes of Dixieland.

Dixieland at Disneyland served as a preview of New Orleans Square, a highly detailed replica of the French Quarter that became Disneyland's first new land when it opened in 1966. The earliest ideas for New Orleans Square included a haunted house, a walk-through pirate wax museum, and a shopping area called the Thieves' Market. By the early 1960s, the pirate museum and the Thieves' Market had been moved to an underground basement, while the space above ground was occupied by the Blue Bayou Mart, an enclosed shopping area containing an elegant restaurant. Ground was broken in early 1962, but construction was delayed when Walt pulled the Imagineers off the project to concentrate on the attractions for the 1964 World's Fair. New Orleans Square cost $18 million, $1 million more than had been expended building the entire park only eleven years earlier. Some of this expense was due to inflation, but it was also a reflection of how much the ambitions of the Imagineers had increased since the mid-1950s.

Image 5.13: Concept art by Herb Ryman of New Orleans Square.

And this bill did not even include all of the work for New Orleans Square's two attractions, neither of which opened along with it in July 1966. As we saw above, a pirate-themed attraction had long been planned for Disneyland. Herb Ryman's 1953 drawings had featured areas in Adventureland labeled the Pirate Shack and Bluebeard's Den, and maps of the park in the late 1950s placed a pirate wax museum in what would ultimately become New Orleans Square. Walt first mentioned that a pirate ride was in development in 1960 during the opening ceremony for the Mine Train Through Nature's Wonderland, and the following year, the name Pirates of the Caribbean first appeared in the Disneyland souvenir book. By 1963, the walk-through wax museum had been upgraded to a "Bayou voyage," using the technology that had been developed for It's a Small World of pushing boats through a water channel using jets hidden beneath the surface. Two years later, the guidebook showed that the ride had continued to evolve, as it now featured audio-animatronic pirates who would "attack, burn and loot a city."

When it opened in March 1967, Pirates of the Caribbean was by far the most complex audio-animatronic attraction that Disney had ever designed. It contained seventy-five human figures that were capable of varying degrees of complex movements, along with fifty animals. The attraction cost $8 million, almost half of what it had cost to build the entire park eleven years earlier. Instead of the usual cramped dark ride that lasted only for a few minutes, Pirates of the Caribbean was a sixteen-minute extravaganza in which the boats floated along a three-level canal that totaled a third of a mile in length. The attraction was so massive in scale, in fact, that one of the two buildings housing it had to be built outside Disneyland's perimeter berm. The ride's two drops were to get the boats below ground level, so that they could pass under the railroad tracks. At the end of the ride, they were lifted back up to ground level by traveling "up a waterfall," using a system adapted from the chain pulls that take roller coasters uphill.

If Pirates of the Caribbean represented something that had never been seen before in an amusement park, New Orleans Square's second attraction was a good example of how Disney turned classic carnival rides into more elaborate showpieces. Haunted-house attractions evolved from early dark rides in which guests rode through maze-like tunnels filled with mirrors and loud noises.[13] By the mid-twentieth century, haunted houses were a staple of amusement parks all over the country. In both Harper Goff's drawings of 1951 and Marvin Davis's drawings of 1953, a creepy old house

---

13   The first haunted house was the Orton and Spooner Ghost House, which made its debut at an English traveling fair in 1915.

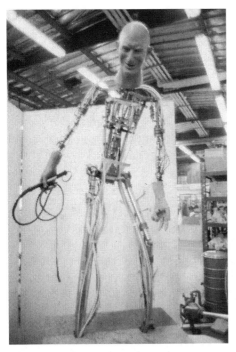

Image 5.14: The "skeleton" of the audio-animatronic auctioneer character from Pirates of the Caribbean, one of the most complex of the seventy-five human figures featured in the attraction.

on a hill had been set off from Main Street, but Walt eventually decided that such a dilapidated structure was not right for that part of the park. He still, however, asked Goff and artist Ken Anderson to keep working on concepts for a walk-through "ghost house." When planning for New Orleans Square began in the late 1950s, the haunted house, now called Bloodmere Manor, was incorporated into it.

Originally, Bloodmere Manor, like Pirates of the Caribbean, was conceived as a walk-through attraction. But when the Imagineers used the sets from the *Zorro* television series to test the movement of several dozen people through a series of rooms, they discovered that there was no way to get them to proceed at a pace sufficient to avoid long lines. The attraction was thus reconceived as a dark ride. The standard type of vehicle used in rides like Snow White Adventures and Mr. Toad's Wild Ride, however, would not work, because it would not have sufficient capacity and because the designers needed to ensure that guests' attention was directed toward the particular effects they wanted them to see. At the time, there was no technology that would make this possible, so the haunted house was again put on hold. Patterned after the nineteenth-century Shipley-Lydecker House in Baltimore, the façade of what was now called the Haunted Mansion was finished in 1963, but the building stood empty for another six years.

In 1966, when a new attraction (Adventures Thru Inner Space) that would pretend to shrink guests down to the size of an atom was being conceived for a Tomorrowland upgrade, a solution to the ride conveyance difficulty was found. Bob Gurr and John Hench were discussing the problem when Gurr picked up a red plastic apple from Hench's desk and began spinning it on its stem. He realized that he could design vehicles linked together in a continuous chain that, like the apple, could rotate to each side as well as tilt backwards. Each vehicle could contain its own speakers and could be hooded so that guests' views were restricted to exactly what the Imagineers wanted them to see. This was the origin of the Omnimover system that is now used in numerous Disney attractions.

Construction resumed on the Haunted Mansion in 1967. The attraction's 131 Omnimovers, or Doom Buggies, gave it a massive capacity of 2600 guests per hour.[14] In addition to its alteration from a walk-through to a ride-through attraction, the Haunted Mansion changed from its original conception as something frightening to a mostly humorous attraction. Imagineer Xavier "X" Atencio wrote the script, and actor Paul Frees, the voice of the Pillsbury Doughboy and Rocky and Bullwinkle villain Boris Badenov, took on the role of the Ghost Host narrator. Disney composer Buddy Baker was assigned to come up with a song that would duplicate the success of "Yo Ho (A Pirate's Life for Me)," which he had written for Pirates of the Caribbean. "Grim Grinning Ghosts" (with lyrics by Atencio) was performed by the Mello Men singers, who included Thurl Ravenscourt, the voice of Tony the Tiger and the uncredited vocalist of "You're a Mean One Mr. Grinch" from How the Grinch Stole Christmas. After it opened in August 1969, the Haunted Mansion quickly became Disneyland's most popular attraction.

New Orleans Square included two other components that were important to Disneyland's history. The Blue Bayou Restaurant, which opened in March 1967, represented a major elevation of the standard of food being served in the park. Its success paved the way for the numerous deluxe restaurants that can be found in Disney theme parks today. The Blue Bayou, which Disney operated itself, also reflected the way in which Walt was taking control of his park. Prior to the mid-1960s, most of Disneyland's restaurants had been operated by outside vendors who had aggressively competed against each other for business; the owner of the Silver Banjo in Frontierland infuriated Walt by boiling onions and using a fan to blow the smell all over the surrounding vicinity. But by the mid-1960s, Disney was providing all of the food service in the park itself.

The other component of New Orleans Square that warrants mention is Club 33, the private club that is entered from a door next to the Blue Bayou. (The name derives from the club's "address," 33 Royal Street.) Club 33 was a rare example of something being put in Disneyland that Walt did not really want. In 1965, Disney was negotiating with General Electric to continue sponsoring the Carousel of Progress after it was moved from the World's Fair to Disneyland. GE executives demanded a corporate hospitality lounge like the one that had been in the company's pavilion at the World's Fair.

---

14   As was the case for Pirates of the Caribbean, the ride building for the Haunted Mansion was so large that it had to be built outside the berm. The famous "stretching room" at the beginning of the attraction is in fact an elevator that takes guests down so that they can pass under the railroad tracks.

To accommodate them, Walt had to break his rule that no alcohol would be served in Disneyland; Club 33 remains the only place in the park where alcohol is available today. Today, the waiting list for Club 33 perennially numbers the maximum thousand names, and a prospective member can expect to wait ten years or more before their name will get to the top.

New Orleans Square was not the only part of Disneyland that received serious attention in the mid-1960s. Tomorrowland had been added to Disneyland very late in the construction process, and Walt had long been frustrated by its failure to live up to his vision. Although a number of attractions had been added, much of Tomorrowland continued to be filled with corporate exhibits that many guests found boring. Walt thus decided to rebuild Tomorrowland almost from the ground up, at a cost of $23 million. The area was expanded to five acres, nearly doubling its size. Focusing on the theme of a World on the Move, the New Tomorrowland, which opened in 1967, featured three new attractions. Two were derived from the 1964 World's Fair: the Carousel of Progress and the PeopleMover, which used the spinning-tire technology adapted from the Ford Magic Skyway.[15]

Image 5.15: The PeopleMover, one of three new attractions added to Tomorrowland in 1967, shown here gliding over Autopia in the late 1970s.

---

15   As he had in the case of the monorail, Walt hoped that the new technology would be adapted for urban mass-transit use. His hopes were to be disappointed, but the Imagineers did succeed in making one sale, to the Houston airport, where the inter-terminal train was designed and built by WED.

The third new attraction was the Monsanto-sponsored Adventure Through Inner Space, which pretended to shrink guests down to microscopic size and take them inside a molecule of water. As we already know, Adventure Through Inner Space's most important contribution to Disney theme park history was the Omnimover system.

Walt Disney did not live to see the opening of Pirates of the Caribbean, the Haunted Mansion, or the New Tomorrowland of 1967. By the mid-1960s, he was suffering from a variety of ailments, including kidney stones, toothaches, and chronic respiratory problems that were aggravated by his lifelong habit of chain-smoking unfiltered cigarettes. Worst of all was an old injury to his neck that he had suffered while playing polo in the 1930s. Over the years, the damaged vertebrae had calcified, causing increasing pain and a noticeable limp. In October 1966, he went to see a specialist, who recommended surgery to relieve the pressure on the nerves in his neck. During the pre-surgery evaluation, however, spots were discovered on his left lung; exploratory surgery confirmed that he had cancer that had metastasized. He was released after ten days in the hospital, but only four days later he was in such intense pain that he had to be readmitted. At 9:35 in the morning on December 15, 1966, Walt Disney died of cardiac arrest caused by lung cancer. His death came as a tremendous shock to the studio, as few employees had known how seriously ill Walt was. His brother Roy issued a public statement declaring that "we will continue to operate Walt's company in the way that he had established and guided it. All of the plans for the future that Walt had begun will continue to move ahead." Roy's promise included the plans for the Florida Project that were already underway, though they would change significantly from Walt's original vision.

six
The Florida Project

Disneyland is in California because that's where Walt Disney Productions was located. In contrast, the company had no ties to Florida, the home of Walt Disney World. Even so, it is tempting to see the choice of location for the second Disney theme park as inevitable. After all, Florida was just about the only place on the East Coast where the weather was warm enough to allow a Disney theme park to operate year-round. In reality, however, a complex sequence of events led Walt Disney to Florida. In contemplating future projects after Disneyland proved a massive success, Walt considered a wide variety of options in a wide variety of locations. In the end, it was not only weather but a host of other factors that caused him to choose Florida. Two of these factors, to be sure, were very similar to the ones that had led Walt to Anaheim: cheap land and good transportation access. These factors were in fact magnified in Florida, for whereas Walt had needed less than 200 acres of land in Anaheim, he now wanted to acquire more than 10,000. And whereas Disneyland had drawn a predominantly local and regional audience, the Florida Project, as it was initially called, needed to attract people from the entire East Coast. But the Florida project was not conceived as merely a pumped-up version of Disneyland. Instead, Walt was planning to build something very different, and much more ambitious.

The previous chapter showed how Disneyland faced two key issues in its first decade of operation: capacity and competition. By the end of that period, the park had to confront a third issue: control. Inside the berm, Disneyland was Walt's universe, and almost anything that he asked for would be made to happen. But outside the berm was a very different story. At the time Disneyland was built, Anaheim's zoning code dated from the days when Orange County had been largely agricultural, and thus there were few development controls in place. Initially, Walt saw this as something positive, because it imposed minimal restrictions on what he could do. But after the park opened, it proved to be a double-edged sword, as uncontrolled development outside the berm quickly threatened to destroy the pristine atmosphere that Walt wanted Disneyland to have.

This development even threatened to intrude into the park itself. In 1961, the Disneyland Hotel built an eleven-story tower, requiring New Orleans Square to be positioned to block it. In late 1963, Sheraton-West Hotels submitted a plan to the city of Anaheim to build a twenty-two-story tower, and in May 1964 another developer submitted a proposal to build a ten-story office building that would be located directly across from the park's entrance. These two proposals prompted Walt to ask the Anaheim City Council to impose a height limit, so that external buildings would not be visible from inside the park. "I don't want the public to see the world they live in while they're in the park," he told them. "I want them to feel they're in another world." The city reduced the height of the Sheraton tower from twenty-two to fourteen stories, but soon afterwards another developer announced plans to build an Angel Spire, a 750-foot-high tower modeled on the Space Needle in Seattle. This thoroughly alarmed everyone, and Walt was able to convince the City Council to pass a height limit that was on a sliding scale depending how close a structure was to the park. Buildings immediately adjacent, for example, could be no higher than seventy-five feet.

Many people in Anaheim, however, opposed such limits on economic development; the *Anaheim Gazette* protested that Disneyland was not a "sacred shrine." This meant that additional development restrictions were going to be difficult to put into place. In July 1965, Walt expressed his frustrations about his lack of control of the area surrounding Disneyland at the tenth anniversary celebration in the Disneyland Hotel. "If we could have bought more land, we'd have bought it," he said, "and it wouldn't look like a second-rate Las Vegas around here."

Images 6.1 and 6.2: (*Opposite page*) Top, an aerial view of Disneyland in 1955, when it was entirely surrounded by agricultural land. Bottom, an aerial view from 1962, in which the encroaching sprawl along Harbor Boulevard is clearly visible at the top of the image.

This was not only an aesthetic but also a financial issue. As others built hotels, restaurants, and tourist attractions that he saw as parasites on Disneyland, Walt felt they were siphoning off money that rightly belonged to him. In its first ten years of operation, Disneyland made $273 million, while the peripheral development that surrounded it made $555 million.

The lack of control over development in Anaheim was not the only, or even primary, reason that Walt Disney investigated the possibility of building a second theme park. He was also interested in attracting a new audience and in generating new revenue. There were plenty of possibilities, for as soon as Disneyland had proven a success, Walt was bombarded with questions about whether he would build another, similar park somewhere else in the country. He received hundreds of proposals. "We had them from all over ...," he recalled. "They wanted us to do one in Egypt. They wanted us to do one in Japan. They wanted us to do one in Brazil—at the capital there."[1] The East Coast of the United States, however, was always Walt's primary target. Market surveys showed that only 2 percent of Disneyland's visitors came from east of the Mississippi, where three-fourths of Americans lived. As early as 1958, Disney began conducting studies of potential East Coast locations for a second Disneyland.

The idea that initially drew the most interest from Walt was for a park in or near New York City, which offered the obvious advantage of a massive population. In 1960, one out of every twelve Americans lived in the New York metropolitan area. But building a park in the New York area would be extremely expensive: Disney's real-estate consultant Buzz Price estimated that it would cost over $45 million, almost three times the price of Disneyland, with much of the added expense coming from the high price of land. Walt knew that he needed a partner to offset this massive up-front investment. And, as had been the case with Disneyland, television was a potential option. David Sarnoff, who was the president of NBC's parent company RCA, was aware that Walt was disenchanted with ABC, as the network had canceled *The Mickey Mouse Club* and *Zorro* in 1959, though they both remained popular.[2] Sarnoff knew that after Disney's contract with ABC expired in 1961, Walt would be looking to move the studio's television

---

1   Joe Fowler, Disneyland's general manager in its first decade, claimed that Walt dismissed these proposals out of hand, but this was not entirely true. About the Brasilia proposal, for example, a Disney executive wrote in a memo that "Walt is interested and might come to Brazil personally if the whole thing looks promising." A quarter-century before the opening of Tokyo Disneyland, Disney was already contemplating the construction of a park outside of the United States.

2   After ABC refused to allow the shows to be broadcast on any other network, Walt sued. Disney was awarded damages, but *Zorro* never returned to the air and *The Mickey Mouse Club* did so only in syndication.

programming to another network. He offered an added enticement that he knew Walt would find difficult to resist: NBC would broadcast the Disney program in color.[3] And to sweeten the pot even further, Sarnoff offered to underwrite much of the cost of building a second Disneyland in the New York area. He presented Walt with a feasibility study for a park in the New Jersey Meadowlands that claimed it would be profitable.

When Walt commissioned his own real-estate expert Buzz Price to take a look, however, Price found that the weather would only allow the park to operate for 120 days a year. Walt was adamantly opposed to the idea of a park that could only operate seasonally, not only because it would generate smaller profits, but also because he feared that having a temporary workforce would lead to a "carny" atmosphere. He considered the possibility of covering the park with a dome, but the cost proved exorbitant. Price's study also showed that visitors to New York differed from those to Los Angeles, as they were more often there on business rather than for pleasure and tended to stay for a shorter time. Price concluded that the combination of these factors did "not point to a profitable venture."[4]

But even if New York was not feasible, Walt remained interested in doing a project on the East Coast. Initially, however, he was thinking of something on a smaller scale than Disneyland. In August 1963, Walt visited Niagara Falls, Ontario, to meet with its mayor Franklin Miller and local business leaders about the possibility of collaborating on a project in the recently completed 325-foot-high Seagram Tower. Walt suggested two attractions: a copy of the Rocket to the Moon ride at Disneyland and a Circle-Vision theater. Circle-Vision films were made by mounting cameras on a moving vehicle in a circular pattern; the films were then shown on nine screens arranged around the interior of a cylindrical theater. The first Circle-Vision film, *A Tour of the West*, was an opening-day attraction at Disneyland in 1955. The theater at Niagara Falls was part of Walt's plan to build a series of Circle-Vision theaters around the country that would show travel films similar to Disney's *People and Places* documentaries of the 1950s. After *A Tour of the West* (1955), Disney made two other Circle-Vision films, *America the Beautiful* (1958) and *Italia '61* (1961), and a third, a railway tour of Europe called *Magic of the Rails*, was in production. With an eye toward

---

3   This was not mere generosity on Sarnoff's part: RCA was the only manufacturer of color television sets at the time, and he hoped that a color Disney program would boost sales. The program, titled *Walt Disney's Wonderful World of Color*, premiered in 1961.

4   This would not be the last time that Walt would be asked to consider building a park near New York. In the mid-1960s, Robert Moses, the driving force behind the 1964 World's Fair, offered Walt a good deal on the land in Queens that the Fair had occupied in an effort to entice him to build a theme park there, but Price once again warned Walt against accepting, primarily due to the weather.

the 1967 Universal and International Exposition (commonly called Expo 67) in Montreal, Walt was interested in making a film about Canada.[5] But the Seagram Tower project never came to fruition, for two reasons. First, Disney and Seagram could not come to an agreement over licensing fees. Second, the overabundance of tourist attractions near Niagara Falls reminded Walt too much of Anaheim.

At the same time as he was exploring the Seagram Tower idea, Walt was looking to turn the forty-five-acre farm in Marceline, Missouri, where his family had lived between 1906 and 1910 into a tourist attraction. Walt discussed this possibility with Marceline's mayor Rush Johnson, and they came up with a plan to create a working farm that would attempt to replicate turn-of-the-century life. Buzz Price's economic feasibility study found that the project would not turn a profit, but Walt continued to explore it as a non-profit venture. Johnson even formed a dummy corporation that purchased the land secretly, with the intention of reselling it to Disney. But the Marceline project was still in development when Walt died in 1966, and Roy Disney later abandoned it. Another idea came from Kansas City, where Walt lived between 1910 and 1923. His friend J.C. Hall, the founder of the Hallmark Greeting Card Company, wanted Walt to join in the re-development of a one-hundred-acre site surrounding Hallmark's headquarters in a part of Kansas City called Signboard Hill, which had become economically depressed by the 1960s. But beyond offering advice to acquire sufficient land to create a buffer zone around the project, as he had failed to do in Anaheim, Walt did not get involved with Hall's plans, which ultimately became the mixed-use Crown Center development.

Although he was looking to other parts of the country, Walt also considered several West Coast projects in the early-to-mid-1960s. One possibility was a collaboration with Samuel Morse, the conservationist and developer of the Pebble Beach Resort on the Monterey Peninsula in northern California. In 1963, Disney commissioned two studies of the feasibility of a project in Monterey but ultimately dropped the idea. Another possibility—which came much closer to becoming a reality—was a ski resort in the Sierra Nevada Mountains. Walt became interested in this idea after he was invited to design the opening and closing ceremonies for the 1960 Winter Olympics in Squaw Valley. At the Olympics, Walt met the famous German skiing champion Willy Schaeffler, whom he later delegated to assess sites in Colorado and California as potential ski resorts. Walt considered Mount San Gorgonio near Palm Springs and Mammoth Mountain east of San Francisco, but was not able to make a deal for either site.

---

5   The film, titled *Canada '67*, was presented in the Telephone Association of Canada pavilion at Expo 67.

Image 6.3: The Mineral King Valley in northern California, where Walt Disney planned to build a ski resort in the mid-1960s.

Walt then turned to the Mineral King Valley, 230 miles north of Los Angeles. In the 1950s, the federal government had tried to attract developers to the area, but there had been little interest. In 1965, Walt offered a massive $35 million to build a "self-contained Alpine village" that would attract 2.5 million visitors a year. The offer was swiftly accepted, and over the next several years, Disney developed a master plan for the site. But opposition from conservationists grew, forcing Disney first to reduce the size of the project and then to commit to the construction of a cog railway to reduce automobile traffic. Even so, the Sierra Club and other environmental groups continued their efforts to stop the project, and ultimately Disney opted to abandon Mineral King in the mid-1970s.[6]

Of all these Disney projects of the early-to-mid-1960s, only Mineral King got past the discussion stage. There was one possibility, however, that came much closer to becoming a reality. By the 1930s, the area along the Mississippi Riverfront in St. Louis was socially and economically blighted. To revitalize the area, city officials obtained funding via New Deal programs to establish the first national historic site, which would commemorate the

---

6   In 1978, Mineral King was incorporated into Sequoia National Park, putting an end to any plans to develop it as a resort. Disney also explored the possibility of building a ski resort at Independence Lake near Lake Tahoe, but the company could not acquire the necessary land from the Southern Pacific Railroad and the federal government.

westward expansion of the United States. Progress on the monument was slow, however, and it was not until 1948 that architect Erno Saarinen's design for a stainless-steel 630-foot-high arch was selected. Ground was finally broken in 1959, and the arch opened to the public in 1967. By that point, it had been joined by a second redevelopment project, Busch Memorial Stadium, which opened in 1966. It was estimated that these two attractions would draw five million people a year to the riverfront. But the city had further plans for the area, including a shopping, dining, and entertainment complex called Riverfront Square. They wanted the complex to have an historical theme; according to the publicity materials, it would derive "its character and charm from the most romantic period of St. Louis—when it faced its river and was the Gateway between the old World and the New, our settled East and our new West."

Image 6.4: The St. Louis riverfront in the early 1940s, following the demolition of the existing buildings in preparation for the construction of the Jefferson National Expansion Memorial, which included the Gateway Arch.

As Riverfront Square's planners brainstormed, they came up with an intriguing idea: why not invite Walt Disney, who had grown up in Missouri, to produce a film about the history of St. Louis that would be shown in one of Riverfront Square's theaters? In early 1963, Mayor Raymond Tucker and the Civic Center Redevelopment Corporation (CCRC), which was over-seeing the Riverfront Square project, approached Walt about making such a film. Intrigued, Walt began formulating plans not only to produce the film but also to build a Circle-Vision theater in which it could be shown. Soon, another Disney attraction was added into the mix: a transportation system that "would have an economic potential as an amusement ride in addition to its primary transportation function." (This sounds similar to the PeopleMover system that was concurrently being developed for the Ford pavilion at the 1964 World's Fair.)

As he became more involved, Walt grew more enthusiastic about the Riverfront Square project. Like Anaheim, St. Louis was well-connected to the new interstate highway system, making it accessible to a large portion of the American population, and Walt thought that it might support a larger-scale Disney attraction. In April 1963, Walt dispatched Buzz Price and Disney's business manager Donn Tatum to take a look. Their preliminary report was sufficiently positive that the following month Walt and Lillian Disney traveled to St. Louis, where they met with the mayor and the CCRC and toured the riverfront district. Impressed by the potential of what he saw and by the commitment that the city had made to the project, Walt began to contemplate developing Riverfront Square as a Disney entertainment complex.

Due to St. Louis' sweltering-in-the-summer, freezing-in-the-winter weather, the complex would have to be entirely indoors. This required a five-story, 160,000-square-foot building able to accommodate 25,000 guests per day. As the Imagineers set to work, a more specific vision began to emerge: the indoor space would be divided into two Mississippi-River-themed halves, one focusing on St. Louis and the other on New Orleans. The former would contain a Jungle-Cruise-type ride that would replicate Lewis and Clark's westward journey and an animatronic bird show similar to the Enchanted Tiki Room, which here would celebrate the ornithologist John James Audubon, who had settled in Missouri in the early nineteenth century. The New Orleans section would contain a boat ride through a Louisiana bayou and a replica of Jean Lafitte's pirate ship. Walt also wanted to incorporate the human audio-animatronic figures that he was developing for the 1964 World's Fair, which eventually evolved into a concept for a stage show about the history of St. Louis. As the project developed, the Imagineers came up with other ideas, including a Matterhorn-style roller coaster themed to Meramec Caverns, a famous Missouri cave, and a dark ride focusing on the great St. Louis fire of 1849 or bank robbers Frank and Jesse James.

So why did Disney invest so much time into developing ideas for Riverfront Square and then not build it? The most frequent explanation is that August Busch, the owner of the Anheuser Busch Brewery, demanded that Walt sell alcohol and Walt refused. There is some truth to this story, but it is not the full picture. Busch did view the prospect of having Riverfront Square be alcohol-free as a snub both to his business and to local culture. Both sides then dug in their heels: the CCRC made it clear that Disney's plans were unlikely to be approved if provision for the sale of alcohol was not made, while Walt appeared on local television to press his case that Riverfront Square should be "something for the whole family." This was not, however, what ultimately scuttled the project. In March 1964, Walt proposed a compromise solution: the top floor of Riverfront Square would contain a restaurant and lounge in which alcohol would be served, while the other floors would be alcohol-free. The presentation met with an enthusiastic response, and the Disney team left believing that an agreement had been reached.

There was one final hurdle: money. When Buzz Price's economic study came back, it reported that a modest profit of 5 percent a year was possible, but only if the CCRC or the city of St. Louis absorbed a significant portion of the $30 to $50 million cost of construction. This was the issue that ultimately stopped Riverfront Square. After flying to Los Angeles in July 1965 to make a last-ditch attempt to save the project, CCRC vice-president Preston Estep conceded that it was a "dead deal." Shortly afterwards, Walt stated that "we were asked to try to develop a major attraction having the impact on the St. Louis area of a Disneyland. We suggested at the outset that a project of that scope, in size and cost, might well prove difficult to accomplish, due to a number of imponderable factors. Such has proved to be the case."[7]

The failure of Riverfront Square did not, as some Disney histories claim, drive Walt to Florida. Instead, the process of determining where a "second Disneyland" would be located proceeded on several fronts simultaneously, and Walt had been evaluating Florida as a possible location for a Disney project for at least a decade. In early 1955, while Disneyland was still under construction, he told a reporter from the *Los Angeles Times* that "the only other place" that he could see where it would be possible to build another Disneyland was Florida. In 1959, he told the press that "Florida would be better than California in many ways" for a second Disneyland. Florida offered one obvious advantage: weather. In the vast majority of

---

7   Disney later recycled some of the ideas for Riverfront Square. The rotating side stages that had been conceived for the audio-animatronic show, for example, later became central design components of the Country Bear Jamboree, while plans to use audio-animatronic figures of Mark Twain and Will Rogers to tell the story of St. Louis' history were revived in the early 1980s for Epcot's American Adventure attraction. August Busch, meanwhile, was inspired by his experience with Disney to expand the "gardens" that were located next to his breweries into full-scale amusement parks. Busch even tried to convince Walt Disney to design a park adjacent to his brewery in Houston, but Walt refused to get involved in something that was so directly associated with alcohol. In 1971, Busch opened an amusement park in Houston anyway, and he also built parks next to his breweries in Van Nuys, California, and later in Williamsburg, Virginia, and he significantly expanded the number of attractions in Busch Gardens in Tampa, which had opened in 1959. The Houston and Van Nuys parks did not last long, but the ones in Williamsburg and Tampa are still going strong, though they are no longer owned by Anheuser-Busch, as in 2009 they were purchased by SeaWorld Entertainment.

the country east of the Mississippi, a theme park could only remain open for part of the year, unless it was indoors, which massively increased the costs of construction, reduced the size, and therefore took a big bite out of potential profits. The further along the process of identifying a site moved, the more weather became an essential precondition, as the difficulties of trying to build in a less advantageous climate became apparent. Weather was not, however, the only factor. A more specific set of circumstances led Walt to Florida, and to Orlando in particular

Walt's first foray into Florida occurred in the southern rather than central part of the state. In 1959, RCA/NBC head David Sarnoff introduced him to John D. MacArthur, an eccentric insurance billionaire. MacArthur owned 12,000 acres of land in northern Palm Beach County that he was interested in developing as a "garden city," or planned, self-contained community, called Palm Beach Gardens. But he was only intending to use 4000 of his acres for the town, so plenty of land would be left over. It seemed a perfect match: MacArthur would provide the land, NBC would help foot the bill, and Walt's Imagineers would design a theme park. The three partners agreed to chip in $100,000 each for a feasibility study, and Walt assigned WED's Marvin Davis to prepare drawings.

In late 1959, Buzz Price flew to Florida to see the potential site. Price concluded that "the area offers a theme park attendance potential which equals or exceeds that experienced by Disneyland in southern California." Soon afterwards, Walt flew to Florida himself, staying in the Palm Beach Hotel under an assumed name in order to keep the potential project a secret. He and MacArthur hit it off—one story even claims that they went skinny dipping together on a secluded beach beside a lake that MacArthur owned. They informally agreed that Disney would use 320 acres of MacArthur's property for a theme park. This was a moment of considerable significance for the future, as it marked the first appearance of the concept of a planned community that was linked to a theme park.

So why did the MacArthur-Disney collaboration fail? There were three reasons. First, in the late 1950s and early 1960s, NBC's parent company RCA was engaged in the development of some very expensive technology, including color television and communications satellites, and it had little cash to spare on theme park development. Second, Roy Disney was not happy when he learned that Walt had obtained MacArthur's permission to use only 320 acres. Aware of the problems that the relatively small amount of land that Disney owned in Anaheim had caused, Roy wanted to create a much larger buffer zone around the Florida park. But when Roy pressed for more land over dinner in Palm Beach, MacArthur became so angry that he left the table, telling his real-estate advisor Jerome Kelly that "I have to get the hell out of here, or I'll hit that goddamn beagle right in the nose."

Third, and most significantly, Walt wanted to build more than just a copy of Disneyland.[8] He was now becoming interested in building a City of Tomorrow, a planned community in which new technologies could be tested. This idea was not necessarily incompatible with MacArthur's vision for Palm Beach Gardens. Buzz Price's initial report on the feasibility of the site was titled *The Economic Setting of the City of Tomorrow*, which made it clear that from the beginning the theme park was only a small part of the overall concept. But MacArthur saw Palm Beach Gardens as his baby, while Walt would merely contribute the theme park as one of its amenities. Walt, on the other hand, was unwilling to cede so much control to MacArthur; he wanted a prominent role in the entire project. Disneyland in Palm Beach Gardens did not fail, as it is sometimes argued, because Walt wanted to build a city and MacArthur wanted to build a theme park; rather, they each wanted to build both, and to have control over both. In the end, even with the large amount of acreage that was available, there was not enough room in Palm Beach Gardens for both men's ambitious plans.[9]

Even after the Palm Beach Gardens negotiations collapsed, Walt continued to believe that Florida was the right location for his new project. In 1961, he hired Buzz Price's Economics Research Associates to "evaluate specific locations for future recreation facilities" in the state. Price dispatched a freelance researcher named Robert Lorimer, who criss-crossed Florida for two weeks evaluating potential sites. Lorimer recommended Ocala, eighty miles north of Orlando, which shifted the focus from south to central Florida. In November 1963, Walt, Price, and a contingent of Disney executives flew to Florida. Following Lorimer's recommendation, they landed in Orlando on the 21st and drove north to Ocala. The next morning, they flew back to California, but Walt instructed the pilots of Disney's private plane to fly over as much of Florida as possible so that he could see it from the air. According to Disney legend, he looked down and saw the point where the newly completed Florida Turnpike and the still-under-construction Interstate 4 were going to meet, about twenty miles southwest of Orlando. Walt supposedly exclaimed, "That's it!" That evening, when they landed in New Orleans to refuel, they learned that President Kennedy had been assassinated in Dallas earlier that day. After

---

8   Walt's aversion to sequels went all the way back to the 1930s, when he regretted having been convinced to produce three sequels to the popular cartoon *The Three Little Pigs*. In 1966, he said, "I don't believe in sequels... I have to move on to new things... I could not possibly see how we could top pigs with pigs. But we tried, and I doubt whether one member of this audience can name the other cartoons in which the pigs appeared."

9   After the negotiations with Disney failed, MacArthur continued to develop Palm Beach Gardens as a residential community. By 1970, it had a population of 7000, though even today its population has not quite reached the 55,000 that MacArthur envisioned.

they resumed their journey west, Walt announced that central Florida would be the location of his new project.

In reality, the decision was not quite that simple, as Walt continued to consider a range of different Florida sites. But gradually, he was honing in on Orlando. When Price assigned a researcher named William Lund to tour both Ocala and Orlando, his conclusion was clear: Orlando offered "greater potential," in particular its south side, because, as Walt had seen from the air, that was where Interstate 4 and the Florida Turnpike were going to meet.[10]

Image 6.5: Florida's Governor Ferris Bryant (center, with raised shovel) leads the groundbreaking ceremony for the extension of the Florida Turnpike from Fort Pierce to Orlando in 1961. The turnpike's proximity was a key reason why Walt Disney selected a site that was southwest of Orlando.

The turnpike provided a link to Interstate 75, which runs from Miami to Michigan's border with Canada, while Interstate 4 linked to Interstate 95, the main highway route up and down the East Coast from Miami to Maine. This meant that whether tourists were coming from the Northeast or the Midwest, they would have easy access to Orlando.

---

10   The location of this intersection was no accident. In the 1950s and 1960s, a roup of local businessmen had sought state funding for roads to make Orlando a transportation hub. Construction of the Florida Turnpike, part of the state highway system, began in the mid-1950s. The first section, from Miami to Fort Pierce, was completed in 1957, but it was not until 1964 that the extension to Wildwood, which included Orlando along its route, was finished. The federally funded Interstate 4, which cuts diagonally across the state from Daytona Beach to Tampa, was built around the same time: the section from Tampa to Plant City was completed in 1960 and the extension to Orlando two years later.

Orlando had more in common with Anaheim than warm weather and good highway access, however. They shared key aspects of their respective histories as well, aspects that made them both attractive sites for a Disney-type development. Both Florida and California had been Spanish colonies, and they joined the union only five years apart, in 1845 and 1850, respectively. Like Anaheim, Orlando began as an agricultural settlement, though in its case the settlers were cattle ranchers and cotton farmers rather than vintners. Also as in Anaheim, the arrival of the railroad in the late nineteenth century was crucial in linking the town to a wider economic world. In 1880, the South Florida Railroad made Orlando a stop on its line from Tampa to Jacksonville, making it possible for farmers to get perishable crops to market. Early experiments had shown that Florida's warm climate and sandy soil were ideal for citrus growing, but only now could local farmers expand into full-scale production, as an orange picked in Orlando could be on a table in New York City within three days.[11] In 1893, Florida produced five million boxes of fruit annually. Just two decades later, that number had doubled, and by 1950, 100 million boxes of citrus fruit were being shipped out of Florida each year. The Orlando area was the center of the state's production; by 1920, one out of every four Florida oranges was grown there, and by 1950 nearly one in two.

Image 6.6: An orange grove on Lake Concord near Orlando, c.1900-1910.

Another similarity between Anaheim and Orlando was their location in regions of major population growth in the twentieth century. Between 1900

---

11   Reflecting this promise, the county surrounding Orlando had been named Orange in 1845, forty-four years before southern California's version got its name.

and 1950, California ranked first in population growth among American states, and Florida third. It was after World War II, however, that central Florida's population truly began to boom. A key factor was air conditioning, which was first installed in public buildings in the late 1930s but not affordable for private homes until the 1950s. Between 1955 and 1980, the percentage of air-conditioned homes in Orlando jumped from 20 to 80 percent. In 1950, Orlando was the 135th largest metropolitan area in the United States, with a population of 115,000. Today, it ranks seventeenth, with a population of 2.3 million, a twenty-fold increase. And just like in southern California, this surge in population meant a shift away from agriculture. In the mid-1950s, 40 percent of Florida's oranges were produced in the Orlando area; by 1990, only 6 percent were.

But despite all the similarities, there were some key differences between central Florida and southern California as prospective locations for a Disney theme park. Whereas Disneyland drew predominantly upon the 5.5 million people who lived in the Los Angeles metropolitan area and the thirteen million people who lived in California in the 1950s, a central Florida location needed to draw from far beyond the Orlando area's 400,000 inhabitants and even Florida's five million in the 1960s. It would have to attract visitors from hundreds of miles away, the Northeast in particular. Walt thus had to take into account not only highway but air access as well. Here, too, Orlando offered advantages, as McCoy Air Force Base, which was also located on the south side of the city, had been converted to a joint civil-military airport in 1961.[12]

Because most of his guests would be tourists rather than locals, Walt also had to ensure that Florida could offer a highly developed tourist infrastructure with ample hotels and other facilities. In the early 1960s, Florida had just begun to commit its economic future to tourism rather than agriculture, a development that was made possible by the rising affluence of postwar American society, by improved methods of mosquito control, and by the spread of air conditioning. By 1965, sixteen million tourists came to Florida annually. Most of them headed for the beach, but along the way many of them were enticed by the wide variety of roadside attractions—alligator farms, tropical gardens, dolphin shows, and quirky museums of all kinds—that sprang up all over the state. In the years before Disney arrived, Florida tourism was democratized: whereas previously it had been relatively inaccessible and therefore reserved for

---

12   In 1975, the air force closed the base, making McCoy exclusively a civilian airport; it was renamed Orlando International Airport the following year. This history is why the call letters of Orlando International Airport are MCO. Today, around half of Disney World's visitors arrive by air, as opposed to only a quarter of Disneyland's.

an elite clientele, now a much broader spectrum of people, including in particular young families with children, both found the idea of traveling to the state attractive and could afford to do so.

Without these developments in the Florida tourist industry, the weather alone would not have been enough to lure Disney there. But in combination with the weather, they were a powerful draw as Walt searched for an East Coast site for his next project. In early 1964, with the focus now on the south side of Orlando, the Disney team swung into action, with attorney Robert Price Foster taking the lead. Foster went to great lengths to keep the identity of his employer a secret: he used a false name, Bob Price, when he was in Florida, and he never flew to the state directly from California.[13] Foster hired a Florida-based attorney named Paul Helliwell to provide local legal advice. Helliwell came highly recommended by Disney's New York attorney Bill Donovan, who had served as head of the Office of Strategic Services (OSS), the predecessor to the CIA, in the Second World War. Donovan knew that Helliwell could keep a secret, because during the war he had served as the head of the OSS's Secret Intelligence Branch in Europe.[14] Disney's desire to conceal its identity was so great that even the Florida real-estate expert whom Foster hired, Roy Hawkins, initially did not know who was employing him. This created problems as Hawkins searched for appropriate parcels of land, because he could not take into account the specific requirements of a theme park. So, for example, he identified a parcel near Sebring, eighty-five miles south of Orlando, but when Foster flew out to look at it, he realized that there were no major highways nearby. Helliwell eventually convinced Foster to reveal their client's identity to Hawkins, so that he could ensure that the properties he looked were suitable for Disney's purposes.

In April 1964, Foster traveled to Florida to look at several properties that Hawkins had identified. One was a 12,000-acre tract near the intersection of Interstate 4 and the Florida Turnpike that was owned by the brothers Jack and William Demetree, who were Jacksonville-based home-builders. The Demetrees had purchased the property in 1960, but now a $90,000 payment was about to come due, and they were eager to sell. They were having trouble finding a buyer because they owned only the surface rights to the property, while the mineral rights to whatever lay underneath belonged to Tufts University in Massachusetts. Bequeathed

---

13   Because Foster sometimes stopped in St. Louis to see his mother, speculation grew rife that the mystery company that was buying so much land was McDonnell Aircraft, which was based there.

14   After the war, Helliwell headed the Far East Division of the War Department's Strategic Service unit. He joined the CIA when it was created in 1947. At the same time as he was assisting with the Disney project in the mid-1960s, Helliwell was also involved in covert operations against Cuba. He handled much of the money-laundering for the ill-fated Bay of Pigs invasion in 1961.

the land by a wealthy alumnus, Tufts had in the 1940s sold the surface rights to rancher and state senator Irlo Bronson, who grazed his cattle on the land. Bronson in turn sold the surface rights to the Demetrees, but they had been unable to acquire the mineral rights, which meant that the land was largely valueless for development, because the university could demand that anything built on the property be torn down if they decided to drill for oil or search for minerals.

Foster and Helliwell knew that the issue of the mineral rights had to be resolved before Disney could purchase the property. They investigated the likelihood of there being anything valuable beneath the surface and discovered that explorations for oil and phosphorous had found nothing. Foster, Helliwell, and the Demetrees then traveled to Boston to meet with the Tufts Board of Trustees, who were initially reluctant to sell the mineral rights. Helliwell, however, had learned that one of the trustees was a vice-president of the First National Bank of Boston. This was important because the president of the bank was an old World-War-II buddy of his. When the negotiations stalled, Helliwell asked to speak to the trustees privately, and then told them something—to this day, no one knows what—that convinced them to sell the mineral rights at a bargain-basement price of $15,000. Now, Disney could pursue the purchase of the Demetrees' land. On June 18, 1964, Helliwell contracted with the Demetrees to purchase a six-month option on their land for $145 an acre, or a total of $1.8 million. This was Disney's first land acquisition in central Florida, and as such it can be regarded as the company's first commitment to Orlando as the site for its new project.

The purchase of the Demetree tract marked the beginning of Disney's complex, cloak-and-dagger acquisition of land in central Florida; strict secrecy had to be maintained to keep the price of the additional land that Disney needed from soaring. To keep the identity of the purchaser a secret, Helliwell set up five dummy corporations: Bay Lake Properties, the AyeFour Corporation, Reedy Creek Ranch, Tomahawk Properties, and the Latin American Development and Management Corporation.[15] No one at the Disney company in California was permitted to speak directly with anyone in Orlando; all communication was routed through Disney's lawyers in New York. Using the dummy companies as a façade, Disney quickly purchased options on two more tracts, an 1800-acre parcel for $250,000 and a 2700-acre parcel for $625,000, and then negotiated a larger purchase of 8500 acres from Irlo Bronson for $900,000. (This was the one parcel that Disney purchased outright rather than first obtaining an option on it.) Disney paid an average of $180 an acre for these

---

15   In late 1966, these companies were merged into a single entity, the Compass East Corporation.

purchases, which totaled 25,000 acres.[16] Within all of these large tracts were smaller, separately owned parcels called "outs." Finding the owners of all the outs and convincing them to sell took months; these piecemeal acquisitions were tracked on a map on the wall of a conference room in the Disney studio in Burbank. Because the outs were smaller parcels, they were also more expensive: Disney paid an average of $300 an acre for them. Obtaining clean title to the land also involved the identification and disbandment of any subdivisions, which required Disney to petition the Orange County government. It was a complex, time-consuming strategy, but ultimately successful. By June 1965, Disney had paid a little over $5 million—or an average of $182 an acre—for a total of 27,258 acres, covering an area eleven miles long by four miles wide, about twice the size of Manhattan.[17]

Image 6.7: In 1964 or 1965, Roy Disney inspects the Orlando property.

---

16   A decade earlier, Disney had paid over twenty times that, or $4000 an acre, for the property in Anaheim.

17   As Disney attempted to acquire the final parcels of land, a few owners refused to sell. Willie Goldstein, who owned thirty-seven acres on the shore of Bay Lake, initially resisted Disney's offer, as his property offered excellent hunting and fishing and a hundred-year-old cabin for him to live in. It was not until local business leaders put pressure on him, and Disney upped its offer to $194,000, or over $5000 an acre, that he gave in. Another owner of 482 acres never sold. The identity of that owner was long a mystery, but in the year 2000 a reporter from the *Orlando Sentinel* discovered that he was a Taiwanese businessman named Ling Kai Kung, who had bought the property in 1962. After Ling died in 1992, Disney and the property's new owner, the World Union Industrial Corporation, worked out design criteria and other issues such as road access so that the property could be developed. Bounded on three sides by Walt Disney World and on one side by Interstate 4, it currently contains the time-share Wyndham Bonnet Creek Resort along with the Wyndham Grand, Hilton, and Waldorf-Astoria hotels.

Even with all of Disney's efforts to hide its identity, there was rampant speculation in the local press. In the fall of 1964, rumors began to swirl around central Florida that a mysterious purchaser was seeking to buy a large amount of land in Orange and Osceola counties. Concerned that such speculation would drive up the price of the remaining acreage that Disney wanted to buy, Helliwell met with the *Orlando Sentinel's* publisher Martin Andersen. Andersen, who swore until his death in 1986 that he was not told the identity of the mystery company until it was announced publicly in October 1965, promised that he would do his best to help keep the secret. The *Sentinel* continued to print speculation, but nothing more. In May 1965, gossip columnist Charlie Wadsworth reported that "there has been one consistent rumor that the land is being purchased for a second East Coast Disneyland attraction." Wadsworth's story did not particularly alarm Disney, however, because he dismissed the rumor as false due to the fact that Walt Disney himself had denied it, and he also cited a number of other companies that could be the potential purchaser, including three automobile manufacturers (Volkswagen, Chrysler, and Ford), three aircraft manufacturers (McDonnell, Republic, and Lockheed), and a chemical company (Hercules Powder). The following month, Wadsworth suggested that the land might be used for "a huge, life-sized model of the city of the future," for which Walt Disney would "furnish the ideas and put the overall package together," but he continued to favor other possibilities, such as Douglas Aircraft, John D. Rockefeller, and Howard Hughes. (He claimed that Hughes was running as a "three-to-one" favorite among local oddsmakers.) More stories appeared in the *Sentinel* later in June and July that mentioned Disney as the possible mystery purchaser, but they also listed alternatives such as General Electric and the United States Air Force, which would use it for their Manned Orbiting Laboratory project.

By this point, Disney had already acquired the vast majority of the land that it needed, and company officials were less nervous about the consequences of the news getting out. On October 1, Helliwell announced that the identity of the purchaser would be revealed at a press conference on November 15. Ironically, it was Walt Disney himself who ended up revealing the secret prematurely. Unaware of what was going on in central Florida, Disney's public-relations team invited reporters from the *Orlando Sentinel* to Anaheim to attend the celebration of the tenth anniversary of Disneyland. Martin Andersen sent Emily Bavar, who was the editor of the newspaper's Sunday magazine. After the tour of the park, Bavar asked Walt point-blank whether it was his company that had been purchasing land in the Orlando area. She recalled that he "looked like I had thrown a bucket of water in his face." He then explained why central Florida would be a terrible location for a Disney theme park, but in the process revealed that he knew an awful lot about the region. Recognizing that Walt was "not a good liar," Bavar became suspicious. On October 17, 1965, her story, titled "Disney Hedges Big Question," made it clear that she thought Disney was the mystery company, but it was presented as mere speculation and buried on page twenty-three.

After Bavar returned to Orlando, she discussed her suspicions with Martin Andersen. Andersen realized that the evidence was so compelling that to ask Bavar to suppress it would be overt censorship; he may also have known, or at least suspected, that by this point little serious harm could be done by revealing the mystery purchaser's identity, as Disney had completed its land acquisitions. On October 20, the *Sentinel* printed a follow-up story that asked, "Is Our Mystery Industry Disney?" It included a postscript in which the editors apologized for "underplaying" the original story, which they asserted "did not have the importance or impact it should have had." They made it clear that they concurred with Bavar's suspicions: "The new project is really going to be a new type of entertainment built by the world's greatest cartoonist, movie producer, showman and world's fair exhibit maker. After talking to Mrs. Bavar, the *Sentinel* is convinced the mystery industry's author, architect and builder is Walt Disney." Three days later came the bombshell: a front-page story headlined "We Say: 'Mystery' Industry Is Disney."

When he saw the story, William Potter, the retired army major-general and former governor of the Panama Canal Zone who had been appointed to direct the development of the Florida Project, rushed to a pay phone to call Burbank and inform Walt that the story was out. He was nervous that he would be blamed, but Walt, aware that he had been responsible for raising Bavar's suspicious, reassured him. Governor Haydon Burns' office was quickly on the phone to Burbank as well, demanding to be told if Disney was the mystery company. Walt knew that the official announcement could wait no longer. Potter and Bob Foster flew to Miami, where the governor was speaking to the Florida League of Municipalities Convention. On October 25, 1965, to a huge roar of applause, the governor announced that Disney was coming to Florida.

SEVEN
De-Centering the Magic Kingdom

Most Disney guests who stand in front Cinderella Castle in the Magic Kingdom probably imagine that they are standing at the center of Walt Disney World. In fact, they are standing close to the far northern edge of Disney's massive Florida property. Instead, it is Spaceship Earth, the giant sphere that stands near the entrance to Epcot, that is located far closer to the center of the property. The peripheral position of the Magic Kingdom and the central position of Epcot on Disney property are no accidents. Instead, they reflect Walt Disney's original vision for the Florida Project, in which EPCOT, which was not a theme park but the Experimental Prototype Community of Tomorrow, was the core element, and the Magic Kingdom was merely an ancillary component that was going to help pay for EPCOT and draw visitors to come and see it. This is why this chapter is titled "De-Centering the Magic Kingdom," because that is precisely what we have to do in order to understand how Walt Disney World began.

EPCOT—the all-capital-letters acronym for Experimental Prototype Community of Tomorrow rather than the "Epcot" with only the "E" capitalized that Disney uses today, was Walt Disney's last big idea in a chain that stretched back to synchronized sound for animated films, technicolor animated films, full-length animated features and, of course, Disneyland's radical alteration of the notion of an amusement park. Unlike the others, it never became a reality, but its ambition and scale led to the creation of the Walt Disney World Resort; without that original vision, Walt Disney World would have ended up being something very different.

To be sure, a second theme park, an East Coast Disneyland, was always part of the plan. Walt was never such an idealist that he ignored the bottom line, because he knew that it was money that made it possible for him to do what he wanted. Plus, he knew that a theme park was necessary to keep Roy happy, because without it an East Coast venture would be too risky. But Walt saw a second Disneyland as a means to an end, not an end in itself. With his innate aversion to sequels, he was now interested in doing something that was breathtaking in scope: he wanted to build a city of 20,000 residents that would feature the latest technology and the latest ideas about urban planning. He wanted to show that American corporations could solve the most pressing urban problems through innovation, and he hoped that the people who came to visit would take what they learned back home with them and apply the lessons to their own lives.

These grand plans, ironically, were not because Walt liked cities: he didn't. While they were on their way to the Chicago Railroad Fair in 1948, he told animator Ward Kimball, "I can't figure out why in the hell everybody lives in the city where they don't have any room and can't do anything. Why don't they come out here where they have this great empty land, filled with opportunity and silence?" But by the 1960s, Walt was eager to move beyond entertainment and tackle some of the biggest social problems of the day. And urban decay was very much at the top of the agenda. Beginning after World War I, the migration of blacks from the rural south to midwestern and northeastern cities prompted many white Americans to move to the suburbs, as they began to see cities as places of crime and danger. This phenomenon, which urban planners called white flight, reached a peak between 1940 and 1970.

But there were more factors at work than race. After World War II, massive federal investment in highways, along with the provision of low-interest housing loans to returning servicemen, drew many people to the suburbs. In the 1960s, the population of suburbs grew six times faster than that of cities. At the same time, manufacturers based in northeastern and midwestern cities sought cheaper sources of labor in the American South and, later, overseas. As cities lost population and industry, their tax base declined, and blight and high rates of unemployment became growing problems. Early efforts to eradicate blight resulted in neighborhoods being razed for new highways and high-rise public-housing projects, but by the 1960s, this kind of modernist urban planning was being blamed for exacerbating the decay, and new solutions were being sought. Walt thought that he could provide them.

In the late 1950s, Walt read everything he could find about urban planning. One book that he particularly liked was Ebenezer Howard's *Garden Cities of To-morrow*, the revised version of Howard's *Tomorrow: A Peaceful Path to Real Reform*, which had been published in 1898. Howard was British, and he was responding to the slum-like conditions that existed in many cities in Britain in the late nineteenth century. As a solution, he proposed the "garden city," a self-contained community with a pattern of development in concentric rings, surrounded by a greenbelt. Each garden city would specialize in a different type of economic function; they would be linked to each other and to a larger central city by rapid transit. The first garden city in Britain was Letchworth, about thirty-five miles from London, which was designed in 1904. It was followed by Welwyn fifteen years later.

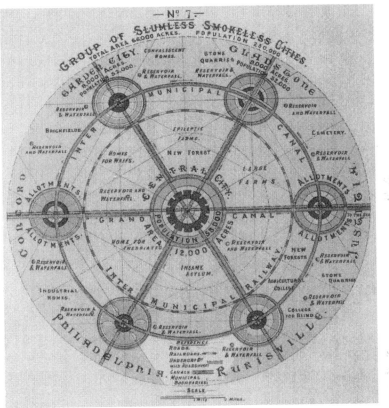

Image 7.1: Ebenezer Howard's garden-city concept, from his *Garden Cities of To-morrow* (1902).

After World War II, garden cities evolved into "new towns," which featured carefully planned designs that were walkable and efficient, with a broad range of housing for all socioeconomic levels as well as commercial, industrial, and leisure facilities. In the 1960s, Walt Disney visited two American new towns: Reston, Virginia, comprised of five small "villages" and high-density housing in order to encourage walking, and Columbia, Maryland, which featured ten residential "villages" surrounding a central office and shopping district. He also looked at a European city, Stockholm, Sweden, which had recently seen the addition of four planned satellite towns, each of which had a high-density core surrounded by rings of residential development that were linked to the core via radial highways and an underground subway.

Another influence on Walt's thinking was the 1964 World's Fair. Not, however, the real fair in New York, because he found many things about it frustrating, in particular the transportation scheme. He felt that in order to be enticed to go to the fair's peripheral zones, such as the recreational area funded by the developer Angus Wynne, visitors needed a special form of transportation that would itself be an attraction. He even tried to convince Goodyear to fund a PeopleMover-type system, but the Fair's organizer Robert Moses went with a cheaper hanging monorail system built by AMF. In the end, Walt was proven right: few visitors went to the recreational area, and Wynne was bankrupted as a result. In fact, the World's Fair as a whole lost nearly $20 million, with some people attributing its financial failure to its poor layout and transportation system.

Instead, it was another 1964 World's Fair, one that never happened, that had a bigger influence on Walt's thinking. In the late 1950s, architect Victor Gruen was hired to draw up plans for a World's Fair in Washington, D.C. Gruen used his concept of cellular urban design, which featured clusters of buildings that mixed residential, commercial, office, and entertainment uses, thus eliminating the need for people to drive. He believed that making a space pedestrian-friendly required keeping the cars out of it, and so his plan called for the fair's central core to be built on a raised, pedestrian-only platform with a network of utility corridors beneath it. Gruen wrote that "the World's Fair will be enriched by the inclusion of structures which will permit the visitor actually to experience elements of the City of Tomorrow in accordance with the newest scientific, sociological and technological concepts." After this fair was over, its structures would be used to create a community of 200,000 people, with concentric rings of housing that became higher density as they got closer to the center. This housing would be interspersed with stores, workplaces, and green spaces; Gruen even proposed the inclusion of an amusement park that would be "developed along the lines of the successfully operated Disneyland near Los Angeles, California."

Even though the Washington World's Fair never happened, Gruen's plan had a lasting impact. In May 1960, the prominent architecture critic Ada Louise Huxtable published an article entitled "Out of a City, Out of a Fair" in *Horizon* magazine. In it, she complained that World's Fairs had become "tired" and predicted that the upcoming New York example would be no exception. She had high praise, however, for Gruen's plan, about which she wrote that "the familiar bugaboos of international expositions have been anticipated and dealt with in this farsighted project," primarily because it "offered a contribution of permanent value." Imagineer Marty Sklar believed that Walt Disney derived many of his ideas for EPCOT from Huxtable's article. Later, Walt acquired a copy of Gruen's book *The Heart of Our Cities*, which was published in 1964.

All of these ideas—about garden cities, new towns, and world's fairs—went into Walt's thinking about EPCOT. He gained confidence in his ability as an urban planner from the fact that many experts had high praise for Disneyland. Victor Gruen referred to Disneyland as a "social center," while James Rouse, the developer of Columbia, Maryland, said that it was "the greatest piece of urban design in the United States today":

> It took an area of activity—the amusement park—and lifted it to a standard so high in its performance, in its respect for people, in its functioning for people, that it really does become a brand-new thing. It fulfills all the functions it set out to accomplish—unselfconsciously, usefully and profitably to its owners and developers. I find more to learn in the standards that have been set and in the goals that have been achieved in the development of Disneyland than in any other piece of physical development in the country.

Walt began to conceive a plan for a city of the future that featured a central commercial core surrounded by residential areas, with a transportation network to move people between the two. In 1965, he drew a very rough rendering of his ideas, with a circular, flower-like EPCOT in the center and a theme park at the top left. Walt then tapped an old friend, architect Welton Becket, to draw up a proper plan for EPCOT. Becket had some experience with this type of project, as he had designed Century City, a 176-acre mixed-use development that had been built on the former 20th Century Fox backlot in Los Angeles. Century City included office space, entertainment venues, a shopping center, and a hotel, and its pedestrian and automobile traffic were kept strictly separate.

But once again, Walt could not obtain what he wanted from a professional architect; he found Becket's drawings too cold and uninviting. So, as he had done for Disneyland, he set up his own team of Imagineers, installing them in a secret project office whose main feature was a sixteen-foot-wide aerial image of the Florida property. In June 1965, the team assembled for a four-day seminar to discuss the implementation of the Florida Project. This would require a massive planning effort, as the project would contain not only entertainment and commercial but also residential, administrative, and industrial components, along with all of the infrastructure to support them. Walt was determined to control the project in every way, to prevent what had happened in Anaheim from happening again. It was during the seminar that Florida real-estate attorney Paul Helliwell first suggested the possibility of Disney creating its own municipality, which would streamline the review process for all the permits and licenses that the project would require and would allow the company to provide its own utility services. Someone raised the objection that the residents of a municipality would have voting rights, but Helliwell countered that Disney could limit voting rights to landowners and then lease rather than sell the residential units to the occupants. Walt initially thought that this approach would create more problems than it would solve, but as the rest of the group thought about Helliwell's suggestion, they began to realize that creating a municipality was the best means of ensuring that Disney retained total control over the project. Soon after the seminar, Imagineer Marvin Davis drew up the first comprehensive plan for the Florida property. It included plans for a city, a theme park, resort hotels, and golf courses, along with the infrastructure that would support them. It also showed how the development would be surrounded by a large greenbelt in order to avoid the encroachment of outside development as had happened in Anaheim.

In November 1965, Walt gave the public a preview of Disney's ideas in a press conference at the Cherry Plaza Hotel in Orlando. The press conference was invitation-only, and tickets were highly coveted. But if the attendees were expecting many details about Disney's plans, they were disappointed, as Walt told them little beyond that his vision for the project included both a working city and a theme park. The Florida Project did not even have an official name yet; when Walt was asked to confirm that it would be called Disney World, he said that they were still working on the title. He was equally cagey in describing the project. "The concept here will have to be something that is unique," he said, "and so that there is a distinction between Disneyland in California and whatever Disney does—and notice I didn't say Disneyland in Florida—whatever Disney does in Florida." He hinted that he might build two different communities, one called Yesterday and based on an older vision of America and one called Tomorrow that would look toward the future. It was clear, however, that he was most interested in tomorrow. "I would like to be part of building a model community, a City of Tomorrow...," Walt continued, "because I don't believe in going out to the extreme blue-sky stuff that some architects do. I believe that people still want to live like human beings. There's a lot of things that could be done. I'm not against the automobile, but I just feel that the automobile has moved into communities too much. I feel that you can design so that the automobile is there, but still put people back as pedestrians... I'd love to work on a project like that."

Image 7.2: (*Opposite, top*) Flanking Florida Governor Haydon Burns, Walt and Roy Disney introduce the as-yet-unnamed Florida project to the press in Orlando in November 1965. At this point, the project was still focused on Walt's EPCOT concept of building an experimental city.

A few months later, Walt charged the Imagineers with producing a film about EPCOT and building a model of it, so that he would have a more detailed means of explaining it to the public, the media, and, most importantly, the state and local officials whose approvals he would need. The script of the film was written by Marty Sklar. Walt recorded his part on October 27, 1966, only seven weeks before his death. The model, meanwhile, was designed by Herb Ryman, while Marvin Davis led the team that constructed it. Built at a scale of one-eighth inch to the foot, it was huge: 115 feet by 60 feet, with over 4500 individual components.[1] The model's "urban core" featured the thirty-story Cosmopolitan Hotel at its center, surrounded by a landscaped recreation deck with tennis courts and walking and jogging paths. Beneath the hotel was an international shopping village, an updated version of the International Street that had been proposed for Disneyland in the late 1950s. It included shops selling goods from all over the world, a variety of global restaurants, shows, and roving entertainers.

On the edge of the urban core was an area of high-density housing, comprised of around fifteen four-to-five story buildings that were linked to the other parts of the city by PeopleMover. Moving outwards, the next concentric ring was a greenbelt, which contained schools, churches, recreation centers, public services, cultural, and athletic venues, and even a Tiki-themed restaurant beside a lake. Next came a ring of low-density

---

1   A portion of the EPCOT model can still be seen along the route of the Tomorrowland Transit Authority PeopleMover in the Magic Kingdom. The remainder of the model was destroyed when it was moved along with the Carousel of Progress from Anaheim to Orlando in 1975.

housing, which in the model consisted of 258 single-family homes in nine different designs. The concept for EPCOT also called for a separate 1000-acre industrial park that would be linked to the city by monorail, as well as smaller industrial areas on the outskirts. Power was generated by a nuclear plant located on the edge of the model. And finally, the model featured its own small amusement park, intended for its residents, in contrast to the larger, separate theme park that would draw tourists to Disney World. All the parts of EPCOT were linked by an extensive transportation network, which included monorails, PeopleMovers, automobiles, moving sidewalks, electric carts, and an airport. All of these forms of transportation converged in a multimodal hub beneath the urban center.

Two days after Walt's death, Roy Disney announced that the Florida Project would be officially named Walt Disney World in his brother's honor. But at this point, it was not even clear that the project was going to continue. Seventy-three years old, Roy had been thinking of retirement, and it was unclear what the future of the Disney company would be without either of its founding brothers. But Roy ultimately decided to stay on, because he felt that he owed it to Walt to make sure that his last dream became a reality. And when he polled his top executives, they, too, wanted to continue with the Florida Project.

Roy's first experience of being the public face of Disney came at a press conference on February 2, 1967, at the Park East Theater in Winter Park, near Orlando, before an audience of business leaders, government officials, and reporters. The purpose of this event was different from its predecessor in November 1965. Then, Walt had provided a vague description of his plans for Florida, as he knew that the magic of the Disney name and the promise of a $100 million budget would ensure a warm reception. But now, it was time to get down to business. After screening the EPCOT film, which packed an extra emotional punch because of Walt's death, Roy announced that Disney was going to spend far more than the $100 million that Walt had mentioned fourteen months earlier. That sum would only cover the theme park; another $500 million would be spent on the rest of the project. In return for this massive expenditure, Roy made it clear what Disney expected from state and local agencies; at one point, he even slipped and referred to these expectations as "demands." First, he cited Buzz Price's estimate that 12,000 cars would visit the property each day. While Disney was willing to build all the roads that would be on their property, he wanted the state to build two new interchanges, one connecting Interstate 4 and State Road 530, and another connecting State Road 530 to Disney property. Both requests were granted; the Florida State Road Board allocated $5 million for improvements in the vicinity of Walt Disney World.

The second thing that Disney wanted was for the state to create an "improvement district" that would cover the entire property. This would allow Disney to sell bonds to finance the development of the property. Disney agreed to provide all the services that the district required in return for almost complete control over what they could do with it. The provision of services was no small matter. The nearest high-voltage power line was over fifteen miles away, and neither Orange nor Osceola County had the capacity to supply the large amount of water that Disney needed. Disney's willingness to take on these problems seemed like a good deal to state legislators. On May 12, 1967, Governor Claude Kirk signed legislation creating the Reedy Creek Improvement District, which gave Disney authority over drainage, waste treatment, utilities, roads, bridges, fire protection, and emergency medical services. But there was one problem: according to Florida law, only a democratically elected government could regulate building codes and land use. So Disney also convinced the state to create two municipalities, Bay Lake and Lake Buena Vista, that together covered the entire improvement district. Voting rights were limited to property owners, of whom there were only forty-seven, all Disney employees. Disney's power over its property was so great that Governor Claude Kirk joked to Roy when he signed the legislation that "it's very comprehensive. I noticed only one omission. You made no provision for the crown."

Image 7.3: With Roy Disney at his side, Governor Claude Kirk signs legislation creating the Reedy Creek Improvement District on the 12th of May 1967.

The Reedy Creek Improvement District had some powers that went beyond those that a local government would typically have. One was the right to operate an airport. The original plans for EPCOT had called for an airport to be built on the southern end of the property. This never happened, but Disney did build a short-take-off-and-landing airstrip. After the Magic Kingdom opened in October 1971, three airlines, Shawnee, Executive, and VQ, operated commercial flights to Walt Disney World from Tampa, Orlando, Fort Lauderdale, and West Palm Beach, though they had all ceased to operate by the end of 1972. There was also a private airstrip and a heliport near EPCOT; only the latter remains today. Another power that Disney was granted was the right to explore "new and experimental sources of power and energy," including nuclear power.[2] But there were some things that Disney could not do, including the construction and operation of schools. Although Disney had included a School of Tomorrow as part of its EPCOT plans, company executives assured local and state authorities that they had no intention of opening their own schools. Instead, they offered to design experimental education programs for use in existing schools.

In the months after Walt's death, Roy maintained a public commitment to the EPCOT idea, because it allowed him to make arguments for Disney to gain extensive powers over its property. A state senator's aide recalled that "we all thought they were going to build EPCOT, a model community. That's what they talked about." But internally, the vision for Walt Disney World was beginning to alter. In a meeting in early 1967, Marvin Davis began by outlining Walt's most recent ideas for EPCOT. After he finished, Roy said, "Marvin ... Walt's gone." Roy had already decided to suspend planning for the rest of the property and concentrate on building the Magic Kingdom theme park and its resort hotels. To be sure, the Magic Kingdom had always been supposed to come first, as the revenues it generated would help pay for EPCOT, but bringing the planning for EPCOT entirely to a halt sent a clear message about Roy's new priorities.

Ground was broken on the Orlando property on May 30, 1967, but for the next two years little happened beyond clearing and preparing the land. Some local legislators were growing impatient with the apparent lack of progress. In April 1969, Disney held a four-day-long press event in Ocoee, Florida, in order to present its detailed plans. The company rented out the entire Ramada Inn and set up a big tent outside that was filled with drawings and models. Guests were escorted through the tent by attractive young hostesses, who read from a script written by Marty Sklar. Such was the

---

2   This power was never exploited, but Disney did build a natural-gas-fired power plant that generated about a third of the power that the Walt Disney World required.

nationwide interest in Walt Disney World that 350 members of the press attended the event from out of state, along with dozens of reporters from Florida, state and local officials, and executives from some of America's biggest corporations. The entire group was bussed to the Parkwood Cinema Theater, where Governor Kirk gave a brief introduction and then Donn Tatum, Walt Disney World's first president, announced that the "Vacation Kingdom" would open in October 1971. Roy Disney spoke last, telling the audience that "this is a big day for our company. I know Walt would like what his creative team is doing, because these are the ideas and plans he began. Everything you will see here today is something Walt worked on and began in some way." The presentation concluded with a seventeen-minute film called *Walt Disney World—Phase 1*, after which the guests were transported to the site to see how construction was proceeding. This was the first time that non-Disney employees had been permitted on the property since Disney had purchased it.

Although the original vision for EPCOT was abandoned soon after Walt's death, it left some important lasting legacies at Walt Disney World. The initial phases of development closely adhered to the master plan that had been developed while Walt was still alive, with the Magic Kingdom, the first two hotels (the Contemporary and Polynesian Resorts), and EPCOT all essentially in their original locations. All of these components were, as Walt had planned, linked by monorail.

In addition, Disney has made several attempts over the years to build residential communities on the Orlando property. In 1972, Disney unveiled plans for a master-planned community that was divided into four themed areas: golf, tennis, boating, and Western/equestrian. Named Lake Buena Vista after the Disney-created municipality in which it was located, the first phase of the community was to consist of townhomes that would be rented to vacationers or leased to corporations. Later phases, however, would have included apartments and single-family houses for permanent residents. In keeping with EPCOT's vision of urban planning, Lake Buena Vista was to have been energy-efficient and pedestrian-friendly, with cars kept well away from the central areas. The project also included a golf course, a shopping village, and a fifty-acre office park. As Disney confronted the problem of how to deal with the fact that permanent residents would have to be given voting rights, however, the plan began to change. Several groups of townhouses, a golf course, and the shopping village were actually built, but only one of the office buildings and none of the permanent residences were ever constructed. But although Lake Buena Vista never became a true residential community, it did retain some elements of the EPCOT vision. The Fairway Villas that were built in 1976, for example, were highly energy efficient, with double-glazed windows and heat pumps rather than air-conditioners.[3]

Lake Buena Vista never had a permanent population, but two other Disney developments currently do. First, there is the town of Celebration, which sits on the southern edge of the property. Built in the 1990s, Celebration shares EPCOT's commitment to extensive master-planning, as it was designed to be pedestrian friendly, mixed use, and human scale. What it does not share, however, is EPCOT's futurist aesthetic; instead, Celebration attempts to replicate an American small town from the early twentieth century, using a traditional grid layout. From the beginning, Celebration has divided opinion: some people see it as too planned, controlled, and sterile, while others see it as an attractive and walkable example of new urbanism.[4]

Walt Disney World's most recent residential community is the luxury subdivision Golden Oak.[5] Its 450 houses, which range in size from 3000 to 12,000 square feet, cost between $1.5 and $8 million. Though Golden Oak duplicates the residential function of the original EPCOT, there is little else about it that embodies that vision, as it is entirely suburban, with no mass transit, shopping facilities, or places of work on site.

There are many people who regard the current, theme-park incarnation of Epcot as a betrayal of Walt's intentions, and who fervently wish that Disney had actually built a city. But in reality, Walt's ideas for his next major project after Disneyland were constantly in flux. There is little doubt that EPCOT would have taken a different form than it ultimately did had Walt lived longer, because every project that he undertook had his personal stamp on it. But there is equally little doubt that it would have

---

3   Although plans were in place for the continued expansion of Lake Buena Vista, no major additions took place after the late 1970s. In the 1990s, several Disney hotels—Old Key West, Port Orleans, and Dixie Landings (now Port Orleans Riverside)—were built on the site previously slated for that expansion, and beginning in 2001, the townhouses and clubhouse were torn down and replaced by the Saratoga Springs Resort. The Shopping Village, meanwhile, was converted to Downtown Disney. Today, virtually all that remains of Lake Buena Vista are the Treehouse Villas at Saratoga Springs.

4   Celebration's population is currently around 7500. Disney dealt with the problem of having a large number of residents who would be able to vote in local elections by de-annexing the town from the Reedy Creek Improvement District.

5   The development is named after the Golden Oak Ranch in Placerita Canyon, about thirty miles south of Los Angeles, which Disney purchased in 1959. Walt had plans to develop part of the ranch into a residential community complete with golf course and shopping village, all linked by a train. Marvin Davis even designed homes there for Walt and Lillian Disney and for Roy and Edna Disney, but the residential side of Golden Oak never came to fruition, according to some sources because Lillian did not want to live so far from Los Angeles. Or at least it never came to fruition in California. Now called Disney/ABC Studios at the Ranch, it is still in use as a film and television shooting location today.

evolved considerably from his original vision. There is evidence, in fact, that Walt understood that building a city full of permanent residents was likely to prove impractical. When in May 1966 Paul Helliwell sent Walt a memo about a possible governing structure for EPCOT that referred to "permanent residents," Walt crossed the phrase out and replaced it with "temporary residents/tourists." Even Walt knew that EPCOT would end up being something very different from what he had originally envisioned. In the EPCOT film, Walt stated that "the sketches and plans you will see today are simply a starting point, our first overall thinking about Disney World. Everything in this room may change time and time again as we move forward."

Disneyland had been Walt's baby. He had overseen every detail of the design, construction, and operation of the park. But, even while he was alive, Walt's role in the Florida Project was very different: he was not a member of the main planning committee, and at the key planning seminar in June 1965, he was present for only the opening and closing sessions. Already, Walt seemed to sense that the Florida Project would be left to others to develop. Walt Disney World may have borne his name, but it was not his vision that would ultimately determine its future.

EIGHT
The Vacation Kingdom of the World

Disney planned to dedicate 2500 of the more than 27,000 acres that it owned in Orlando to Phase 1 of Walt Disney World. This was ten times the size of Disneyland, which allowed for ideas to be conceived on a much larger scale. It is inaccurate, however, to think of Walt Disney World as simply a bigger version of Disneyland. From the beginning, the Magic Kingdom was only a part, and not even the most important part, of the project as a whole. After the abandonment of the original EPCOT concept, Disney decided to build the "Vacation Kingdom of the World," a full-scale resort that would offer a variety of leisure activities, which would in turn entice people to stay longer than the day or two that they spent at Disneyland. This meant, ironically, that Walt Disney World ended up having to perform some of the functions of a city after all, because it had to support a large population of temporary residents who stayed in its hotels, ate in its restaurants, and used its infrastructure.

Walt Disney World was the largest private construction project in American history. The Disney company directly oversaw the building of the Magic Kingdom theme park, while the Reedy Creek Improvement District (RCID), led by its president General William Potter, handled the construction of the infrastructure for the property, including the power plant, sewage treatment works, and drainage system. All of this work had to be done on swampy land that many people thought was undevelopable. And to add to the challenge, it was supposed to follow the principles of the original vision for EPCOT, including energy efficiency, environmental responsibility, and sound practices of urban planning.

Drainage was the first and most essential task, as nothing else could begin until the water that inundated the property was under control. The excavation work for the drainage system took sixteen months—a third of the total time it took to construct Phase 1—with crews working nearly around the clock to build fifty miles of canals and eighteen miles of levees.

A flood-prevention method had to be devised that would not damage the area's fragile wetland environment; the water had to be managed, not simply removed. Disney created a system in which, if the water rose on one part of the property, a float mechanism would open gates that would allow the water to flow into the next section. There were nineteen sets of gates in all; when the water level decreased, they closed automatically as well.

In places that would be visible to the public, the canals were designed to look like natural water features. (When you see water on Disney property in Orlando, it is most likely part of the drainage system.) Admiral Joe Fowler, who had previously directed the construction of Disneyland, took on the same role for the Magic Kingdom. One of his last memories of Walt Disney was of a moment when he saw an early canal that Potter had laid out from Bay Lake to the southern end of the property. It ran, Fowler recalled, in a line "as straight as an arrow": "I was with Walt when he first saw it. Walt never raised his voice. The only way you could tell he was angry was when he raised his right eyebrow. He raised it now and said, 'Look, Joe, I don't want any more of those Corps of Engineers canals.'" After that, the canals were designed to look more like rivers, with graceful curves and meandering routes.

By the spring of 1969, the drainage system was complete, and construction of the Magic Kingdom, the two original hotels, the transportation system, and other infrastructure could begin. To oversee the construction process, Disney hired the J.B. Allen Company, the California-based firm that had carried out the work for Disneyland's "second opening" in 1959. Allen was responsible for managing 10,000 workers from eighty-seven different subcontractors.[1] The work was focused on the far northern end of the property, where the Magic Kingdom was located, as the original EPCOT plan had called for. After Walt's death, there had been some discussion about moving the theme park to a more central location, but eventually it was decided to leave it where Walt had wanted it to be. This required the Reedy Creek Improvement District to build a four-lane parkway running five miles from the main entrance to Walt Disney World to the Magic Kingdom's parking lot.[2] It also meant, however, that Disney could incorporate the natural Bay Lake into the plans for Phase 1. The lake was drained so that the decaying organic matter at the bottom that turned it dark brown could be removed; the engineers were surprised to find beautiful white sand underneath. Bay Lake was then refilled with clean, clear

---

1   Fed up with the delays and lax attitude of the workers, Disney fired J.B. Allen in early 1971 and formed its own contracting company, called Buena Vista Construction.

2   Originally, there were about seventy miles of roads on Disney property. Today, there are 167, some of which are six lanes wide. It is highly unusual for private roads in the United States to be so large.

water and stocked with 70,000 fingerling bass, which helped to control the property's rampant mosquito population. But if Bay Lake had harbored a pleasant surprise with the discovery of the white sand, the land in front of the proposed site for the Magic Kingdom contained an unpleasant one: it was too swampy to support a parking lot. Disney turned necessity into invention, and decided to create a second water feature, the Seven Seas Lagoon, in front of the Magic Kingdom. This made the entrance to the theme park more visually appealing and fully isolated it from the "real world," as Walt had wanted.

The existence of the Reedy Creek Improvement District and the Disney-controlled municipalities of Lake Buena Vista and Bay Lake meant that Disney was able to develop and implement its own building codes and zoning regulations. The RCID was responsible for the building codes; its eleven building inspectors worked closely with the Imagineers at WED headquarters in Glendale to ensure that everything was in compliance. This allowed for both efficiency and flexibility; for example, when it was discovered that epoxy held better and was easier to use than traditional mortar to hold bricks together, the code was quickly adjusted to take this into account. Standards could also be quickly developed for the unusual situations that a theme park created, such structures made of fiberglass and the marking of exits in dark buildings, for which no traditional codes existed. The process, recalled RCID district director Tom Moses, meant that "we saved [Disney] money, and we saved ourselves a whale of a lot of time."

This flexibility also allowed Disney to fulfill some of the more techno-logically innovative ideals of the original EPCOT concept. Potter made the rounds of some of America's biggest corporations, including Westinghouse, Bell Labs, Bell Telephone, IBM, Allied Chemical, RCA, Rockwell, and Union Carbide, in order to solicit ideas. A few were actually implemented. The Swedish-built Automated Vacuum Assisted Collection (AVAC) system, for example, collected trash at several points around the Magic Kingdom, and then drew it at sixty miles an hour every fifteen minutes through pneu-matic tubes to a central compacting station. In partnership with the United Telephone Company of Florida, Disney developed an electronic telephone system that was the first to offer entirely touch-tone dialing and the abil-ity to connect international calls without the aid of an operator. It was also the first telephone system to have all of its lines buried underground. Other ideas, however, fell by the wayside. RCA, for example, planned to build an advanced communication system for guests and employees, but the plan fell through when the company's computer division was sold to Univac in 1970.

The construction of the Magic Kingdom offered Disney a chance to correct some of the flaws of Disneyland. According to Disney legend,

Walt had been dismayed to see a Frontierland cowboy walking through Tomorrowland to get to his job, and so he demanded that his next park have a means for cast members to get from one section to another without being visible to guests. Disneyland, in fact, had already experimented with a limited system of tunnels beneath New Orleans Square and the New Tomorrowland, which opened in 1966 and 1967, respectively. In Walt Disney World, this concept was taken much further: an extensive network of corridors called Utilidors was installed underneath the entire Magic Kingdom. Although the Utilidors are often referred to as being underground, they are not, because Florida's high water table makes it impossible to build below ground level. Instead, the "floor" of the Magic Kingdom had to be elevated fourteen feet, using the dirt excavated from the Seven Seas Lagoon. Guests thus walk on the second story, while the Utilidors that guests walk on top of are at ground level. In addition to allowing cast members to get from one part of the park to another, the Utilidors contain offices; a cafeteria, bank, salon and break rooms for the cast members; kitchens for the park's restaurants; service access entry points; and utilities such as the AVAC garbage-collection system. They also contain the park's Digital Animation Control System (DACS), which controls all of the audio-animatronic attractions.[3]

The construction of all this was not cheap; the Utilidors alone added $5 million to the Magic Kingdom's cost. In total, Phase I of Walt Disney World cost $400 million, or twenty-five times what Disneyland had originally cost. To help offset this massive expense, Roy Disney considered merging with a larger corporation—Litton Industries, Gulf and Western, and Westinghouse were all interested—but he knew that Walt had rejected a similar deal with General Electric a few years earlier, and so he too determined to maintain Disney's independence. Instead, to pay for Disney World's Phase I, Disney sold convertible debentures, or bonds that were automatically converted to stock when the share price reached a certain level, to fund Disney World. Disney issued $190 million in convertible debentures, which, combined with a $72 million stock offering, gave them over $200 million in capital for Walt Disney World. The remainder of the cost was met by a common stock issue in 1971, which allowed Disney World to open debt-free. [4]

The Magic Kingdom opened on October 1, 1971. As the date drew closer, the pace grew more frantic: holes were filled in with dirt or concrete, whichever

---

3   There are smaller Utilidor systems under part of Epcot's Future World and under Disney Springs.

4   Because it resulted in the issuance of more stock, this strategy diminished the Disney family's ownership stake in the company. The overall value of their shares, however, doubled.

was faster, and construction walls were slapped up to hide things that were unfinished. One of the last tasks to be completed was the laying of four-and-a-half acres of sod on the barren ground surrounding the Contemporary Resort, which was done by everyone who could be rounded up, including Disney executives. They finished at 6am on the morning of opening day.

Guests competed to be the first to enter the park, and technically the first person to make it through the turnstiles was a University of Florida student and former high-school track star named Jack Sherrod, who sprinted in as soon as the gates opened. The officially designated winners, however, were William and Mary Windsor and their two young sons, three-year-old Jay and one-year-old Lee, from Lakeland, Florida. The Windsors had spent the previous night in their car at a nearby rest area so that they could be first in line. As they stood in front of the entrance gates, they were picked out of the crowd by Director of Marketing Jack Lindquist. Lindquist recalled that he "picked a family with a father who looked like Jack Nicklaus and a mother who looked like Mrs. Brady [the character played by Florence Henderson on The Brady Bunch television series]." As cast members applauded, they were escorted in by Mickey Mouse and driven up Main Street in the fire engine to Cinderella Castle.

The opening of the Magic Kingdom was much less chaotic than that of Disneyland. Only 10,000 guests were on hand, as Disney had deliberately scheduled the opening for a school day during a time of year when crowds were likely to be light. Even though this was the number that Disney both expected and wanted, some press accounts reported that the park's opening was a failure, and the price of Disney stock dropped nine dollars a share overnight. Disney designated the entire first month of the Magic Kingdom's operation as a "preview" in order to provide an opportunity to work out any bugs and glitches. The official opening ceremony did not take place until October 25, when more than 40,000 guests were present. Roy gave a brief address, but he spent much of the day on a boat in the Seven Seas Lagoon. When he was asked why he was not in the Magic Kingdom with the press and public, he replied, "Today is my brother's day. I want them to remember my brother today."

The fears about lack of attendance swiftly dissipated, as Disney found itself with the opposite problem. Within a few weeks of opening day, it was a common occurrence for the Magic Kingdom to reach capacity and close temporarily; guests would simply wait in their cars on the grass outside the parking lot for space to open up.[5] And once they made it into

---

5   In 1972, the parking lot was expanded from 9000 spaces to 12,000.

the parking lot, Disney struggled to get them to the Magic Kingdom. At Disneyland, guests simply parked their cars and walked or took a tram to the park entrance, but to reach the Magic Kingdom, they had to be transported around or across the Seven Seas Lagoon. The centerpiece of the transportation network was a 3.5-mile-long monorail loop that carried visitors from the Ticket and Transportation Center, the central collection point to which guests were brought by the parking-lot trams, to the Magic Kingdom.

The construction of the monorail proved to be an enormous challenge. The only company that could produce the fifty-five-ton beams for the track was located in Tacoma, Washington; it cost almost $1 million to ship the 337 beams across the country by rail. The beams were installed on top of a series of concrete pylons, but central Florida's landscape was studded with sinkholes, which meant that every pylon had to be a different height, requiring them to be cast individually on site. Copied from Learjet airplanes by Imagineer Bob Gurr, Disney World's Mark IV monorails, which cost $6 million each, represented a radical design departure from their predecessors at Disneyland.[6] Only three trains were ready in time for opening day, and as park attendance increased they were far from sufficient to handle the crowds. Three more monorails were under construction, and Disney quickly ordered four more, but before they arrived, other modes of transportation had to be pressed into service. The six steam launches that had been designated to ferry guests back and forth to the Contemporary and Polynesian Resorts and the houseboats that had been intended for guests to rent were instead used to transport guests to and from the Magic Kingdom. Two paddlewheel steamboats that were supposed to be used for private parties were also used, but they proved to be slow and prone to mechanical breakdowns, and two double-decker ferryboats were swiftly ordered to replace them. One story even claims that Disney was so desperate for additional transportation capacity that the Mike Fink Keelboats were temporarily transferred to the Seven Seas Lagoon.

These watercraft helped to ease the strain, but their capacity was limited, and so six of the twelve parking-lot trams were also commandeered. Disney had initially planned to build trams that would be driven by powerful compressed-natural-gas engines, but as construction costs for Phase 1 soared, they were replaced by off-the-shelf units built by United Tractor. The road from the Transportation and Ticket Center, however, had a 5 percent

---

6   Today, the Disney World monorails are Mark VI, while at Disneyland new Mark VII trains intended to look more like the original 1959 version were introduced in 2008. Fifty million people a year, or 150,000 a day, ride the Walt Disney World monorail, making it the second-busiest monorail system in the world, after only the system in Chongqing, China.

uphill grade after it passed under the canal that linked the Seven Seas Lagoon to Bay Lake. The trams constantly overheated on the hill, leaving disgruntled passengers stranded by the side of the road. Disney quickly designed new trams that were powerful enough to make it up the hill, but it was six months before they were ready for service.

Once guests made it into the Magic Kingdom, what did they find? The new park shared many attributes with Disneyland: guests entered via Main Street, U.S.A. and walked towardsthe castle. The park was arranged in the same hub-and-spoke pattern, with Adventureland, Frontierland, Fantasyland, and Tomorrowland in roughly the same places that they are in Disneyland. But there were some significant differences as well. Most obviously, the Magic Kingdom was significantly larger than Disneyland, with wider walkways and spaces to alleviate congestion. Originally, Disneyland covered about 60 acres, while the Magic Kingdom covered 107.[7] This greater scale was obvious as soon as guests entered, as the Magic Kingdom's Town Square and Main Street were much larger than Disneyland's. Though both Main Streets are set in the same time period, around 1900, the Magic Kingdom's represents a bigger, more prosperous East Coast town, with a more ornate style of architecture that Disney refers to as "eastern seaboard Victorian," in contrast to Disneyland's smaller midwestern town. On both Main Streets, the buildings are two stories high, but in the Magic Kingdom they appear to be three stories high, thanks to the use of exterior architectural details and forced perspective to trick the eye. A second place where the Magic Kingdom's larger scale is immediately apparent is its castle. At 198 feet, Cinderella Castle is two-and-a-half times taller than Disneyland's Sleeping Beauty Castle. It might have been taller still, but Florida law requires any structure higher than 200 feet to have a red airplane-warning light on top. So the Imagineers once again used forced perspective to make the castle look even taller than it is. The stones and windows get smaller as they go up; the railing of the balcony from which Tinkerbell begins her flight before the Wishes fireworks show, for example, is only two feet high.

---

7   Today, Disneyland covers around 80 acres, while the Magic Kingdom covers 120.

Image 8.1: Concept art by Herb Ryman of Cinderella Castle. Dated 1967, Ryman's drawing shows how early plans for a castle that was significantly larger than Disneyland's took shape.

On opening day, the Magic Kingdom featured three unique attractions: the Mickey Mouse Revue in Fantasyland, an audio-animatronic extravaganza of classic songs and scenes from Disney animated films; the Country Bear Jamboree in Frontierland, a humorous show featuring singing audio-animatronic bears that had originally been conceived for the Mineral King ski resort in the mountains of northern California; and the Hall of Presidents, the product of Walt Disney's long-cherished dream of bringing American history to life using audio-animatronics, in this case with figures representing all thirty-seven presidents of the United States. The Hall of Presidents was located in Liberty Square, which had evolved from the idea for Liberty Street in Disneyland in the late 1950s. The idea was revived for the Magic Kingdom partly because it was something Walt had very much wanted to do, but also in anticipation of the patriotic sentiment that was expected to accompany America's bicentennial celebration in 1976.

Image 8.2: Liberty Square, the Magic Kingdom's only unique land. It represented an updated version of the idea to add a Liberty Street to Disneyland in the late 1950s. This image shows its main attraction, the Hall of Presidents, which evolved from Walt Disney's concept for a show called One Nation Under God, with audio-animatronic presidents in the place of waxwork ones.

Other attractions, if not entirely new, were given a makeover that made their theming unique to the Magic Kingdom. Disneyland's Submarine Voyage, for example, was retitled 20,000 Leagues Under the Sea and themed to the 1954 Disney live-action film, with submarines that copied the steampunk look of the film's *Nautilus*. And some ideas for unique attractions were dropped altogether. In Fantasyland, the Imagineers originally planned to create an entirely new set of dark rides. A Mary Poppins ride was proposed as a replacement for Peter Pan's Flight; an Ichabod Crane/ Headless Horseman ride as a replacement for Mr. Toad's Wild Ride; and a Sleeping Beauty ride as a replacement for Snow White's Adventures. Roy Disney quashed these ideas, however, because he was worried that East Coast guests would be disappointed if they did not get to enjoy the same attractions that were featured at Disneyland.

Image 8.3: Cinderella Castle (seen from the back) and Fantasyland in the mid-1970s, with Main Street, U.S.A. and the Seven Seas Lagoon in the background. The Imagineers originally intended the Magic Kingdom's Fantasyland to feature different attractions from its Disneyland equivalent, but Roy Disney decided to copy the originals instead.

As Disney desperately sought to increase guest capacity, the early years of the Magic Kingdom saw the introduction of a number of new attractions. Although many of these, such as the Circle-Vision film America the Beautiful and Flight to the Moon, already existed at Disneyland, some did not. A slow-paced boat ride, the Swan Boats, was installed in the moat surrounding the castle in May 1972, and the Eastern Air Lines-sponsored dark ride If You Had Wings arrived the following month. The Magic Kingdom's biggest need, however, was for a thrill ride. Expecting guests to be predominantly families with young children, Disney was surprised when a significant number of teenagers and young adults came through the turnstiles of the Magic Kingdom. Like Disneyland in its early years, the park did not have an attraction more thrilling than the Mad Tea Party to appeal to them.[8] To remedy this deficiency, Disney revived an idea that had been

---

8   Land had been set aside in Fantasyland for a version of the Matterhorn, but it was never built. Florida never did get its own Matterhorn, though there were later discussions about installing a version of it in a Switzerland pavilion at Epcot or in Hollywood Studios.

in development since the mid-1960s. As part of the New Tomorrowland project at Disneyland, the Imagineers had designed a new roller coaster that was called at different points Space Port, Space Voyage, and Space Venture, until it was finally given the name Space Mountain in 1966. In order to simulate space flight, Walt Disney proposed putting the ride in the dark, which required it to be entirely indoors. In the late 1960s, the project was temporarily shelved because the technology was not yet available to build it and because the construction of Walt Disney World was consuming all of Disney's ready cash. But after the Magic Kingdom opened, Space Mountain returned to the front burner. By the early 1970s, computer technology had improved so that roller coasters could now utilize a "zone system" to operate multiple trains on a single track. This system allowed more trains to operate on the same track, eliminating the need for multiple tracks and therefore reducing the footprint of the building. Even so, the building to house Space Mountain was so massive—its 72,500 square feet of floor space could hold a football field—that even in the capacious Magic Kingdom it had to be located outside the boundary of the park. (That's why guests go down—to get under the railroad tracks—as they enter.) Construction began in December 1972. Half of the $20 million cost was paid by RCA, in fulfill-ment of its contract to provide a communications system for Disney World, which included a commitment to pay $10 million toward the sponsorship of "an attraction of interest." Space Mountain opened on January 15, 1975.[9]

Other attractions were conceived for the Magic Kingdom but never built. Among them was what is probably the most famous unbuilt attraction in Disney history: Thunder Mesa. Designed by Imagineer Marc Davis, Thunder Mesa was a giant artificial mountain patterned after a mesa, or flat-topped hill with steep sides, in the American Southwest. A runaway-mine-train-themed roller coaster would have circled the exterior, which would also have included a canoe-themed log-flume ride and various walk-through exhibits such as a pueblo Indian village. Inside Thunder Mesa would have been a restaurant called the Mesa Terrace, a western-themed version of Disneyland's Blue Bayou. The Mesa Terrace would have overlooked Thunder Mesa's star attraction: the Western River Expedition. The Imagineers thought that Disneyland's wildly popular Pirates of the Caribbean would be boring to Florida audiences because the real Caribbean was so nearby. To replace it, they conceived of a western-themed boat ride, some of the

---

9   After it proved a huge hit, Space Mountain was reconfigured for Disneyland's smaller space. Not only did the Imagineers have to double the width of the cars because there was room for only one track in Anaheim instead of Orlando's two, but they also dug a hole fifteen feet deep for the foundation so that the building would not be visible from Main Street. A version of Space Mountain currently exists in all six Disney resort locations.

ideas for which derived from the Lewis and Clark attraction that had been proposed for the Riverfront Square project in St. Louis in the mid-1960s.

Thunder Mesa was immense, and immensely expensive, and so, although the land for it was cleared, it was delayed until the end of Phase I of Walt Disney World's construction. In the meantime, everything was done to get the Western River Expedition ready to build: a script was drafted, a detailed scale model was built, theme music was written, and some of the audio-animatronic figures were even sculpted. But after the Magic Kingdom opened, guests frequently asked cast members about the pirate ride at Disneyland that they had heard so much about. Disney's president Card Walker decided to go the safe route and build a version of Pirates of the Caribbean in Florida. It opened in 1973 and cost $30 million, half of what had been budgeted for Thunder Mesa. The Thunder Mesa concept lingered for several more years, but the Western River Expedition was ultimately jettisoned due to its high cost and the difficulty of depicting American Indians in a humorous but non-offensive way. Only one part of Thunder Mesa was ever built. The runaway mine train concept gradually evolved into Big Thunder Mountain Railroad, which opened in Disneyland in 1979 and in the Magic Kingdom in 1980.[10]

Image 8.4: The runaway-mine-train-themed roller coaster Big Thunder Mountain Railroad, the only part of Thunder Mesa that was ever built, under construction in the Magic Kingdom in 1979.

---

10   The name Thunder Mesa lives on as the name of the fictional town Disneyland Paris' Frontierland.

The differences between Disneyland and the Magic Kingdom are important in understanding the two parks, but they pale in comparison to the differences between Disneyland and Walt Disney World as a whole. Until recently, Disneyland was a theme park with a single adjacent hotel. Disney World, on the other hand, was designed from the beginning to be a full resort, with multiple hotels and entertainment options, all linked by an efficient mass-transit system. Central to this plan were the two original hotels, the Contemporary and Polynesian Resorts. Disney had never run its own hotels before; to learn the business, it signed a consulting contract with Western International, the predecessor of the Westin hotel chain, which allowed Disney executives to observe its flagship property, the Century Plaza Hotel in Los Angeles. Later, Disney used the Hilton Inn South in Orlando as a training facility. Owner Finley Hamilton had built the 140-room hotel on a dirt road about ten miles north of Walt Disney World; he paved the road himself, calling it International Drive because, as he put it, "it sounded big and important."[11] Disney agreed to manage the hotel for him until the Magic Kingdom opened, and for some months afterward. It was consistently close to full occupancy due to all the Disney executives who needed a place to stay while they were in Orlando.[12]

This was all in preparation for the opening of Walt Disney World's two hotels. The design of the Contemporary Resort evolved from the futuristic hotel that had stood at the center of the original EPCOT plan. Some elements were retained, such as the integration with the transportation network, which was accomplished by having the monorail pass through the hotel's lower floors. But after the surrounding city was eliminated, a thirty-story tower standing in isolation in central Florida's flat landscape would have looked ridiculous, and so in the late 1960s the design changed to a lower structure with an atrium in the center.[13] The hotel was given the nickname "Contemporary" during the design process, but in 1971 it was officially designated the Tempo Bay. When Roy Disney heard about the change, however, he thought the new name was "phony and plastic," and so it reverted to its original name.

Intended as a luxury hotel with rooms costing a then-pricey $29 to $44 a night, the Contemporary was built as a collaboration between Disney and the United States Steel Corporation. One of U.S. Steel's subsidiary

---

11   Today, International Drive is Orlando's main tourist strip and is lined with restaurants and hotels.

12   The upper-level executives, including Roy Disney and Joe Fowler, stayed in five cottages that Disney built in Bay Hill, about five miles north of the Disney World site.

13   The design was inspired in part by the Hyatt Regency Hotel in Atlanta, which opened in 1967. Designed by architect John Portman, the Hyatt had a twenty-two-story atrium in the center.

companies, American Bridge, had been experimenting with a new building technique called modular construction, in which the frame of a building was erected on site but the components assembled off-site and then slotted into the frame. This building method had previously been used for the Palacio del Rio Hotel in San Antonio, which had been built in only 202 days. Imagineer Marvin Davis altered the Palacio del Rio's design to an A-frame shape to make it less of a shoebox. The thirteen pairs of 150-foot-high steel frames that comprised the building's skeleton were constructed on site, but the hotel's thousand rooms, at a pace of around forty per week, were built off-site at a nearby assembly plant, trucked in, and lifted into place by a crane.[14] This was supposed to decrease the cost of construction, but the process turned out to be more complicated, and expensive, than predicted. The room modules, which were supposed to cost $17,000 each, ended up costing closer to $100,000. One problem was that they had to be loaded one at a time into alternating sides of the frame so as not to unbalance the weight. Weighing 4.5 tons each, the modules were extremely difficult to maneuver when they were hanging from the cranes, and they rarely slid into their designated openings easily. Plagued by construction delays, the Contemporary was not finished until January 1972, three months after the Magic Kingdom opened. The original arrangement had been for Disney to retain ownership of the land and for U.S. Steel to own both of the original hotels, but as construction fell further behind schedule, relations between the two entities grew increasingly tense. Roy Disney eventually decided to buy out U.S. Steel's interest for $50 million and have Disney operate the hotels itself.

The second original hotel at Walt Disney World was the Polynesian Village Resort, which was positioned across the Seven Seas Lagoon from the entrance to the Magic Kingdom. The original design for the Polynesian was inspired by modern Hawaiian hotels such as the Ka'anapali Beach Hotel on Maui, but as it evolved, the hotel came to be inspired by the same Tiki culture as the Enchanted Tiki Room (or Tropical Serenade, as it was originally called in the Magic Kingdom). The Polynesian's design featured a central Great Ceremonial House, surrounded by eight longhouses containing the guest rooms. Specific design elements were inspired by architectural features that the Disney team saw on research trips to Hawaii, Tahiti, and Samoa. Like the Contemporary, the Polynesian was built by U.S. Steel using modular construction: the rooms were assembled off-site and then trucked in. In the Polynesian's case, however, instead of being

---

14   One of many Disney urban legends claims that after the rooms were loaded into the frame the building settled, making it impossible to remove them. In reality, the rooms were never intended to be removed, as they were sealed with concrete and welding once they were loaded in.

loaded into a preexisting steel frame, the rooms were simply stacked, and then the hallways and entryways were built around them.

From the beginning, both the Contemporary and the Polynesian were rarely less than completely full. And because their rooms were occupied by families rather than by business travelers, they were overflowing with people: normal occupancy rates for hotels were 1.5 persons per room, but the Disney hotels averaged over three. This created massive jams in the restaurants, as the dining rooms could only accommodate a fraction of the guests at any given time. The wear-and-tear on the facilities was intense, and already by the fall of 1972, less than a year after the hotel had been completed, Disney carried out a thorough refurbishment of the Contemporary Resort.

Image 8.5: An aerial view of Phase 1 of Walt Disney World in the early 1970s, from the south shore of the Seven Seas Lagoon. The Magic Kingdom is at the center of the image, with the Contemporary Resort to its right and the Polynesian Resort and Transportation and Ticket Center at the bottom. The rectangular patch of land jutting into the west side of the lagoon was originally intended for the Asian Resort; today, the site is occupied by the Grand Floridian Resort.

There was thus an immediate need for more hotel capacity. The original plans for Walt Disney World called for three more hotels—the Asian, Venetian, and Persian resorts—to supplement the first two. Inspired primarily by Thailand, the design for the Asian Resort featured a three-sided courtyard surrounding a 160-foot-high central building with a restaurant on top. A square plot of land, clearly visible in early aerial shots of Walt Disney World, was prepared for the hotel on the northwestern side of the Seven Seas Lagoon, where the Grand Floridian is today. The Venetian Resort was supposed to be located between the Transportation and Ticket Center and the Contemporary Resort, while the domed Persian Resort was to be on the shore of Bay Lake. So what happened to these plans for additional hotels? They were scrapped due to events far beyond central Florida. In 1973, Egypt and Syria launched a military campaign against Israel in an attempt to gain back the territory that had been lost in the Six-Day War of 1967. When America agreed to supply arms to Israel, the Arab-dominated Organization of Petroleum Exporting Countries (OPEC) imposed an oil embargo on the United States. Gasoline prices doubled, sharply reducing the Magic Kingdom's attendance, which saw 800,000 fewer people come through the turnstiles in 1974 than in the previous year. The crisis caused Disney to drastically curtail its plans for expansion. Not only the three additional hotels but new attractions such as the Western River Expedition were canceled, while others, such as the Big Thunder Mountain Railroad, were significantly delayed.[15] The construction of Space Mountain continued only because its foundation had already been built, but even its completion was delayed by over a year.

Disney did add one hotel in the early 1970s, the Golf Resort, but it contained only 153 rooms. It was not only smaller but less popular than the other hotels; while they were usually close to full, its occupancy rate hovered at less than 75 percent. Its lack of appeal was due not only to its lack of theming, but also to the fact that it was not on the monorail loop.[16] Additional hotel capacity was supplied by outside companies. In January 1970, Disney had opened the Walt Disney World Preview Center near the intersection of Interstate 4 and State Road 535, on the southeastern edge of Disney property near what is now Disney Springs. Intended to show

---

15   In the late 1970s, the idea for the Persian Resort was revived when Disney entered into discussions with the Shah of Iran about funding it, but the Iranian Revolution of 1979 put an end to these plans. The Venetian Resort was also revived when in the 1990s Disney CEO Michael Eisner became interested in building a hotel that was even more luxurious than the Grand Floridian. The project eventually evolved into the Mediterranean Resort, but it was abandoned for a second time when it was discovered that the land on which it was supposed to be built was extremely swampy, which would have required very deep, and very expensive, foundations to be dug.

16   In the mid-1980s, the hotel was renamed the Disney Inn and given a *Snow White* theme in an effort to increase its appeal; its size was doubled to 300 rooms at the same time. But it still lagged in popularity, and in the early 1990s, Disney contracted to lease the hotel to the armed forces, which had been looking to build a resort for current and retired servicemen. Renamed Shades of Green, it proved so successful in this incarnation that the armed forces purchased the hotel outright in 1996 for $43 million, though Disney still owns the land beneath it. Expanded further between 2002 and 2004, it now contains nearly 600 guest rooms.

curious visitors what they could expect, it no longer had a purpose after Phase 1 opened, and it closed at the end of September 1971. The area surrounding it was designated the Motor Inn Plaza, and Disney recruited two major hotel chains, Travelodge and Howard Johnson, and two smaller ones, Royal Inns and Dutch Inns, to build high-rise, mid-level hotels, which when they opened in 1972 added 1600 rooms to Disney World's capacity, doubling the existing amount.[17] The final accommodation option in Disney World's early years was the Fort Wilderness Campground, which originally contained 232 campsites, but was expanded after it proved popular.

In the early 1970s, Walt Disney World was a different place than it is today. Now, people expect to spend long hours in the parks; the Magic Kingdom in particular is often open past midnight. But during Disney World's first decade, the Magic Kingdom was its sole theme park, and it was only open for limited hours each day, typically 9am to 6pm. Much of Disney's entertainment focus was thus on providing guests with things to do outside the park. Each of the three resorts had at least one bar or night club that was open until 2am. The latter included the Magnolia Room at the Golf Resort and Captain Cook's Hideaway at the Polynesian Village Resort. The most famous of Disney World's early 1970s nightspots, however, was the Top of the World Dinner Theater on the top floor of the Contemporary Resort. Famous performers, including Rosemary Clooney, Sammy Davis, Jr., Duke Ellington, and Phyllis Diller, all played there. It was not profitable, but Disney kept it open in order to keep guests happy and increase the resort's prestige.[18]

In the daytime, Walt Disney World guests could swim, fish, or sail on Bay Lake, or they could play a round of golf. The two original golf courses, both located adjacent to the Golf Resort, were Palm and Magnolia, each of them championship caliber.[19] There were also more creative entertainment

---

17   The hotel buildings are still there, though they are no longer on Disney property and have all changed ownership.

18   According to some sources, the live entertainers did not always promote the kind of family values that Disney wanted, and so in 1981 a show called Broadway at the Top was installed. It ran until 1994, when it was closed to make room for the California Grill restaurant, which opened the following year. The Top of the World is often referred to as the Top of the World Lounge, but that in fact was a separate fourteenth-floor space that was originally called the Mesa Grande Lounge. There, guests could enjoy a drink without paying the cover charge for the theater, and it quickly became a popular fireworks-viewing spot, as the California Grill remains today. Bay Lake Tower, the Disney Vacation Club property next to the Contemporary that opened in 2009, features on its top floor a new Top of the World Lounge, which is reserved for the exclusive use of Bay Lake Tower guests and Disney Vacation Club members.

19   A PGA event was played on a Disney course annually between 1971 and 2012. Palm and Magnolia both hosted these events, as did Disney's World third golf course, Lake Buena Vista, which opened

options. In 1974, an 11.5-acre island in Bay Lake was renamed Treasure Island in order to link it to the 1950 Disney live-action film. Guests could visit either by boat from the Magic Kingdom, which cost $1.50, or while they were on the World Cruise, a journey around the Seven Seas Lagoon and Bay Lake that cost $2.50. Most of the planned pirate-themed elements were never built, however, and instead the island's most prominent feature came to be its displays of exotic birds and animals. In 1977, Treasure Island was renamed Discovery Island, and an even greater emphasis was placed on the zoological displays.[20]

In the early 1970s, the Imagineers drew up plans to create an Old West-themed town at Fort Wilderness that would feature shops and restaurants, but only Pioneer Hall, built of 1283 pine logs shipped in from Montana, was ever completed. The original concept for Pioneer Hall, which opened in 1974, was for guests to purchase food from a cafeteria-style restaurant and then enjoy a nature lecture or a screening of one of Disney's *True-Life Adventure* documentaries while they ate. Disney executives soon realized, however, that this would generate few profits, as guests would not be willing to pay extra for such low-key entertainment. The restaurant was thus upgraded to the full-service Crockett's Tavern, and a ticketed show was devised to bring in extra revenue. But because this was at the time when Disney World attendance was suffering due to the oil crisis, instead of paying professional performers, Disney recruited students from the California Institute of the Arts who were enrolled in a summer internship program to stage a musical show with a backwoods theme. The show, called the Hoop Dee Doo Musical Revue, proved so popular that when the students went back to school in the fall, they were replaced by professionals. Tens of thousands of performances later, the Hoop Dee Doo Revue continues today.

But there was a limit to how much additional revenue could be squeezed out of the campground, and so Disney abandoned the remainder of the plans for the Old West town and built a hard-ticketed attraction instead. In 1976, Walt Disney World's first water park, River Country, opened. Located on the shore of Bay Lake, River Country was themed as an "old swimming hole" that was loosely tied to Mark Twain's Tom Sawyer stories. Occupying

---

in 1972 and which also hosted LPGA events. In the early 1990s, Disney added two other courses: Eagle Pines, designed by Pete Dye, and Osprey Ridge, designed by Tom Fazio. Eagle Pines closed in 2007 to make room for the new Four Seasons Resort and the Golden Oak residential development. The ownership of Osprey Ridge, meanwhile, was transferred to the Four Seasons; it reopened in 2014 as the Tranquilo Golf Club. Finally, there is a nine-hole course called Oak Trail at Walt Disney World; originally called the Wee Links and oriented towards younger golfers, it opened in 1980.

20   After Disney's Animal Kingdom opened in 1998, Discovery Island became redundant, and it closed the following year.

six acres, it was designed to appear as if there were no separation between it and Bay Lake. Water from the lake was sucked into a large pipe, filtered, and then pumped up into an artificial mountain at the center of the park, from which it was forced into the park's flumes at a rate of 8500 gallons a minute. A rubber barrier separated Bay Lake from River Country's Bay Cove, and special sensors prevented lake water from spilling into the water park's filtered pools. The filtration system, however, proved faulty, and in 1980 an eleven-year-old boy died after being infected by an amoeba that caused a rare form of encephalitis. Nonetheless, River Country continued to operate for another decade, even after Disney opened two other water parks, Typhoon Lagoon in 1989 and Blizzard Beach in 1995. But after the 9/11 attacks led to a decrease in Disney World's attendance, River Country failed to reopen in the spring of 2002, and it has remained closed ever since.

By the mid-1970s, Walt Disney World had thus developed into a true "vacation kingdom," with not only a theme park but three resort hotels, a campground, daytime leisure activities, and nighttime entertainment options. It was a massive success: annual attendance rose from 10.7 million in 1972 to 13 million by the mid-1970s. (Disneyland attracted between 9 and 10 million visitors a year in the same period.) In the future, Walt Disney World would have a major impact on other Disney resorts, as it became the model for a Disney "destination resort." Disneyland would evolve to look more like it, and two international resorts, in Tokyo and Paris, would copy the Vacation Kingdom of the World as well.

NINE

EPCOT Center and Disney's First International Park

The early 1980s saw the opening of two Disney theme parks: EPCOT Center, the first Disney theme park to depart from the Disneyland model, and Tokyo Disneyland, the first park to be built outside of the United States. Although Orlando and Tokyo are over 7000 miles apart, the histories of the two parks were intertwined. As the cost of designing and building EPCOT soared, Disney was eager to find additional sources of revenue. This led its executives to respond favorably when the Oriental Land Company approached them about partnering in the construction of a Disneyland-type theme park in Tokyo. EPCOT and Tokyo Disneyland both went on to become successful and popular additions to Disney's theme park portfolio. Today, they are, respectively, the sixth- and second-most visited theme parks in the world. But in both cases, the path to opening day was a complicated one.

By the mid-1970s, Disney considered the building of Phase I of Walt Disney World to be complete. The definition of "complete" had been somewhat of a moving target. Originally, the company had stated that an annual attendance of ten million guests, which they assumed would take five years, was the goal, but the Magic Kingdom had met this mark in its first year of operation. So instead the target was shifted toward capacity: Disney wanted the Magic Kingdom to have enough attractions to equal Disneyland's daily capacity of 70,000 guests. This was achieved in 1975, and so Disney could now return its attention to developing the rest of the Florida property. But this brought back to the front burner a difficult question: what to do about EPCOT, the idea that had been the centerpiece of the original plans for the Florida Project?

Through the early 1970s, although EPCOT was rarely mentioned by Disney executives, it remained on the agenda as something for the future. But by the mid-1970s, Disney had abandoned any notion of building a city, and images from the EPCOT film and model no longer appeared in the company's promotional literature. In May 1974, Disney's president Card Walker announced that the company would be proceeding with the "phased program" for the development of Walt Disney World, which included the "concept" for EPCOT. But in this instance "concept" was a slippery word. Walker made it clear that EPCOT was now being assessed "from the point of view of economics, operations, technology, and market potential." Though he was vague about specifics, Walker stated that Disney was no longer seeking "the commitment of individuals and families to permanent residences." In July 1975, a Disney spokesman confirmed to a reporter that "the concept that was originally envisioned is no longer relevant."

The abandonment of EPCOT as a city, however, did not mean that Disney had thrown the idea out altogether. There were three reasons why Disney maintained a commitment to build a version of EPCOT that could at least be somewhat linked to the original vision. First, Disney had used its promise to build a city to gain numerous concessions from the Florida state government that had given it nearly total control of the Orlando property. Some legislators were therefore pressing the company to do what it had said it was originally going to do. Second, the public remained keenly interested in the EPCOT idea. Floridians, who had been barraged with publicity about the "city of tomorrow" in the mid-to-late 1960s, wanted to know when it would be built, and visitors from other states frequently asked about the project as well. And finally, Disney executives maintained a degree of commitment to Walt's original vision for EPCOT, even if they knew that it would only be built in a much-altered form.

To blunt some of the pressure to build EPCOT as it had been conceived, Disney advanced the argument that many of the ideas behind it had been implemented in Phase 1 of Walt Disney World, so that in essence the entire Florida Project was the embodiment of Walt's idea. Whenever he was asked when Disney was going to start working on EPCOT, Joe Potter, the head of the Reedy Creek Improvement District, would point out all of the technological breakthroughs on Disney World property, like the AVACs trash system, the clean power plant, and the linear-induction motors on the PeopleMover, and say, "That's the spirit of EPCOT." This argument was not particularly convincing, however, because in reality few of EPCOT's most important concepts were ever implemented on the Florida property. Employee transportation depended on cars and buses rather than energy-efficient PeopleMovers, and over time guest transportation came to rely on them more heavily as well. Little of Walt Disney World was pedestrian-friendly, as it was nearly impossible to walk from one part of the resort to another.

But Disney was unwilling to give up on EPCOT altogether. In 1973, Imagineer Marty Sklar began convening the Wednesday Morning Club, a group of members of the original EPCOT design team. Bob Gurr recalled that they would discuss "What's EPCOT? How are we going to do this?" The following year, Card Walker announced that the company would be moving ahead "in a phased program" with EPCOT. Instead of a city, however, it would now take the form of "satellites," or demonstration sites scattered throughout Walt Disney World that would display new technologies, including some of those used on the property. The first satellite was to be something called the World Showcase, which was an adaptation of Walt's idea for the international shopping area that was to have been part of the original EPCOT. The World Showcase was touted by Disney as "the first major step in the evolution of EPCOT."

By 1975, Disney was finally ready to get serious about EPCOT. In February of that year, Walker announced that "we are really getting it off the ground." He continued, "We think we can do it, and if we can, it'll be one of the most exciting things the company has ever done. It's bigger than us, but because we're us we might be able to get it done." But what was the "it" that Walker referred to? At a press conference in July, he described the plans in more detail, making it clear that Disney was no longer going to build a city:

> We believe we must develop a community system oriented to the communication of new ideas, rather than to serving the day-to-day needs of a limited number of permanent residents. EPCOT's purpose, therefore, will be to respond to the needs of people by providing a Disney-designed and Disney-managed forum where creative men and women of science, industry, universities, government and the arts—from around the world—can develop, demonstrate and communicate prototype concepts and new technologies, which can help mankind to achieve better ways of living.

Walker explained that this new version of EPCOT would have three parts. First, there would be the EPCOT Institute, "an independent organization which will provide the administrative structure necessary to facilitate participation in EPCOT and its 'satellite' research activities by all interested parties. Its goal will be to guarantee that the maximum benefits from EPCOT-related research will flow to both the sponsors of EPCOT activities and the public, and to establish the technical credibility of projects undertaken through a series of expert advisory boards."

Second, there would be the satellites, "which will be engaged in researching, testing and demonstrating prototype products and systems in such fields as energy, agriculture, education, medicine and communications, in locations best suited for the particular program." The satellites would be located both on- and off-site and would "undertake projects funded by one sponsor or joint programs funded by industry, government, foundations and universities." The first satellite was still going to be the World Showcase, now with the addition of an International Village, in which the employees from all over the world who would staff the World Showcase would live. The vision for the World Showcase had expanded considerably since the initial announcement the previous year: instead of occupying a small site near the Transportation and Ticket Center, it was now going to be located on one hundred acres of land located near the center of the property, close to where EPCOT is today. It was no longer a shopping village, but rather a series of pavilions celebrating different countries that would be sponsored by national governments. A Disney spokesman estimated that it would "reach dimensions and expenditures similar to that of the current Magic Kingdom theme park." Construction of the World Showcase was supposed to begin in 1976, with a target opening date of 1979.

The third and final component of EPCOT circa 1975 was the Future World Theme Center, "a high-capacity visitor facility which will employ advanced communications techniques, including motion pictures, models, multi-media exhibits and ride-through experiences, to inform millions of people each year about what is being done in the creative centers of science and industry around the world. Most importantly, it will demonstrate how these new technologies and ideas can be applied in a practical way to improving the environment for living in existing communities throughout American and the world." Both the Theme Center and the World Showcase would be linked to the Magic Kingdom and the resort hotels by an expansion of the monorail. Disney estimated that it would spend $650 million on this new version of EPCOT, a figure roughly equivalent to what it had spent on Walt Disney World thus far.

By 1975, EPCOT thus contained the two core elements of the theme park that it eventually became: Future World and World Showcase, though they had not yet been combined into a single entity. It still included, however, a much heavier dose of science and technology research and demonstration than the version of EPCOT that was eventually built. In the mid-1970s, Disney spent considerable time and energy promoting this aspect of EPCOT to government officials in an effort to attract support. Disney even made a presentation to Secretary of State Henry Kissinger, who arranged meetings for the Disney marketing department in Amsterdam, Athens, Copenhagen, Brussels, and Paris in order to promote the World Showcase idea. Disney also opened a field office in Washington, D.C. At the same time, Disney representatives met with executives from a variety of American corporations in an effort to convince them to participate in the Future World Theme Center and the EPCOT satellites.

The Imagineers were tasked with trying to make these disparate ideas work together in a way that would attract guests. This was crucial because Disney needed EPCOT to take the pressure off the Magic Kingdom, which at peak times became very crowded. An appealing EPCOT would also help to convince guests to stay at Walt Disney World for an extra day or two, therefore improving the resort's bottom line. So how could EPCOT be designed in a way that met all of these demands? What became the EPCOT that opened in 1982 gradually evolved between 1975 and 1978. As is the case with so many things Disney, a legend explains the crucial step. Supposedly, in late 1976, Imagineers Marty Sklar and John Hench were under pressure to make a presentation to Disney executives. Desperate to create something that would make sense from both a creative and business standpoint, they pushed the previously separate models of Future World and the World Showcase together, and EPCOT the theme park was born.

There is probably some truth to this story, but the full explanation for what happened is more complicated. Although Future World and World Showcase had been combined by the end of 1976, it was not until the following year that what Disney referred to in its annual report as a "conceptual breakthrough" was achieved in determining what EPCOT would ultimately look like. This breakthrough went under the rather mundane name of Master Plan 5, in which Future World and World Showcase were installed in adjacent pavilions positioned in a circular arrangement, with the former serving as a "showcase for prototype concepts" and the latter as an "international people-to-people exchange." Master Plan 5 included many elements that would ultimately become part of EPCOT. Future World contained an attraction called Spaceship Earth, though it was housed in a dome at this point rather than a sphere, and an educational exhibit focusing on computers called Communicore, as well pavilions labeled Life and Health, The Land, Transportation, Space, The Sea, and Energy. The America pavilion in World Showcase included an attraction called the American Adventure, although it was located at the southern end of the lagoon closest to Future World, rather than at the northern end where it would eventually be located.

At the same time as Disney was refining its plans for EPCOT, however, it was also reducing them. In the late 1970s, global economies were faltering, and national governments were not eager to pony up the money to sponsor theme-park attractions. Disney approached around fifty national governments about building pavilions, and models of EPCOT from this era show between twenty and thirty national pavilions ringing the World Showcase Lagoon. The response was so lackluster, however, that Disney quickly revised the number downwards to seventeen and then further to between eight and ten. World Showcase pavilions that were discussed but never built included the United Arab Emirates, Iran, Denmark, Costa Rica, and Australia. After EPCOT opened, Disney widely advertised a Phase II that was supposed to include pavilions representing Spain, Venezuela, Israel, and Equatorial Africa. Later, Disney negotiated with Switzerland and Russia about new pavilions, and there were preliminary discussions with India, but these efforts also came to naught. Disney executive Pete Clark recalled that "a lot of time and money was spent on trips, but they didn't get us much."

In most cases, the pavilions were not built because a financial agreement could not be reached. Around 1990, for example, Disney proposed to the Soviet Union an idea for a pavilion that would include a replica of the onion-domed St. Basil's Cathedral, an audio-animatronic show called Russia: The Bells of Change, and a dark ride based on the folk tale *Ivan and the Magic Pike*. But the collapse of the Soviet Union in 1991 badly damaged the Russian economy, eliminating any possibility of public or private sponsorship. Money was not the only issue, however. The Equatorial Africa pavilion was going to be shared by Kenya, Senegal, and the Ivory Coast, but negotiations collapsed when the three countries could not agree on which one would get top billing on the signage. Israel actually signed a contract in 1980 to underwrite a pavilion, but Disney grew nervous about the possibility of its becoming the target of terrorism or protest and backed out of the deal.[1]

Image 9.1: Herb Ryman's concept art for an Equatorial Africa pavilion in EPCOT's World Showcase. The pavilion was never built because the three participating countries, Kenya, Senegal, and the Ivory Coast, could not agree on which one would be listed first on the signage.

---

1   These fears were confirmed in 1999, when an Israel display was included in the Millennium Pavilion, a temporary exhibit between the Canada and United Kingdom pavilions. Israel's presence led the Arab League and several Arab-American organizations to threaten to boycott Disney.

The lack of enthusiasm on the part of national governments forced Disney to change its approach: instead of trying to convince governments to fund the pavilions, they focused on private corporations. Bass Brewery, Pringle of Scotland, and Royal Doulton China all made contributions to the United Kingdom pavilion, while Mitsukoshi supplied a smaller-scale version of one of its department stores for the Japan pavilion. But these contributions paid for only a small portion of the total cost of the pavilions, and so most of the major attractions that they were supposed to contain were eliminated. A proposed Rhine river cruise for the Germany pavilion was abandoned, as was an audio-animatronic show called Winds of Change and a bullet-train ride for the Japan pavilion.[2] The United Kingdom pavilion was supposed to feature a Victorian music-hall-style dinner theater, and Italy was to have a boat ride. The dearth of attractions in World Showcase caused a major change to Disney's ticketing policy. Executives realized that they could not charge separate admissions for each pavilion when they contained no rides, only shops and restaurants. They therefore decided to replace the ticket books with an unlimited "passport," a single ticket that would admit guests to all attractions.

In the end, World Showcase opened with nine pavilions and only one attraction, the El Rio del Tiempo boat ride in Mexico, along with films in the China, France, and Canada pavilions. A Morocco pavilion was added in 1984; paid for by the king of Morocco, it was the only World Showcase pavilion to be fully funded by a national government. Norway arrived in 1988, bringing the total to eleven. The story of the Norway pavilion provides a microcosm of the complexities of the development of World Showcase. In its quest to attract a Scandinavian sponsor, Disney had initially negotiated with Denmark, and as late as 1983 discussions were ongoing with the LEGO toy company about contributing to a pavilion. Disney was so confident that an agreement would be reached that a set of restrooms in World Showcase was built in a Danish style. But the negotiations with LEGO fell through at the last moment, and Disney now tried to attract other Scandinavian sponsors. NorShow, a consortium of eleven Norwegian companies, put up $33 million. Disney paid the remainder of the pavilion's $45 million cost. The pavilion included the World Showcase's second ride, Maelstrom, as well as a conference center called the Norway Club. The first $3.2 million in profits from the pavilion's shops and food concessions went to NorShow, and the next $400,000 to Disney. After that, NorShow kept 60 percent of the profits and Disney 40 percent. In 1992, four years after the pavilion opened, the Norwegian investors sold

---

2   Both pavilions still contain the large show buildings that were built for these attractions.

their stake to Disney for $26 million, which meant that Norway lost $7 million on the deal. Until 2002, the Norwegian government continued to contribute $200,000 annually to the pavilion's cost of operation. After that, it became the only World Showcase pavilion to be entirely owned and operated by Disney, which explains why it has recently been converted to the kingdom of Arendelle from the wildly popular film *Frozen*.

Image 9.2: The United States pavilion from the Universal and International Exposition, or Expo '67, in Montreal. A geodesic dome designed by the architect Buckminster Fuller, who had devised the mathematical calculations for such structures, the pavilion was one of the inspirations for Spaceship Earth, the iconic attraction that stands at the entrance to Epcot. The Imagineers, however, wanted to offer a more dramatic entranceway than walking through a doorway on the side of a dome could provide, and so they came up with the idea to create a complete sphere rather than only half of one. To design a geodesic sphere, which had never been done before, they turned to the new architectural tool computer-aided design, which produced a plan for two domes joined together. Piles were driven 160 feet into central Florida's swampy ground until they hit bedrock in order to provide a foundation for six legs that support a steel ring. The upper dome sits on top of this ring, while the lower dome hangs from it.

Disney was more successful in obtaining corporate sponsorships for Future World. The company opened a corporate preview center in New York where potential sponsors could be wooed. Its first "big catch" was General Motors, which agreed to sponsor a transportation-themed pavilion called The World of Motion for $35 million over ten years. Other corporations swiftly followed, and when EPCOT opened in 1982, it had over twenty different sponsors who paid Disney between $10 and $50 million each. Spaceship Earth, the iconic attraction that stands near the main entrance to Epcot, was sponsored by the Bell System, while the other original Future World pavilions were the Universe of Energy (Exxon), Journey into Imagination (Kodak), and The Land (Kraft). Three more pavilions joined them later: Horizons (General Electric) in 1983, The Living Seas (United Technologies) in 1986, and Wonders of Life (MetLife Insurance) in 1989.

Image 9.3: Future World's Horizons pavilion, which opened in 1983, contained a dark ride that displayed visions of the future and then allowed guests to choose one of three different endings. Despite the fact that some fans consider it to be the greatest ride in Epcot history, it closed in 1999.

EPCOT Center, as it was now called, opened on October 1, 1982, eleven years to the day after the Magic Kingdom. At 300 acres, EPCOT was more than twice the size of the Magic Kingdom; 10,000 construction workers had labored for three years to build it. The original budget of $600 million had ballooned to somewhere between $1 and $1.5 billion. The scale of the project had forced to Disney to hire an outside contractor, Tishman Construction, which had previously built many high-profile projects, including the World Trade Center in New York City. When construction began in 1979, few sponsors had signed on, which meant that pavilion designs were constantly in flux. Disney originally designed the Land pavilion, for example, for Georgia-Pacific, with a main attraction that took guests on a hot-air balloon ride through different global environments, including a swamp, a desert, and a frigid mountaintop. When Kraft took over, however, the Imagineers had to hurriedly create a food-production-themed ride called Listen to the Land.

Image 9.4: EPCOT Center's Future World in 1983, the year after the park opened. The image shows (left to right) Spaceship Earth, the Universe of Energy, and the new Horizons pavilion.

EPCOT was an immediate success. 25,000 people—twice as many as predicted—came to the opening, and throughout the first months of operation, lines were long and restaurants were jammed. The latter problem was exacerbated by the fact that the full-service restaurants in World Showcase had been designed to have an intimate feel, in order to make guests feel as though they were actually dining in that country. The spillover effect caused the counter-service locations to be overwhelmed as well; the patisserie in the France pavilion had expected to sell five hundred pastries a day, not the five thousand that it actually did. More counter-service locations, such as a fish-and-chips shop in the United Kingdom, were quickly added, and snack carts were positioned everywhere. EPCOT was the first Disney theme park in which alcohol sales to the public were permitted, and this entailed a steep learning curve, as cast members had never had to deal with a significant number of tipsy guests before.

Another early problem was the tendency of the biggest attractions to break down. Spaceship Earth's Omnimover system struggled with a track that first went sharply uphill and then sharply downhill, while the complicated systems that ran the Universe of Energy's giant ride vehicles and the American Adventure's complex audio-animatronics rarely functioned properly. Guests also complained bitterly about the long distances that they had to walk due to the park's immense size. To deal with this, Disney rushed additional modes of transportation into service, including double-decker buses in Future World and boats in World Showcase.

But even with all its problems, from Disney's perspective, EPCOT had perfectly fulfilled its objectives. Guests increased the average length of their stays at Disney World from 1.6 to 2.4 days, and overall attendance grew from 12.5 million to 22.7 million, almost 5 million more than predicted. Previously, Walt Disney World had generated twice as much revenue as Disneyland; now, it produced six times as much. Disney had traditionally treated Disney World as a destination for East Coast guests and Disneyland for their West Coast counterparts, but now the former became a "national" resort for guests from across the country and around the world, while Disneyland was marketed more as a destination exclusively for Californians.

Not everyone was pleased by what they encountered, however. Critics complained that EPCOT had failed to fulfill Walt's original vision and that it took a Pollyanna-ish approach to the world's problems, rather than offering any real solutions. The Land pavilion was typical: while the unorthodox food-production methods that were touted on the Listen to the Land boat ride seemed impressive, in reality they were not practical for large-scale agriculture. Corporate logos were everywhere, making some pavilions seem like giant advertisements. Anything negative was banished; Disney only grudgingly, for example, added a brief reference to the Vietnam War to the American Adventure after historians complained.

But if some guests found EPCOT devoid of any serious educational content, others thought it had too much. A frequent complaint was the lack of classic Disney characters, who were banned from the park, while only EPCOT-specific ones like Journey into Imagination's Dreamfinder were permitted. World Showcase was populated by the People of the World dolls, whose wire costumes were recycled from the America on Parade celebration that had been featured in both Disneyland and the Magic Kingdom for the bicentennial in 1976. The eight-foot-high characters, however, had been designed to be seen from a distance; close-up, their large size often terrified small children. Disney's Bill Hoelscher recalled that "the dolls did not go over that well. Children were frightened of them. They thought they were monsters."

Since opening day, EPCOT has changed more profoundly, and more controversially, than any other Disney theme park. In 1994, it became the first Disney park to undergo a name change, when the acronym, all-capital-letters EPCOT was dropped and the park became simply Epcot with only the initial "E" capitalized. But the changes went much further than that. Of the seven Future World pavilions of the 1980s, two no longer exist. The Wonders of Life pavilion, which opened in 1989, contained a simulator ride through the human body called Body Wars, a show about the human brain called Cranium Command, a film called *The Making of Me*, and several other minor attractions. But Body Wars made a significant percentage of guests feel queasy, limiting the pavilion's popularity. After MetLife gave up its sponsorship in 2001, Disney failed to persuade another corporation to come on board. By 2004, the pavilion was only open during peak attendance periods, and in January 2007, it closed permanently. The second lost pavilion was much more lamented by Epcot fans. Sponsored by General Electric, Horizons contained a dark ride that displayed various visions of the future and then allowed guests to choose one of three different endings. After GE gave up its sponsorship in 1993, it closed the following year. After reopening temporarily in 1995, it closed permanently in 1999. The pavilion was then demolished to make room for the Mission: SPACE attraction.

The transition from Horizons to Mission: SPACE is indicative of Epcot's evolution since the 1980s. In broad terms, the educational content of the park has been supplanted by thrill rides and Disney-related content. To be sure, some of the original elements remain, albeit in altered form. Spaceship Earth has been updated several times but still features the original audio-animatronic figures and a narrative focusing on communication. Listen to the Land in The Land pavilion became Living with the Land in 1993, but the ride saw only minor changes. The Universe of Energy became Ellen's Energy Adventure in 1996, with new narration by Ellen DeGeneres and Bill Nye the Science Guy, but it still focuses on the search for energy resources. Many other things have changed, however. Epcot now has three thrill rides: the General Motors-sponsored Test Track, a high-speed ride that allows guests to design their own cars and test them on a "Sim Track"; Mission: SPACE, which simulates space travel so realistically that it has replaced Body Wars as the Disney attraction most likely to make people barf; and Soarin', a simulated hang-glider flight over California. At the same time, Epcot has been Disneyfied. In 2007, The Living Seas became the *Finding Nemo*-themed The Seas with Nemo and Friends and El Rio del Tiempo became the Gran Fiesta Tour Starring the Three Cabelleros. Norway's Maelstrom was closed in 2014 in order to be converted to Frozen Ever After, an attraction based on Disney's enormously successful animated film *Frozen*. These changes to Epcot are fiercely debated by Disney fans. Though some people are happy to see it become more of a conventional theme park, others would prefer a return to the vision at the time of its opening, with a greater focus on education and technological innovation.

The second theme park that Disney built in the early 1980s was Tokyo Disneyland. From the time that the first Mickey Mouse cartoon, *Opry House*, was released in Japan in 1929, Disney has been very popular there. Although animated features such as *Snow White and the Seven Dwarfs*, *Pinocchio*, and *Bambi* were banned, along with all American films, during the Second World War, they gained a wide audience after they premiered in the 1950s. Disney cartoons and films, *Snow White* in particular, were major influences on the Japanese animation style known as anime, which assumed its modern form in the 1960s. The leading anime artist of the era, Osamu Tezuka, was a huge fan of early Disney animation. Tokyo Disneyland could thus take advantage of the large number of Disney fans in Japan.

As a Disney theme park, it was distinctive for two reasons: it was the first park to be built outside of the United States, and it was the first not to be owned by Disney. Tokyo Disneyland is owned by the Oriental Land Company (OLC), a partnership between two companies, Mitsui Real Estate Development and Keisei Electric Railway. The original purpose of the OLC, which was formed in 1960, was to reclaim a part of Tokyo Bay in Chiba Prefecture in order to develop it for industrial purposes. Once the reclamation project actually started four years later, however, local authorities required that the land be reserved for recreational use. In the early 1970s, as they were assembling a proposal for a "recreational facility" that would fulfill the requirement, OLC officials visited leisure facilities and tourist sites in America and Europe. Their travels included stops at Disneyland and Walt Disney World. They were so impressed by the Disney theme parks that they decided to ask Disney to partner in building a version of Disneyland in Tokyo.[3]

In February 1974, the OLC invited Disney executives to come to Tokyo to discuss the project, and in June OLC president Chiharu Kawasaki traveled to California to meet with Disney's president Card Walker. These meetings were positive, and in December, Ron Cayo, Disney's vice-president for business affairs, visited Japan to assess the idea more thoroughly. After presenting extensive data about the Japanese market, the OLC took the Disney team on a helicopter tour of the proposed site. Cayo was impressed, and a "basic agreement" was signed in which Disney and the OLC committed to continue to pursue the project. In 1975, Disney produced a concept document touting the site's suitability for a Disneyland-style theme park and a preliminary site development plan. The following year, the project

---

3   The OLC was not the only Japanese company that was attempting to woo Disney in this era, as Mitsui's archrival Mitsubishi also approached the company about partnering on a theme park project to be located near Mount Fuji. But Mitsubishi ultimately backed off, perhaps due to pressure from the Japanese government.

entered the development phase, and soon thereafter it was officially given the name Tokyo Disneyland.

The financial arrangements for funding the project had yet to be worked out in detail, however, and it was at this point that things began to get more complicated. The estimated cost of construction ballooned from the original estimate of 50 billion yen, or about $250 million, to 120 billion yen, or $750 million. The government of Chiba Prefecture, which was eager for the project to succeed, agreed to rezone some of the land so that residential and commercial buildings could be built on it, which substantially increased the land's value. The prefecture also granted the OLC permission to sell some of the land if it proved necessary. These two decisions allowed the OLC to secure a much larger loan than it would have been able to do otherwise. The loan was so large that twenty-two Japanese banks had to join together to finance the massive project.

Negotiations with Disney, meanwhile, proved equally challenging. The process of working out a deal was tense and nearly broke down at several points. Immersed in the design and construction of EPCOT, the costs of which were continually rising, Disney was uninterested in taking on an ownership stake in Tokyo Disneyland. Instead, the company wanted to pay $2.5 million in return for 10 percent of the entrance fees and 5 percent of the revenues from food and merchandise sales. Disney wanted this arrangement to last for fifty years, but the Japanese Ministry of Finance had set a maximum duration of twenty years for licensing agreements with foreign companies. In the end, Disney agreed to settle for forty-five years, so after 2028 Disney will receive no revenues from Tokyo Disneyland. But even though this turned out to be one of the worst deals in Disney history, the OLC's team balked. Disney's negotiators were convinced that they wanted the deal to collapse so that they could develop the site for other purposes. But in the end, OLC president Masatomo Takahashi decided that he wanted to build something that would leave its mark on Japan, rather than just another real-estate development. The contract between Disney and the OLC was finally signed in 1979.

Construction of Tokyo Disneyland began on December 3, 1980. WED Enterprises was paid a flat fee for designing the park and retained complete control over all aspects of the design. Tokyo Disneyland ultimately cost 180 billion yen ($1.3 billion), three-and-a-half times the original estimate. After a month of previews, the park officially opened on a rainy April 15, 1983. Instantly very popular, it attracted 10 million guests in its first year of operation, and within five years was attracting over 13 million guests annually. Today, it attracts 17 million guests a year, making it the world's second-most-popular theme park after the Magic Kingdom. This is particularly impressive when it is taken into account that the guests are almost entirely Japanese—less than 4 percent of them come from outside Japan, and 70 percent come from the Kanto region of the island of Honshu, which includes Tokyo and its environs. Tokyo Disneyland's popularity created another potential problem—congestion—but the Disney design team and the OLC had anticipated and carefully planned how to deal with the crowds. The park, which is 50 percent larger than Disneyland and slightly larger than the Magic Kingdom, was given more open spaces and wider walkways. Even so, on busy summer days, Tokyo Disneyland often reaches its capacity of 85,000 guests by noon.

Image 9.5: Concept art for Tokyo Disneyland by Imagineer Herb Ryman.

Not only did Tokyo Disneyland attract a large number of visitors, but they spent more per person than at any other Disney park, which made it the most consistently profitable of any Disney theme park. It proved such a success that in 1988 plans for a second Tokyo park were announced. Originally called Disney Hollywood Studios Theme Park at Tokyo Disneyland, it was going to have a movie theme similar to Disney-MGM Studios in Orlando. But in 1992, the theme was altered to the seven seas, in keeping with Tokyo Disneyland's bayside location. Construction began in 1998, and the park, called Tokyo DisneySea, was completed three years later, at a cost of 333 billion yen. Although it shares some attractions with other Disney parks, a number are unique to it, including Journey to the Center of the Earth, which uses the same slot-car technology as Epcot's Test Track, and an updated version of 20,000 Leagues under the Sea.

Despite its distinctiveness, DisneySea features several ideas that were recycled from abandoned projects. In the 1970s, Imagineer Tony Baxter had conceived of a new land for Disneyland called Discovery Bay, which would focus on the futuristic ideas of the late-nineteenth-century science-fiction writer Jules Verne. (Today, we would call Baxter's industrial, retro-future aesthetic "steampunk," but at the time that term did not exist.) Discovery Bay was going to feature a ride in a dirigible based on the 1974 Disney film *The Island at the Top of the World*, another aerial ride called the Great Western Balloon Ascent, a water ride called the Lost River Rapids, and a roller coaster called the Spark Gap. But when *The Island at the Top of the World* flopped and Disney began devoting most of its theme park resources to the construction of EPCOT Center, Discovery Bay, which was estimated to cost more than $55 million, was shelved. Some of Baxter's ideas, however, were incorporated into Tokyo DisneySea. The Mysterious Island section of the park recalls his love of Jules Verne, while the Port Discovery section adopts Discovery Bay's steampunk aesthetic.

In the new millennium, Tokyo Disneyland expanded into the Tokyo Disney Resort, as three Disney-licensed hotels were built: the art-deco-style Tokyo Disney Ambassador Hotel (2000), the Tokyo DisneySea Hotel MiraCoasta (2001), and the Tokyo Disneyland Hotel (2008). In addition to the three official Disney hotels, there are six other affiliated hotels on the Tokyo Disneyland site, along with a shopping, dining, and entertainment complex called Ikspiari.[4] A three-mile-long monorail system called the Disney Resort Line links together all of the attractions and amenities on the site.

Tokyo Disneyland was Disney's first park outside of the United States, but OLC president Takahashi felt emphatically that guests did not want something Japanese, but rather a near-exact copy of the American original. In the early 1990s, a company spokesperson said that the OLC had "really tried to avoid creating a Japanese version of Disneyland. We wanted Japanese visitors to feel they were taking a foreign vacation by coming here, and to us Disneyland represents the best America has to offer." Disney was happy to go along with this, as it was immersed in building EPCOT and had few creative resources available to dedicate to Tokyo. John McCoy, a member of the Tokyo Disneyland design team, recalled that the park "was to be based on existing attractions with minimal design work." The overall park layout and most of the individual attractions were based on Disneyland, while the castle was a close copy of Cinderella Castle in the Magic Kingdom. One attraction, the Mickey Mouse Revue, was even packed up lock, stock, and barrel in Orlando and shipped to Tokyo for installation there. Only a single attraction, Meet the World, an audio-animatronic show that traced the history of Japan's interaction with the outside world, was unique to Tokyo Disneyland, and even it had originally been conceived for the Japan

---

4   According to the OLC, Ikspiari is a term coined from "the name of a good, warm-hearted fairy of Persian myth." The complex contains 140 shops and restaurants along with a cinema.

pavilion in Epcot's World Showcase.[5] The park's soundtrack featured mostly American music, and most of the restaurants originally served American food. There were no vending machines, a staple of Japanese life, inside the park, and Caucasian actors were employed to portray the characters whose faces were visible.

Image 9.6: Concept art by Herb Ryman for Meet the World, Tokyo Disneyland's only original unique attraction.

Over time, however, Tokyo Disneyland has become more Japanese. After guests complained, more Japanese restaurants were introduced, and the stores began to sell more items specifically intended for Japanese consumers, in particular items intended to fulfill the Japanese tradition of *omiyage*, or gifts purchased for friends and family back home. The park now stages an elaborate celebration of Japanese New Year, or *shogatsu*, in which Mickey and Minnie Mouse appear in traditional kimonos. A good example of the "Japanification" of Tokyo Disneyland is provided by the story of a character called Duffy the Disney Bear. Disney originally introduced Duffy in 2002 for the launch of the Once Upon a Toy Store in Orlando's Downtown Disney. Nameless at the time, he was supposed to be Mickey Mouse's teddy bear who had been magically brought to life by Tinker Bell's fairy dust. But he did not catch on with American Disney fans, and stuffed bears were quickly relegated to Disney outlet stores.

In 2004, however, the bear was re-introduced as part of the Christmas celebrations at Tokyo Disneyland. He proved immediately popular, and the following year the OLC decided to launch a full-out marketing blitz. Now named Duffy, he was given a new backstory claiming that he was a special, hand-made gift that Mickey carried in his duffel bag (hence his name) when he traveled. The Cape Cod-themed part of the American Waterfront section of Tokyo DisneySea was turned over almost entirely to Duffy merchandise, and photo points were set up around the park for

---

5   Meet the World closed in 2002.

guests to take photographs of their bears. Japanese fans were soon making their own costumes for their Duffy bears in addition to purchasing the official Disney ones. Today, Duffy appears in other Disney parks, but he continues by far to be most beloved in Japan. As an example of the aspect of Japanese popular culture known as *kawaii*, which roughly translates to "exaggerated cuteness," he represents one of the most obvious ways in which Japanese guests have adapted their version of Disneyland to their own culture.

In many ways, EPCOT Center and Tokyo Disneyland were two very different theme park projects. EPCOT was the long-awaited, much-evolved realization of Walt Disney's original idea for the Florida property. It bore little resemblance to its two predecessors, Disneyland and the Magic Kingdom. Tokyo Disneyland, in contrast, was deliberately conceived as a near carbon copy of the original Disney park in Anaheim. But despite their differences, the two parks shared something very important: they were the first two Disney theme parks to be entirely designed and built after Walt Disney's death. They thus represented the Disney company's earliest efforts to redefine what the future of its theme parks was going to be, with one paying homage to the legacy of its older siblings and the other something entirely new. Over the next decades, Disney theme parks would continue this path of evolution: there would be three more variations on Disneyland—in France, Hong Kong, and Shanghai—but also five entirely new parks with themes based on the movies, animals, California and, as we already know, the seven seas. The success of EPCOT and Tokyo Disneyland paved the way for this major expansion of the Disney parks, in both the United States and around the world.

TEN
The Eisner Years

By 1989, there were four Disney theme parks. Over the next sixteen years, seven more parks opened on three continents. Walt Disney World in Orlando gained two parks, along with three water parks, eighteen hotels, and a new shopping, dining, and entertainment district called Downtown Disney. In Anaheim, Disneyland was expanded into a full-scale resort, with the addition of a second theme park, two hotels, and its own version of Downtown Disney. Disney also expanded globally, with the opening of the Euro Disney Resort, now Disneyland Paris, in 1992 and Hong Kong Disneyland in 2005. These parks were all built while Michael Eisner was CEO of Disney between 1984 and 2004. Eisner's contribution to the parks and to Disney history as a whole remains a source of controversy among Disney fans. But whatever one's opinion of him, there is no doubt that he shaped the theme parks more than any other individual since Walt and Roy Disney.

In the early 1980s, Disney shareholders were deeply discontented, as the company had recently faced several attacks from corporate raiders and hostile takeover bids. After peaking at $120 a share in the early 1970s, the price of Disney shares was hovering at a dangerously low $50 in 1984. Net profits and income were falling as well. Disney's management remained extremely conservative; when some executives attempted to raise Disneyland's parking and ticket prices, which had not been increased in years, the idea was rejected on the grounds that Walt had felt it was crucial for guests to feel like they were getting "good value."

Under the leadership of Walt's son-in-law Ron Miller, who became president of Disney in 1977 and CEO in 1983, the company created the Touchstone imprint, an important step toward broadening its appeal beyond G-rated family films. This led to box-office successes like *Splash*, released in 1984, which starred Darryl Hannah as a voluptuous mermaid alongside a young Tom Hanks. But other Disney films failed to meet box-office expectations, like *Tron* (1982), or were outright flops, like *The Black Hole* (1979) and *The Watcher in the Woods* (1980). Moreover, Disney continued to lag behind other studios in the pace of production. In 1983, it released only three films—*Trenchcoat, Something Wicked This Way Comes,* and *Never Cry Wolf*—which lost a combined $5 million at the box office. In this era, half of the film division's revenues were coming from re-releases of animated classics rather than from new productions.

In 1984, Roy E. Disney, the son of Walt's brother Roy O. Disney, joined with fellow Disney board member Stanley Gold and major stockholder Sid Bass in a campaign that succeeded in replacing Miller with former Paramount Pictures and ABC television executive Michael Eisner, who had never worked for Disney. With a reputation for being hard-nosed and difficult to get along with, Eisner was very different from Disney's previous leaders. But he also had a golden touch that had turned low-budget films like *48 Hours* (1982) and *Terms of Endearment* (1983) into big hits and had produced blockbuster successes like *Raiders of the Lost Ark* (1981), a project he had championed despite the skepticism of his superiors about its box-office potential.

Eisner became Disney's CEO in September 1984. Two other key leaders joined Disney at the same time: former Warner Brothers head Frank Wells became the company's president and Eisner's former president of production at Paramount, Jeffrey Katzenberg, became head of Disney's film division. At first, Eisner focused on what he was most familiar with: live-action films. In his early years at the helm, Disney produced a string of solid hits including *Down and Out in Beverly Hills* (1986), *Ruthless People* (1986), *Three Men and a Baby* (1987), and *Good Morning Vietnam* (1987). Made for modest budgets, these films all performed extremely well at the box office. *Three Men and a Baby*, for example, cost $11 million and made $167 million, while *Good Morning Vietnam* cost $13 million and made $124 million. And the hits kept coming: 1990's *Pretty Woman*, starring Richard Gere and a then-unknown Julia Roberts, cost $14 million and grossed over $460 million, making it the most successful film in Disney history. Disney also had a big-budget success with *Who Framed Roger Rabbit* (1988), a revolutionary combination of live action and animation made in partnership with Steven Spielberg that grossed $330 million. In 1985, Disney began releasing its library of classic films on videocassette; the first three releases, *Pinocchio, Cinderella,* and *Sleeping Beauty*, were both popular and profitable. The opening of a chain of Disney stores in major retail markets was equally successful. The first store opened in Glendale, California, in 1987; by 2000, there were 750 Disney stores nationwide. Disney's annual operating income soared from $300 million prior to Eisner's arrival to almost $800 million in 1987. Eisner found new profits so easy to come by that he referred to himself as "working in the world's biggest candy store."

The success of Disney's live-action films gave Eisner the confidence to revive the feature animation division, which was all but moribund by the mid-1980s. When Katzenberg had his first meetings with the animators, he was dismayed. They had spent ten years and $40 million making a film called *The Black Cauldron*, which Katzenberg thought was too dark to appeal to children, or even to adults. He was proven right: when it was released in 1984, it grossed only $22 million. But despite *The Black Cauldron's* failure, Katzenberg was convinced that feature animation was something unique to Disney and that it could be revived. The next release, *The Great Mouse Detective* (1986), was a modest success, and the one that followed, *Oliver and Company* (1988), a genuine hit. Katzenberg began devoting more and more time to animation, which he now believed could be even more profitable than live action thanks to Disney's virtual monopoly over the genre. *Oliver and Company* had been a musical, and Katzenberg was eager to find similar material. When animator Ron Clements proposed an adaptation of the Hans Christian Andersen fairy tale "The Little Mermaid," Katzenberg loved the idea and hired Broadway composers Howard Ashman and Alan Mencken, most famous for *Little Shop of Horrors*, to write the songs. Released in 1989, *The Little Mermaid* grossed $222 million, making it by far the most successful animated film in history. It was followed by *Beauty and the Beast* (1991), *Aladdin* (1992), and *The Lion King* (1994), which matched and even exceeded its success. Taking in close to a billion dollars at the box office, *The Lion King* became the second-highest-grossing film in history.

In the 1990s, Disney also branched out into a new kind of animation. In 1979, *Star Wars* creator George Lucas launched a computer division of his studio that originally focused on producing computer-generated special effects for Lucasfilm projects. In 1985, Disney and Lucasfilm began collaborating on a project called CAPS, for Computer Animation Production System, to digitize the animation process. The following year, after Apple founder Steve Jobs purchased the technology rights for $10 million, the Lucasfilm division was spun off into a separate company called Pixar. Over the next several years, Disney and Pixar continued to work closely together, and in 1991, Pixar signed a three-film, $26 million production deal with Disney. The first of these films, 1995's *Toy Story*, grossed $360 million and launched a massively successful franchise. The second and third films were *A Bug's Life* (1998) and *Toy Story 2* (1999), which were also very profitable.

Eisner's comprehension of the film industry, however, was matched by his ignorance of theme parks. He had never visited Disneyland as a child, and he had taken his three sons to Walt Disney World only once. And the learning curve was going to be steep: the Walt Disney Outdoor Recreation Division, as it was called at the time that Eisner took over, was the part of Disney over which Walt's legacy held the most sway. The Imagineers, who had exceeded their budget for EPCOT by $300 million, were nervous, as the previous regime had been planning to outsource much of what they did. But when he toured Imagineering headquarters, Eisner was impressed by their creativity. He was also aware that the theme parks were responsible for three-quarters of Disney's income at the time, and thought that their relatively flat levels of attendance could be increased. He was willing to contemplate the addition of new attractions and even entirely new parks. For insight, he relied on his fourteen-year-old son Breck, who attended Eisner's meetings with the Imagineers. Being a teenaged boy, Breck wanted more thrill rides, and so Star Tours, a *Star-Wars*-themed simulator ride, and Splash Mountain, an $80 million log-flume ride that culminated in a five-story drop, were quickly green-lighted.

Image 10.1: Splash Mountain, the log-flume thrill ride that opened in Disneyland in 1989 and the Magic Kingdom in 1992 as part of Michael Eisner's efforts to make the theme parks more appealing to a teenage and young-adult audience.

As Eisner grew more familiar with the theme park business, he came to see it as having the potential to generate large profits. The EPCOT vision of parks serving a predominantly educational purpose made no sense to him. But parks as places of entertainment and profit did. One of the first things he did as Disney CEO was to raise the price of admission, which had no impact on the number of guests but a dramatic one on Disney's bottom line. This was the start of a massive expansion of the Disney theme parks that remains controversial among Disney fans today. On the one hand, it resulted in the construction of seven new parks: one in California, two in Orlando, two in Europe, and two in Asia. More money was poured into the parks than at any other point in Disney history. But on the other hand, some people feel that as the Eisner era went on quality came to be sacrificed to profit. Under Eisner's leadership, the revenue from Disney's theme parks tripled, but many fans do not feel that this was rewarded with a sufficient amount of reinvestment, particularly toward the end of his tenure.

In his early years, Eisner was most interested in the Florida parks, because he saw the greatest potential for expansion there. In the early 1980s, only around 3000 acres of the Florida property had been developed, with an additional 7000 dedicated to conservation and water management, which left over 17,000 acres on which to build. The plans for this expansion were formulated at a "super design charrette" in February 1985, in which Disney executives, along with leading architects, planners, and real-estate developers, met to discuss what should be done with Disney's remaining acreage in Orlando. The overwhelming consensus was that the Walt Disney World Resort should be expanded through the addition of more theme parks, hotels, and leisure and entertainment facilities.

The first step in this expansion was the construction of a third theme park. The genesis of what became Disney-MGM Studios (now Disney's Hollywood Studios) arose from the growth of Disney's film division under Eisner and Katzenberg. Disney's intensified production schedule of both live-action and animated films—Eisner planned to increase feature-film production from around five films a year to fifteen—created a need for additional studio space. The acquisition of land near Los Angeles would be very expensive, and so Disney turned to a location where they already owned thousands of acres of land that was not being used: Orlando. The original idea was to create a working studio that would also allow guests to view the production process, much like a Hollywood studio tour, something that Disney had never offered to the public in Burbank.

Disney was not, however, the only film studio that was thinking along these lines. In 1982, Universal Studios acquired 400 acres of land in Orlando, on which it intended to build a production facility and studio tour that would be similar to Universal Studios Hollywood.[1] The project was slow to get off the ground because Universal was initially unable to find an investment partner, but in 1986 the studio made a deal with the Canadian theater chain Cineplex-Odeon, and so the Orlando concept

---

1   Universal later accused Eisner of directly copying many of their ideas for the Orlando project, which they claimed he had seen when they attempted to convince Paramount to partner with them in the early 1980s.

could now move forward. To compete, Disney decided to expand its idea for a working studio into a film-oriented theme park. In keeping with management's new profit-driven philosophy, however, costs would be kept strictly under control, with no ballooning budgets as had happened with EPCOT. A mere $300 million, a quarter of what EPCOT had cost, was originally budgeted for the movie park.[2] The intent was for it to be a "half-day" attraction that would be just enticing enough to convince guests to stay at Disney World for an extra day in order to visit it.

Because it had only a small library of live-action films, Disney needed to partner with another studio to make the movie park feasible, and so an agreement was signed with Metro-Goldwyn-Meyer (MGM) to use its name, logo, and film library. Construction of Disney-MGM Studios began the following year. As Disney had received numerous complaints that EPCOT was too large, the park was designed on a similar scale to the Magic Kingdom, with a "Hollywood Boulevard" lined with replicas of real buildings from the Golden Age of Hollywood in the 1920s and 1930s leading from the entrance to a "castle," in this case a replica of the famous Grauman's Chinese Theater, home of the Hollywood Walk of Fame.

Disney-MGM Studios opened on May 1, 1989. Because of the rush to beat Universal, which Disney managed to do by a year, the park had only six attractions on opening day: three shows (the Monster Sound Show, SuperStar Television, and Hollywood! Hollywood! A Star Studded Spectacular!), two studio tours (The Magic of Disney Animation and the Backlot Tour), and one dark ride (The Great Movie Ride). What made the park unique, however, was the presence of a real working studio, which had two parts. First, there was Walt Disney Feature Animation Florida, where in the late 1990s and early 2000s Disney produced several animated features, including *Mulan* (1998) and *Lilo & Stitch* (2002). Second, there was Walt Disney Studios Florida, which contained three soundstages that were used primarily for television productions, but also for some live-action films. The soundstages were used both by Disney and by other production companies who paid to lease them.

Disney-MGM Studios saw a steady stream of additions in its early years. Three months after opening day, the Indiana Jones Stunt Spectacular made its debut. Then, 1990 saw the arrival of the park's first thrill ride, the simulator-based Star Tours. In 1991, Beauty and the Beast Live on Stage and Muppet*Vision 3D both arrived, followed in 1992 by the Voyage

---

2   The budget was later increased to $550 million. In response, Universal increased the budget of its project from $200 million to $500 million.

of the Little Mermaid puppet show.[3] That same year, the park added its first nighttime show, Sorcery in the Sky; six years later, it was replaced by the Disneyland import Fantasmic!, which required the construction of a 10,000-seat amphitheater. In 1994, the park saw its first significant expansion with the addition of Sunset Boulevard. It contained a major thrill ride, the Twilight Zone Tower of Terror, an enhanced version of a drop tower ride in which guests plummet thirteen stories. Five years later, the park got its third thrill ride, the Rock'n'Roller Coaster, Disney's first launch roller coaster and its first coaster to take riders through inversions.

These additions reflected the need to increase the number of attractions in Disney-MGM Studios, but they also reflected a more fundamental change in its identity, as it ceased to be a working film studio and became purely a theme park. The idea of moving some of Disney's production to Florida turned out to be impractical, as it proved to be too expensive to fly actors, directors, and other crew members in from California. Orlando's opportunities for shooting on location were very limited, while other southern states, such as Louisiana and Georgia, gave much bigger tax incentives to film studios. By the early 2000s, both Disney and Universal had all but ended film and television production in Orlando. The production of animated films, meanwhile, was drastically altered by the arrival of computer-generated animation in the 1990s, as Disney gradually abandoned the production of hand-drawn films. This led to the closure of the Florida animation studio in 2004.

With the opening of Disney-MGM Studios and the dramatic revival of Disney's feature animation that began with *The Little Mermaid*, 1989 was a banner year for Disney. Eisner was so optimistic about the future that he announced that the next ten years would be "the Disney decade." This message was primarily directed at the company's stockholders, who were promised that the value of their shares would double. Much of this increase was to be on the back of revenue from the theme parks, in which Eisner planned to make a massive investment. To be sure, many of the grandest plans for the Disney decade never came to fruition. EPCOT was supposed to benefit from a major update of Future World and several new World Showcase pavilions. Disney-MGM Studios was supposed to get a land based on *Who Framed Roger Rabbit*, a new area that replicated the first Disney studio on Hyperion Avenue in Los Angeles, and a major new thrill ride based on the film *Dick Tracy* (1990). None of these plans were ever realized.

---

3   Muppet*Vision 3D was originally supposed to be part of an entire Muppet-themed land, but the contract with Disney had not been finalized at the time of Jim Henson's death in 1990. Alienated by Disney's aggressive pursuit of the deal, Henson's heirs would only permit the Muppet characters to be licensed for individual attractions.

Other ideas did not work out in the way that Eisner intended. In his zeal to add thrill rides, he encouraged the Imagineers to come up with something truly scary. That concept eventually evolved into Alien Encounter in the Magic Kingdom's Tomorrowland, in which the monster from the film *Alien* (1979) was unleashed upon terrified guests as they sat pinned into the seats in the circular theater previously occupied by Mission to Mars. After the ride opened in 1995, Disney received thousands of letters from guests complaining that they had never expected to experience something so scary in a Disney park. Alien Encounter lasted for only eight years, before it was shut down in 2003 and replaced by Stitch's Great Escape, essentially a comical version of the same attraction in which Stitch replaced the alien.

Image 10.2: Alien Encounter, which opened in the Magic Kingdom in 1995, was another part of Michael Eisner's effort to make the Disney theme parks more appealing to adult guests. After it proved too scary, however, it closed in 2003.

In other ways, however, the Disney decade had more lasting effects in Orlando. Even before Eisner came on board, Disney was aware that the increased number of guests that EPCOT would attract would strain the capacity of the resort's three hotels, which were almost always close to full. In 1980, the company announced the construction of four new hotels. One, a 600-room low-rise hotel with a "New Orleans feel," was to be built as part of an expansion of Lake Buena Vista Village; the other three hotels were the Grand Floridian Beach Resort, the Mediterranean Resort, and the Cypress Point Lodge. The Grand Floridian and Mediterranean were to be located on the shores of the Seven Seas Lagoon, with the former occupying the site previously designated for the Asian Resort and the latter that of the Venetian Resort. The Cypress Point Lodge, meanwhile, was supposed to be on the shore of Bay Lake near the Fort Wilderness campground. But when EPCOT ran massively over budget, the new hotels were put on hold. Instead, Disney made a deal with John Tishman, whose construction company had supervised the construction of EPCOT, to build two hotels on Disney property, one to be operated by Sheraton and the other by Holiday Inn under its Crowne Plaza imprint.

When Eisner came on board in 1984, he concurred that the number of on-site hotels badly needed to be increased, as Disney was losing profits to hotels that were located off property. The following year, he created the Disney Development Company, a subsidiary that was charged with designing and building hotels and shopping areas on Walt Disney World property. But there was a problem: the deal with Tishman. Intended primarily as convention venues, Tishman's hotels were going to be boring high rises. "I instantly hated the designs," said Eisner. "I associated Disney with fun, theatricality, magic. These [buildings] were ... bland, boxy, and completely unimaginative—typical of the hotels that large chains have put up all across America." Eisner contemplated making a deal with Marriott to own and manage all of Disney's hotels and to build three new Disney World hotels, but when Tishman found out, he filed a $300 million lawsuit for breach of contract. In 1988, Tishman and Disney settled the lawsuit, and the construction of the two hotels moved forward.

Eisner still wanted something other than conventional shoeboxes, however. Ever since the eminent architect Robert A.M. Stern had designed an apartment in New York City for Eisner's parents in the 1970s, Eisner had been very interested in architecture. He wanted to hire star architects to design projects for Disney, and considered two, Philip Johnson and Michael Graves, for the Tishman hotels. In a chance encounter at the Metropolitan Opera, however, Johnson did not know who Eisner was, and so Graves, who was known for his postmodern designs, got the job. He designed one hotel in a triangular shape, the other in the form of a shallow arch.[4] To add the whimsy that Eisner wanted, Graves selected two animals, the dolphin and the swan, to serve as the symbols of the hotels, because they were something that children could identify with and because they had no association with Disney.

---

4   Disney paid for the additional costs of construction that resulted from Graves' unconventional designs.

Image 10.3: The Swan and Dolphin Hotels, designed by Michael Graves. There is no truth to the story that the huge statues of swans and dolphins that top them were placed on the wrong buildings, and since it was too expensive to move them, the names were simply switched.

In the meantime, Disney also returned to building its own hotels. Inspired by the upscale seaside hotels, such as the Breakers in Palm Beach, that were patronized by wealthy travelers to Florida in the late nineteenth and early twentieth centuries, the Grand Floridian Beach Resort opened in 1988, on the site on the western side of the Seven Seas Lagoon that had been proposed for the Asian Resort. The Cypress Point Lodge morphed into the Wilderness Lodge, inspired by the National Parks lodges of the Pacific Northwest, in particular the Old Faithful Inn at Yellowstone, the Ahwahnee Hotel at Yosemite, the Lake MacDonald Lodge in Glacier National Park, and the Timberline Lodge on the slopes of Mount Hood in Oregon. The Wilderness Lodge opened in 1994. Eisner also revived the idea for the Mediterranean Resort, which he envisioned as being more luxurious than the Grand Floridian. But when the land was cleared in the late 1990s, it was so swampy that the pilings necessary to support the building would have to be extremely deep, which massively elevated the cost of construction.[5]

All of these hotels were targeted at an affluent clientele, or, in the case of the Swan and Dolphin, conventioneers. In 1988, however, Disney opened

---

5   Rumors were rife that the Mediterranean Resort would at long last be built when the land was re-cleared in 2010, but this was done to improve sightlines for the monorail drivers.

the Caribbean Beach Resort, described at the time as a "value" hotel, with rates around half of those of other Disney-operated hotels. Caribbean Beach marked a departure in another way as well: it was not located on the monorail route or linked by boat to a theme park, requiring guests to travel to and from the parks by automobile or bus. Then, 1991 saw the addition of another resort, Port Orleans, that was targeted at the same price point as Caribbean Beach; it was joined the following year by a compatriot named Dixie Landings, and in 1997 by another, Coronado Springs. By that point, however, these hotels were no longer labeled as "value" properties. In 1994, Disney began targeting an ever lower and more family-oriented price point with the All-Star Sports Resort. Caribbean Beach, Port Orleans, Dixie Landings, and Coronado Springs were reclassified as moderate resorts, while All-Star Sports now became a value resort, with smaller rooms and staff-to-room ratios of only 0.38, as compared to 1.5 in the deluxe resorts. It was joined in 1995 by another value resort, All-Star Music, and by a third, All-Star Movies, in 1999. But Disney also added more deluxe resorts in the 1990s, including the Yacht Club (1990), the Beach Club (1990), and the BoardWalk Inn (1996). Located near Epcot, all three of these hotels were designed by Robert A.M. Stern, reflecting Michael Eisner's commitment to commissioning star architects to build projects for Disney. And finally, 1991 saw the opening of the Old Key West Resort, the first Disney Vacation Club (time-share) resort on Disney property.[6] That makes fourteen new hotels in all, with a total of 12,000 rooms, that opened between 1988 and 2000.

Nor were hotels the only additions to Disney World's guest facilities during the Disney decade. Other major embellishments included two water parks and an entertainment, dining, and shopping district called Downtown Disney. Disney World already had a water park, River Country, but it was small and its water was unheated, which meant that it had to close during the winter months. In 1986, Eisner decided that the resort needed a larger park that could operate year-round. Ideas for theming included a beached cruise ship and a Florida swamp, but eventually it was decided that the backstory would be about a fictitious storm named Hurricane Connie that had flooded a resort named Placid Palms. The park was called Typhoon Lagoon. After it opened in 1989, Typhoon Lagoon proved so popular that plans were quickly put in place to build a second water park. Called Blizzard Beach, it was based on the premise that a freak snowstorm had blanketed Florida. It opened in 1995, with

---

6   Disney had long resisted getting into the timeshare business, which had an unsavory reputation for intense sales pressure and poor maintenance, but management was tired of losing so much in potential sales to outside vendors.

the 120-foot-high Summit Plummet, at the time the highest and fastest waterslide in the world, as its signature attraction.

Another addition to Walt Disney World was a new shopping, dining and entertainment complex. Originally intended to serve the residences that were planned for the area, the Lake Buena Vista Shopping Village had gradually evolved into a retail and entertainment area for the entire resort. In 1977, it was renamed Disney World Village to reflect this evolution. Eisner wanted to expand the complex's offerings even further in order to entice guests who were staying outside to remain on Disney property in the evenings. He wanted to compete with downtown Orlando's Church Street Station, an entertainment district featuring nightclubs and restaurants that was similar to South Street Seaport in New York City and Fanueil Hall Market in Boston. In 1986, Disney announced that it was adding an area called Pleasure Island to Disney World Village. In 1995, Pleasure Island and the shopping area, now called the Marketplace, were combined into a new complex called Downtown Disney. Downtown Disney also featured a new area called the West Side, which was home to an arena for a Cirque de Soleil show called La Nouba and a video-game arcade called DisneyQuest.

Other changes to Walt Disney World had to do with a new management attitude that focused more closely on profits. Ticket prices, which in the old days had been increased infrequently, were now typically raised three times annually, which meant that they doubled every four years. Attractions that were low-capacity and expensive to operate, such as the Davy Crockett Explorer Canoes and 20,000 Leagues Under the Sea, were closed. Another attraction, Mr. Toad's Wild Ride, fell victim to a new Disney corporate strategy called synergy, or cross-merchandising. Once guests had all-inclusive tickets, theme park attractions no longer made money directly. Rather, they functioned as advertisements for Disney films and merchandise. Mr. Toad offered little value for this purpose, whereas Winnie the Pooh, the rights to which Disney had acquired in the 1960s, was a merchandising juggernaut worth billions annually. The announcement in 1998 that an attraction called The Many Adventures of Winnie the Pooh would replace Mr. Toad was accompanied by the revelation of two other changes to the Magic Kingdom that were also intended to promote synergy. Tomorrowland's Take Flight would be replaced by Buzz Lightyear's Spaceranger Spin, and Adventureland's Tropical Serenade would see the addition of the bird characters Iago and Zazu from the recent animated films *Aladdin* and *The Lion King*.

This trend was repeated all over Walt Disney World. Previously, many retail locations in the theme parks had sold goods that were intended to add atmosphere more than make money. Liberty Square, for example, featured candle and silversmith shops, even though guests had little interest in purchasing these items. But Eisner's team stocked the stores exclusively with high-profit Disney items. The desire to ensure that everything was Disney-branded carried over to EPCOT as well as the Magic Kingdom. Eisner was mystified as to why the Disney characters had been kept out of EPCOT, and Mickey Mouse and his friends were swiftly introduced, albeit in costumes that were appropriate to the particular locations. In Future World, they wore silver spacesuits, while in World Showcase, they donned kimonos, serapes, and berets.

A final development of the Disney decade in Orlando was the decision to build a fourth theme park. The Imagineers had long been interested in developing a park featuring live animals to compete with Busch Gardens in Tampa, and in 1994, the success of *The Lion King* further increased interest in the idea. There were also concerns. Zoos were becoming increasingly controversial, and Disney executives feared that people would not want to see animals in cages. The Imagineers assured them that the animals would be displayed in their natural habitats, with invisible barriers separating them from the guests. They also promised that the park would focus on the theme of environmental conservation. These arguments initially failed to convince Michael Eisner, who harbored doubts that animals would be sufficiently entertaining for Disney guests used to more intense thrills and grander spectacles. It was not until the Imagineers brought a 400-pound tiger into a meeting to prove just how riveting an animal could be that Eisner was converted.

The park was originally supposed to be called Disney's Wild Kingdom, but Disney could not acquire the rights to the name from the insurance company Mutual of Omaha, which had broadcast a television show called *Wild Kingdom* in the 1970s. It became Disney's Animal Kingdom instead. Construction began in 1995, but by the time it got underway, the massive expansion of the theme parks that had begun in the mid-1980s had given way to an equally massive retrenchment. Some attractions that had been conceived for Animal Kingdom were never built at all, while other plans were scaled back. Of the park's four lands, only two—Africa and DinoLand USA—were completed in time for opening day in 1998. Asia, however, was only partly finished; its whitewater rafting ride Kali River Rapids opened in 1999 and its roller coaster Expedition Everest not until 2006. And the Beastly Kingdom, which was supposed to focus on mythical animals, was entirely put on hold and eventually scrapped.[7]

---

7   This was the second time that Disney had abandoned a land based on mythology. In the 1970s, Imagineer Joe Rohde proposed a land called Mythia, the inspiration for which derived from Greek

Image 10.4: Expedition Everest, the roller coaster in Animal Kingdom's Asia section, under construction in December 2004, thirteen months before it opened. Put on hold due to the financial problems of Disneyland Paris, Expedition Everest cost a reported $100 million.

Why was Animal Kingdom subjected to such a dramatic retrenchment? To tell that story, we have first to return to Anaheim to see what had been going on there since the early 1970s. As Disney devoted most of its theme park resources to Walt Disney World, the attention given to Disneyland lagged. To be sure, there were some additions: a $8 million new land called Bear Country opened in 1972, with the Country Bear Jamboree as its centerpiece, the first time that an attraction had been imported from Florida to California. Disneyland also got two new thrill rides: Space Mountain, another export from Orlando, arrived in 1977, followed by Big Thunder Mountain Railroad in 1979, a year before it opened in Orlando. In the 1980s, Fantasyland was given a $55 million makeover that was intended to make it look more like Walt Disney's original vision, before he had run short of cash during Disneyland's construction. All of its classic dark rides were upgraded, and a new one, Pinocchio's Daring Journey, was added.

Many other, more elaborate schemes for Disneyland were abandoned in this era, however. As we saw in the last chapter, Tony Baxter's plan for

---

and Roman myths, for Disneyland. Rohde later became Animal Kingdom's principal designer, and he recycled some of the ideas for Mythia into the Beastly Kingdom.

a Jules Verne-themed land called Discovery Bay was dropped. Other abandoned ideas included Big City U.S.A., a New-York-themed area featuring a Broadway-style theater for live performances, which would have been built where Mickey's Toontown is today, and Dumbo's Circusland, which would have included a dark ride called Circus Disney and a roller coaster themed to immerse guests in the world of classic cartoons.[8] In the early 1980s, discussions began with George Lucas, a Disneyland fan since his childhood, about creating a new land filled with attractions that were based on his films, including *Star Wars* and *Raiders of the Lost Ark*. This idea, too, never came to fruition.

After EPCOT Center opened in 1982, more attention was given to Disneyland. As Disney executives began to draw up a long-range master plan for Anaheim, one question quickly emerged as the biggest: whether to build a second theme park. These preliminary discussions were interrupted when Eisner and the new leadership team arrived in 1984. Eisner saw Disneyland as offering limited prospects for additional profits, and rumors were rampant that he was thinking of selling it. He was eventually convinced that Disneyland was the company's flagship theme park, and he determined to update it in a manner that would increase its appeal to teenagers. This is what led Eisner to green-light Star Tours and Splash Mountain for Disneyland as well as Walt Disney World. While they were still in development, some stopgap measures were introduced. Videopolis, a 5000-square-foot dance floor, was installed in Fantasyland in 1985, and the 3D film *Captain EO*, starring Michael Jackson, premiered in Tomorrowland in 1986.

Eisner felt that it was going to take more than a dance floor and a few new rides to make Disneyland relevant to a new generation of theme park fans. For that, it would take something bigger. The possibility of building a second theme park, or in Disney terminology a second gate, became a topic of intense discussion. Eisner liked this idea because he felt that it would induce guests to stay at Disneyland for multiple days, just like they did at Disney World. But where to build it, given Anaheim's limited space? In the early 1990s, Disney thought it had an answer to this problem. After Jack Wrather, the owner of the Disneyland Hotel, died in 1984, his company began selling off its assets. When Disney, which had wanted for decades to purchase the hotel, heard that a company from New Zealand called Industrial Equity was negotiating to purchase the hotel from the Wrather Corporation, it decided to play hardball. Disney informed Wrather's company that the contract for leasing the monorail stop at the hotel would soon be up, and that they were considering a significant increase in the

---

8   Big City USA later served as an inspiration for the American Waterfront "port of call" at Tokyo DisneySea.

amount they charged. The message was clear: if Wrather tried to sell the hotel to anyone but Disney, Disney would make it so expensive to operate the monorail that the hotel would not be profitable. A deal, not surprisingly, was soon reached. Disney paid $161 million for not only the Disneyland Hotel, but also several tourist assets in Long Beach, the port about twenty miles west of Anaheim. The latter included a sixty-six-year lease on the *Queen Mary*, the retired ocean liner that had been converted into a tourist attraction and hotel, and fifty-five acres of land that was currently occupied by a museum housing the *Spruce Goose*, the massive wooden airplane that had been built by Howard Hughes in the 1940s. But more important from Disney's perspective was that it believed it had obtained the rights to dredge and fill almost 250 acres of land on the Pacific coast. For Disney, this was a potential solution to the question of where to put a second park in southern California. For decades, they had been dissatisfied with the surroundings of Disneyland and with Anaheim's failure to institute stricter planning controls to limit development around the park. In Long Beach, the harbor would serve as a natural buffer, protecting the park from sprawl. In July of 1990, Disney announced that it was planning to spend $2.8 billion developing a resort in Long Beach that would be called Port Disney.

Image 10.5: The R.M.S. *Queen Mary*, the retired Cunard Line vessel, now a floating hotel and tourist attraction in Long Beach, California. Acquired by the Walt Disney Company along with the Disneyland Hotel and other assets of the Wrather Corporation in 1988, the ship was to have been incorporated into the Port Disney concept.

So what was Port Disney going to look like? The *Queen Mary* would have been moved but would have continued to function as both a hotel and the icon of the resort. The rest of the site would have contained a theme park called DisneySea. At its center would have been a futuristic aquarium called Oceana, surrounded by lands called Mysterious Island, Heroes' Harbor, Fleets of Fantasy, Boardwalk, and Adventure Reef. Other components of Port Disney included a waterfront shopping and entertainment complex, five new hotels containing almost 4000 rooms, a marina, and a cruise-ship terminal. The resort's attractions were to be linked together by a monorail system and water taxis, while a shuttle bus would have provided a connection to Disneyland.

There were multiple reasons why the plans for Port Disney never came to fruition. First, Disney ran into problems with the California Coastal Commission, as the 1976 California Coastal Act prohibited the use of landfill for recreational purposes. Disney was also concerned about the possibility of lawsuits by environmental groups like the Sierra Club. But although Disney publicly cited these regulatory and legal hurdles as the main reasons why the project was abandoned, in reality they played only a secondary role, as by the early 1990s they had largely been overcome. Instead, there was another reason why Port Disney never became a reality: it was not the only second-gate project that Disney was considering, as the company had also continued to explore the development of a second theme park in Anaheim.

Preliminary plans for this park, which was to be built on the Disneyland parking lot, were announced in May 1991. It was to be a smaller version of EPCOT called WestCOT. Like its Orlando counterpart, it was to be divided into Future World and World Showcase. The former was to contain three pavilions, the Wonders of Living, the Wonders of Space, and the Wonders of Earth, while the latter would have contained pavilions representing Asia, Africa, Europe, and the Americas. Proposed attractions included a simulator-based update of Disneyland's former Adventure Thru Inner Space ride, a raft ride down a fictitious African river called the Congobezi, and a roller coaster with a Great Wall of China theme. All of WestCOT's attractions were to be linked together by the World Cruise, a boat ride that would stop at each pavilion.

Beyond WestCOT, Disney's plans for Anaheim called for an expansion and upgrade of the Disneyland Hotel, along with three entirely new hotels, all patterned after famous southern California landmarks. The New Disneyland Hotel would be based on the Hotel del Coronado in San Diego, the Magic Kingdom Hotel on the Spanish mission in Santa Barbara, and the WestCOT Lake Resort on the Beverly Hills Hotel. In addition, a 5000-seat amphitheater called the Disneyland Bowl and a new shopping and entertainment district called the Disney Center would be set on a six-acre lake, with buildings inspired by the Casino on Catalina Island, the Boardwalk in Venice, and other local landmarks. The entire area would be off-limits to automobile traffic: several parking garages would be built on the edges of the district, and guests would be transported to its attractions and facilities by a PeopleMover system. Construction on the project was supposed to break ground in 1993 and be complete by 1999.

Plans for Port Disney were announced in April of 1990, and those for WestCOT in May 1991. Disney never intended to pursue both projects, which had an estimated cost of $3 billion each, and ultimately, its leaders decided that Anaheim presented the better option. In December 1991, the company announced that it was no longer pursuing the Port Disney project. In many ways, Anaheim had always had the advantage. There, Disney would have to gain approvals only from city authorities, while in Long Beach consent from twenty-six different federal, state, and local regulatory agencies had to be secured. Moreover, the Long Beach project would require an extra $50 to $75 million in wetlands restoration in order to offset the environmental problems of the landfill. Some Disney historians have concluded that the Long Beach idea was only a ruse to convince Anaheim officials to make hundreds of millions of dollars in infrastructure improvements to accommodate Disney's plans. But Disney did spend several years and millions of dollars in developing plans for Port Disney, so it is unlikely that the company was not at least somewhat serious about them.

Even after Disney decided to pursue the WestCOT option, however, the path forward in Anaheim was far from smooth. Many local residents expressed concerns about the scale of the project and the additional traffic that it would bring. Disney's announcement that the visual focal point would be a 300-foot-high gold globe called Spacestation Earth only added to the protests.[9] A further problem was that Disney had to acquire fifteen privately-owned properties in Anaheim to accommodate WestCOT. They were able to purchase seven of these, but the other eight held out; Disney then began hinting that they would ask the city of Anaheim to use the power of eminent domain to seize them. Worried about all of these issues, a group of Anaheim residents formed a group called Homeowners for Maintaining the Environment (HOME). It quickly grew to over 1600 members, who handed out literature about what a bad neighbor Disney was to people on their way into Disneyland. Faced with this barrage of bad publicity, Eisner called for the plans for WestCOT to be scaled back. The

---

9   The globe, which would have been the tallest structure in Orange County, was 120 feet higher than Spaceship Earth, its counterpart at EPCOT.

300-foot globe became a spike, and the 4600 new hotel rooms were reduced to a thousand. Disney also took most of the parcels of land that they did not own already out of their plans. After these changes were made, the Anaheim City Council approved Disney's plans for WestCOT in June 1993.

By that point, something had happened far away from southern California that had dramatically altered Disney's financial calculations. That something was Euro Disney, which became the greatest failure in Disney theme park history, at least in its early years. A Disney resort in Europe had first been considered as early as 1975, and the success of Tokyo Disneyland helped to convince the company's executives that a second international park was a good idea. When Tokyo Disneyland broke Disneyland's one-day attendance record only four months after opening in 1983, the head of the theme park division, Dick Nunis, said that, "We knew then that we had to go to Europe." Studies showed that there was an enthusiastic European audience for Disney theme parks. Trailing only New York and Los Angeles, Walt Disney World in Orlando was the third most popular destination for European tourists, and over two million Europeans visited one of the American parks every year. Western Europe had other characteristics that seemingly made it an ideal location for a Disney theme park, including a high standard of living and a concentrated population of 370 million, which meant that, relative to the United States, there were 50 percent more people living in roughly the same amount of space. Disney films and characters had long been popular in Europe, and in the 1980s around a quarter of Disney's merchandising revenues came from European markets. For all these reasons, a European park seemed like a no-brainer.

In 1984, Nunis presented Eisner with a list of 1200 potential European locations for a park. The list included sites in England, Portugal, Germany, Italy, Spain, and France. The list was quickly winnowed. No site bigger than 300 acres was available in England near a population center, while all the sites near Italian cities were too mountainous. Germany was ruled out because research showed that Germans preferred to visit other countries for their vacations. By the spring of 1985, the list had been reduced to four sites, two in Spain and two in France. Frank Wells told Nunis to "start negotiating with both countries and see if you can get us a deal." Assuming that a Disney theme park was going to be a tourism cash cow, both countries' governments competed aggressively for the project. The Spanish sites, both of which lay on the Mediterranean coast, one near Barcelona and the other near Alicante, had a major advantage: a warm and sunny climate similar to that of southern California and central Florida. But chilly weather had not deterred guests from visiting Tokyo Disneyland;

that experience had convinced Disney, as one executive put it, that their parks were "weather-proof." Furthermore, France was much more centrally located within Europe, while travel both to and within Spain was relatively difficult, as its rail line was not part of the European network and it did not possess a national highway system. Studies showed that Disney could expect only six million visitors a year to a park in Spain, and between eleven and seventeen million to a French equivalent. Finally, Disney was extremely popular in France; the character of "Monsieur Mouse" was so ubiquitous that many French children thought of him as French, not American. When the French government offered a package that included $750 million in low-interest loans, a price of $5000 per acre for the land (much less than its market value), right of first refusal on 10,000 additional acres surrounding the development that would provide an "exclusion zone" to protect it from encroaching sprawl, a pledge to improve the roads and train connections to the site, and $400 million in infrastructure improvements, it sealed the deal.

But which French site would win out? One was in the south of France, near the town of Toulon on the Mediterranean coast, while the other was near Paris. Further investigation revealed that the Toulon site lay on bedrock, which would make construction much more expensive. Moreover, Paris was a place that tourists visited year-round, as well as a major transportation hub. The city was within a four-hour drive for seventy million people and a two-hour flight for another 300 million. Euro Disney thus ended up on a flat site occupied mostly by beet farms near the town of Marne-la-Vallée, about fifteen miles east of Paris. In December 1985, Eisner flew to Paris to announce plans for the Euro Disney Resort, which would include in addition to the theme park seven hotels containing almost 6000 rooms, a campground, a golf course, and a convention center. The final contract was signed two years later. This time, Disney did not merely take a licensing fee as it had done in Tokyo. Instead, it set up a separate company called Euro Disney SCA, in which Disney had a 49 percent stake, the maximum that the French government would permit. This arrangement meant that Disney had to invest only $250 million of its own money in the project; the rest of the capital came from a public stock offering and debt that was raised on the equity provided by the stock. Accepting Disney's revenue projections without question, the banks estimated that Euro Disney would make a profit of $400 million in its first year.

There were some early warning signs that things might prove more difficult than Disney and the investors anticipated. Despite Mickey Mouse's popularity in France, he quickly became the symbol of a backlash against American cultural imperialism. One cartoon depicted him as Godzilla trampling Paris, while another showed him as the pilot of an American fighter plane targeting the French capital as an "invasion site." French intellectuals decried Euro Disney as "a cultural Chernobyl" and "a black stain on the soul of France." Other French people were upset that hundreds of farmers, many of whose families had worked the land for centuries, would be displaced by the development. Disney was undeterred. Opinion polls showed that the vast majority of the French population approved of the project. In 1989, the launch of Euro Disney SCA shares on the stock markets in London, Paris, and Brussels met with an enthusiastic response: just six days later, the shares were oversubscribed by eleven times.

Disney did not need high stock prices to feel optimistic about Euro Disney's prospects. This was a time when Disney executives were confident that everything they touched would turn to gold. Euro Disney was conceived at a time when Michael Eisner believed that the sky was the limit for theme park profits. Simply by raising ticket prices at Disneyland and Walt Disney World, he had brought millions of dollars into Disney's coffers. He therefore believed that the world was full of people who would pay large sums of money to enjoy a Disney theme park, and that the more he spent building a park, the more profits he could expect back in return. One Disney executive later recalled, "It was like, 'We're building the Taj Mahal and people will come—on our terms.'" In 1990, the fall of the Berlin Wall brought the promise of an inflow of guests from Eastern Europe. Anticipating a massive number of visitors, Disney announced that it was increasing the number of attractions in Euro Disney to accommodate 15 percent more guests, and moved up the construction schedule for a planned second gate.

This meant, inevitably, that the budget had to be increased, but this was not a subject of particular concern. With such rosy attendance forecasts, Disney was confident that the park would be a huge success, and in any event spending on Euro Disney had always been planned to be lavish. Euro Disney was, from the beginning, conceived differently from Tokyo Disneyland. Whereas the latter park had been designed as a near carbon copy of the original Disneyland because that was what Japanese guests wanted, its French sibling was always seen as something that would have a distinctively European flavor. Tony Baxter, who headed the Imagineering team that designed the park, acknowledged that Disney was "building a resort next to one of the most sophisticated, cultured cities in the world, and we're going to be competing with the great art and architecture of Europe. We have to do something unique." This did not mean that all American influences would be eliminated: that would require Main Street, U.S.A. and Frontierland to be axed. But it did mean that they would be more muted than they were in other Disney parks.

Image 10.6: Concept art by Herb Ryman of Euro Disney.

Michael Eisner's personal taste also played a role in the design of Euro Disney. A Europhile, Eisner believed that Europeans would not tolerate cheap replicas. In a country filled with real medieval castles, it would not do to have a fake one made of plaster and fiberglass. Euro Disney's castle thus became the only Disney castle to be built from real stone and to have handcrafted stained-glass windows. Because Eisner and the park's designers believed that the French saw American culture as shallow, they crammed Euro Disney with details intended to convey depth and sophistication: everything was decorated with art and props, and the fiberglass and synthetic fabrics used in other parks were replaced by real wood, bricks, and canvas. Elsewhere in the resort, the world's most prominent architects were commissioned to design buildings: Frank Gehry created a shopping and entertainment complex called Festival Disney, while the Hotel New York was designed by Michael Graves, the Newport Bay Club and Hotel Cheyenne by Robert A.M. Stern, the Sequoia Lodge by Antoine Grumbach, and the Hotel Santa Fe by Antoine Predock. As a result of decisions like these, and of France's high labor costs, the expense of building Euro Disney soared. At the same time, the project fell further and further behind schedule, and when Eisner insisted that it meet its April 1992 opening date, costs rose even higher due to the enormous amounts of overtime that Disney had to pay. In the end, Euro Disney cost a staggering $5 billion, almost four times the original estimate, leaving Disney with $3.5 billion in debt.

Euro Disney opened on April 12, 1992. Prospective visitors were warned about chaos on the surrounding roads, as a poll taken by the French government indicated that as many as 500,000 people might try to attend. But by midday, only 25,000 people had entered the park. This did not particularly dismay Disney executives, who were relieved not to have to deal with a massive crowd, but although attendance picked up somewhat over the ensuing months, it fell off again when the weather turned colder. Pre-opening research had predicted 60,000 visitors a day, but Euro Disney drew an average of only 25,000, forcing estimates of annual attendance to be reduced from 11 million to 9 million. And a lack of attendance was not the only issue; so were different patterns of guest behavior from what Disney was accustomed to in America. Europeans got more vacation time each year than did Americans, but this meant that they had less money to spend per day. This was problematic for Euro Disney, which relied on guests paying a premium to stay in Disney-branded hotels and buying expensive food and souvenirs. Euro Disney's hotel occupancy rates hovered at around 50 percent, instead of the predicted 85 percent, as many guests opted to stay in Paris and only come to the park for the day. Even those who did stay in Disney hotels often only stayed for a single night; the turnover was so rapid that Disney had to install extra computer terminals to handle the number of people checking in and out. European guests also spent far less per person in the parks than their American and Japanese counterparts did.

It quickly became apparent that, given the interest on the park's massive debt and an economic recession that hit Europe in 1992, there was no way for Euro Disney to turn a profit. In December 1993, Disney announced a net loss of $308 million for the fiscal year, which meant that the resort was losing almost $1 million per day. This came as a shock to Disney's leadership team. "We had a generation of executives who had never been around failure," Eisner recalled. "We had this momentum that never seemed to end... Even I got kind of used to it and comfortable with it." In the company's annual report to its stockholders, who had seen the value of their assets decline sharply as a result of Euro Disney's problems, Eisner admitted that the project was "our first real disappointment" and gave it a grade of "D," for "dreadful."

Things did not improve quickly. Euro Disney's losses in the first quarter of 1994 were a third higher than they had been the previous year. In March 1994, Disney issued an ultimatum that the debt had to be restructured or else it would no longer provide sufficient operating funds to keep the park open. "Everything is possible today, including closure," said Eisner in an interview with the French magazine *Le Point*. The banks had little choice: if the park closed and Euro Disney SCA declared bankruptcy, they would be left with an empty theme park, 5000 acres of nearly worthless real estate, and $4 billion in unpaid loans. They thus agreed to write off the next sixteen months of interest payments and to postpone repayments of the principal for three years. For its part, Disney agreed to forego its annual management fee, which was supposed to be 6 percent of net revenue, until 1999, and after that to reduce it to only 1 percent. Disney also forgave $210 million that it was owed in service fees. This was embarrassing, but not nearly as embarrassing as having Euro Disney declare bankruptcy.

In the mid-1990s, Euro Disney finally began to turn an annual profit in some years. Its improving finances allowed the long-delayed second gate in France, the movie-themed Walt Disney Studios Park, to open in March 2002, though its budget was slashed from the original $2.3 billion to a mere $500 million. A modest sixty-two acres in size, with most of its attractions imported from other parks, it currently attracts only 4.5 million guests a year, the lowest total of the eleven Disney theme parks. That same year, Disney renamed the original park Disneyland Paris. Disney CEO Michael Eisner said at the time that for "Americans, the word 'Euro' is believed to mean glamorous or exciting. For Europeans it turned out to be a term they associated with business, currency, and commerce. Renaming the park 'Disneyland Paris' was a way of identifying it with one of the most romantic and exciting cities in the world." This explanation for the change of name was a tacit admission of just how much Disney had failed to understand in opening its first European park.

There are several reasons why Euro Disney / Disneyland Paris struggled so mightily. First and foremost was the massive debt that has burdened the park from the beginning, which has made it difficult to fund major improvements and expansions and at times even basic maintenance. Second was the culture clash between European and American patterns of leisure, which Disney failed to understand or take into account. Third was that Euro Disney, more than any other Disney park, required Disney to appeal to a wide variety of nationalities and cultures. Tokyo Disneyland, the first international park, attracted a homogenous urban and Japanese audience, but Euro Disney had to find ways to appeal to people from all over Europe. The failure to solve these problems accounts for the park's early difficulties, not any failings with the park itself, which contains some of the most beautiful and distinctive work the Imagineers have ever done.

The scale of Euro Disney's problems became apparent just as Disney was reformulating its plans for the second gate in Anaheim. Suddenly, the company's entire philosophy about theme park construction rotated 180 degrees. Instead of sparing no expense to build the best park possible, the idea was now to build on the cheap, or not at all. In late 1993, Eisner declared, "I don't even know if there's going to be a WestCOT. We're at a real crossroads. We had a very big investment in Europe and it's difficult to deal with. This is an equally big investment. I don't know whether a private company can ever spend this kind of money." New Disney parks would have to be built quickly and efficiently, and without incurring large amounts of debt, so that they would be profitable from the day that they opened.

What did this new attitude mean for Anaheim? Disney had made too many promises about building a second park to completely renege, but it was clear that the elaborate plans for WestCOT would have to be significantly reduced. In August of 1995, forty Disney executives gathered at a retreat in Aspen, Colorado, to discuss what was now being referred to as "the Anaheim problem." Their ideas were all over the map: the new park could have a sports theme, or it could be an imaginary trip along Route 66, or it could focus on the natural world. They could do a scaled-back version of the DisneySea park that had been intended for Long Beach, but that park had been so lavish that even a smaller version would still be very costly. They could do a version of Disney-MGM Studios in Florida, but why would people want to come and see a replica of a movie studio when there were real ones just up the road? They could do only the Future World or World Showcase part of WestCOT, but then guests might complain that they had gotten only half a park. After listening to all these ideas, Eisner came up with his own theme: California. "We can do everything we want to do under that umbrella," he said. "People are seeking that perfect, idealized California, and we will be able to deliver it to them." A year later, in July 1996, Disney officially announced plans to build a fifty-five-acre theme park called Disney's California Adventure, along with a 750-room luxury hotel called the Grand Californian.[10] The Disneyland Resort would also get a 300,000-square-foot shopping and entertainment district called the Disneyland Center (later changed to Downtown Disney). Albeit on a more limited scale than the WestCOT plans had called for, Disney was attempting to convert Disneyland into a multi-day resort, in imitation of its Florida sibling.

Construction began on California Adventure in early 1998, and the park opened on February 8, 2001. The estimated cost was $650 million, less than a fourth of what Disney had intended to spend on WestCOT. To hold down costs, Disney had even considered letting its hotel division rather than the Imagineers design the park, but when the latter revolted, management relented. California Adventure featured a few unique attractions, including California Screamin', a steel roller coaster designed to look like an old-fashioned wooden one; and Soarin' over California, a simulation

---

10   This would bring the number of Disney-owned hotels in Anaheim to three, as in 1995 Disney had purchased the Pan Pacific Hotel from its Japanese owners for $36 million. They initially renamed it the Disneyland Pacific Hotel, but in 2000 it was rebranded as the Paradise Pier Hotel after the section of California Adventure that it overlooks.

of a hang-glider ride. But most of its attractions were recycled from other parks or were simple off-the-shelf midway rides. Even the Imagineers were dissatisfied. When asked what he thought about the park, John Hench, who had worked for Disney since 1939, said that he preferred the parking lot that it had replaced. It would take another decade, and a billion additional dollars, for California Adventure to satisfy most Disney fans.

Image 10.7: The original entrance to California Adventure (decorated here for the holidays), which featured a smaller-scale replica of the Golden Gate Bridge. In 2011, the "California" sign was replaced by a replica of Los Angeles's Pan-Pacific Auditorium (the same building that inspired the entrance to Disney's Hollywood Studios in Orlando), and the Golden Gate Bridge by a bridge imitating the one where Glendale Boulevard and Hyperion Avenue cross the Los Angeles River. The change was made in order to have the entrance fit in with the new Buena Vista Street section of the park, which represents Los Angeles at the time Walt Disney arrived there in the 1920s.

Other improvements that were made to Disneyland in the 1990s also reflected this "cheaper is better" philosophy. As part of the Disney decade, Disneyland had been slated for a significant expansion. It did, in the end, get some minor additions. In 1993, the 3.2-acre Mickey's Toontown opened to the north of Fantasyland; the fact that even such a small area had to be located outside the berm shows just how cramped Disneyland was. Intended primarily for young children, Toontown consisted of a Mickey and Minnie Mouse character-greeting area and several play areas, with only a single ride, a kiddie roller coaster called Gadget's Go-Coaster. A year later, it gained more adult appeal with the addition of the dark ride Roger Rabbit's Car Toon Spin. In 1995, Adventureland got a major new thrill ride, the Indiana Jones Adventure. It used new technology called the Enhanced Motion System, which was essentially a motion simulator mounted on a moving vehicle.

As impressive as the Indiana Jones Adventure was, it had been scaled back significantly from the original plans for an Indiana Jones-themed area that included a roller-coaster as well. A 3D film starring the Muppets and a Little Mermaid dark ride were moved to California Adventure, while other attractions were eliminated entirely, including a high-tech dark ride called Dick Tracy's Crimestoppers, two Roger Rabbit-themed attractions (the simulator-based Toontown Trolley and the dark ride Baby Herman's Runaway Baby Buggy Ride), and Geyser Mountain, a western-themed ride that would have functioned like the Tower of Terror in reverse by using powerful elevator motors to send guests shooting into the air. Some of these attractions were intended for a new land called Hollywoodland, which would have shared many attractions with Disney-MGM Studios in Orlando.

Perhaps most revealing of the effects of Euro Disney's problems on Disneyland, however, was the fate of an update of Tomorrowland, which had not been significantly overhauled since 1967. In the late 1990s, the Imagineers decided that, rather than envisioning what the real future would be like, they would focus on creating an imaginary one, or what they called "the future of our dreams." Feeling that people no longer believed in "progress" as optimistically as they had in the 1950s and 1960s, they turned for inspiration to some of the visionaries of the past, such as Jules Verne and H.G. Wells. It was no coincidence that this was reminiscent of the old Discovery Bay idea, because the same Imagineer, Tony Baxter, was in charge of both projects. But Discovery Bay had been conceived on a grand scale, with a budget to match, whereas now Baxter was given only $100 million for the Tomorrowland update. He was forced to recycle existing infrastructure as much as possible, which led to one of the most notorious attraction failures in Disney history. Using the track from the WEDWay PeopleMover, which had closed in 1995, the Imagineers spent $25 million on a thrill ride called the Rocket Rods. Reaching speeds of thirty-five miles-per-hour, it was designed to be the fastest ride in Disney history; whereas the PeopleMover had taken sixteen minutes to make the journey around the track, the Rocket Rods took only three. But there was a problem: the PeopleMover track was flat, which meant that the cars had to decelerate drastically on its unbanked curves and then accelerate rapidly on the straightaways. All of this stopping and starting was extremely hard on the machinery, and the Rocket Rods soon became notorious for being out of commission more often than not. The ride lasted for barely two years. Disneyland president Cynthia Harris admitted that "the problem was a budget-conscious decision to run the high-speed Rods on the PeopleMover's unbanked track."

Image 10.9: The Rocket Rods, one of the shortest-lived attractions in Disney history. The attraction was another victim of the cost-cutting caused by the struggles of Disneyland Paris. Given a budget of only $25 million, the Imagineers were forced to re-use the track from the PeopleMover. This led to the high-speed ride vehicles having to brake sharply to go around the unbanked curves, which caused severe wear-and-tear on the machinery. The Rocket Rods closed in September 2000, after having operated for twenty-nine months.

No tour of the Eisner years is complete without a look at two more projects, one that never got off the ground and one that did. In 1993, Disney announced plans to build a theme park called Disney's America on 3000 acres in Haymarket, Virginia, twenty miles from Washington D.C. With nine themed areas, the park would trace the course of American history, a subject about which Eisner had become passionate after visiting colonial Williamsburg. Proposed attractions included a Lewis-and-Clark-themed river ride (an idea that had been around since the days of Riverfront Square in the mid-1960s), a Civil War fort that would serve as the setting for a nightly battle between the *Monitor* and the *Merrimac*, a musical show about immigration featuring the Muppets, a steel-mill-themed roller coaster, and a simulated World War II military flight. Disney's America would have been part of a resort complex that included hotels, a golf course, and other leisure facilities.

Although the idea gained the support of Virginia's governor Douglas Wilder and other key politicians, many local citizens were outraged. Much of their concern stemmed from the fact that the project would be located only five miles from the Manassas National Battlefield Park, a major Civil War historic site. The fight over Disney's America hinged on two issues. First, there was the regulation of land use so as to maintain a balance between historic preservation and economic development. Although the battle was often depicted in media accounts as a giant corporation versus people from small-town Virginia, in reality the majority of people in the rural county, Prince William, in which the project would have been located, favored it as something that would bring badly needed economic development, whereas most of the opposition came from more suburban Loudon and Fauquier counties. But perception mattered, and this was a battle that Disney lost badly. The opponents of the project formed a group called Protect Historic America and took out a full-page ad in *The New York Times* in which they called Eisner "the man who would destroy American history."

Image 10.9: Manassas National Battlefield Park in Prince William County, Virginia, the site of the First and Second Battles of Bull Run in 1861 and 1862 during the American Civil War. The battlefield's proximity to the proposed location of Disney's America was a major factor in the controversy over the project.

The content of the ad related to the second issue: the representation of American history. Disney was naïve in assuming that the public and professional historians would accept without question the company's ability to depict complex events such as early contacts with American Indians, westward expansion, and the Civil War. The project's opponents enlisted the aid of historian Shelby Foote, who had recently come to prominence in Ken Burns' PBS documentary *The Civil War*. Foote warned that "anything Disney has ever touched—whether it's fantasy or fact, whether it's Davy Crockett or whoever—has always been sentimentalized. And every good historian, every great artist, knows that sentimentality is the greatest enemy of truth." Faced with such vocal opposition, and with research studies that suggested that the park would only be able to operate for eight months a year due to the weather, Disney abandoned the project in 1995.

Four years later, Disney announced a smaller-scale theme park project, but an important one nonetheless because it reflected the company's continuing commitment to global expansion despite the problems with Euro Disney. On a cramped 300-acre site on Hong Kong's Lantau Island, the company planned to build a park in partnership with the Government of the Hong Kong Special Administrative Region (HKSAR). Disney would own 43 percent of the shares and HKSAR 57 percent. HKSAR invested $1.5 billion to build the park plus another $1.7 billion for roads, a rail link, and other infrastructure improvements. Disney invested only $316 million, a huge disparity that the Hong Kong press aggressively criticized. There was only room for four lands—Main Street, U.S.A., Adventureland, Fantasyland, and Tomorrowland—and twenty-one attractions. Two hotels were also squeezed onto the site. Hong Kong Disneyland was built more quickly than any other Disney park: ground was broken in January 2003, and the park opened in September 2005. It struggled in its first year, attracting only 5.2 million visitors rather than the predicted 5.6 million, and by 2007 attendance had dropped to only four million. In recent years, however, attendance has increased to over seven million guests annually.

By 2000, Disney's annual revenues had increased from $1.5 to $8.5 billion, and the company's market value from $2 to $22 billion. But behind the scenes, all was not well. Many Disney historians trace the beginning of the management problems to the death of Frank Wells in a helicopter crash in 1994. This led to two difficulties. First, Wells had been the one person who had been able to rein in Eisner's more extravagant ideas and smooth the many feathers that his abrasive personality ruffled. Second, when Eisner refused to appoint Jeffrey Katzenberg to succeed Wells, it propelled Katzenberg to leave Disney and led to a messy lawsuit that ultimately forced the company to pay a $280 million settlement in order to fulfill the terms of his contract. Katzenberg's departure, in turn, led Eisner to hire his friend, super-agent Mike Ovitz, as president. After clashing sharply with Eisner over management styles and decision-making, Ovitz was fired after only a year on the job, costing Disney another $138 million in cash and stock as a severance package.

Further problems arose when Disney immersed itself in the deal-crazed corporate world of the 1990s and acquired the ABC broadcasting network for $19 billion. Although the deal brought the highly profitable ESPN sports channel into Disney's portfolio, it proved more problematic to generate consistent revenues from ABC itself. The game show *Who Wants to Be a Millionaire?*, which premiered in 1999, briefly elevated the network in the ratings, but the fact that it was soon being broadcast five nights a week showed just how few other hits ABC had. In 2001, Disney made another problematic acquisition when it purchased the Fox Family Channel for $5 billion. The channel was already suffering from declining ratings, and its assets ultimately proved to be worth less than a third of what Disney had paid.

At the same time, both the animated and live-action film divisions began to falter. Though the slate of films that followed *The Lion King*, including *Pocahontas* (1995), *The Hunchback of Notre Dame* (1996), *Hercules* (1997), and *Tarzan* (1999), were all solidly profitable, they did not generate the same level of buzz and box-office success as their predecessors. After 2000, revenues from animation dipped sharply, as only *Lilo & Stitch* (2002) was a true hit, while *The Emperor's New Groove* (2000), *Atlantis: The Lost Empire* (2001), and *Brother Bear* (2003) all performed poorly, and *Home on the Range* (2004) was an outright flop. Only Pixar continued to enjoy consistent success with *Finding Nemo* (2003) and *The Incredibles* (2004). Cumulatively, Pixar's first five films grossed $2.5 billion, the highest average per film for a studio in Hollywood history. But Steve Jobs was growing disenchanted with the relationship with Disney and with Eisner in particular. In 2004, negotiations to renew the agreement between Pixar and Disney broke down, and Jobs announced that he would not deal with Disney as long as Eisner was in charge. On the live-action side, mega-budget films such as *Pearl Harbor* (2001) and *Treasure Planet* (2002) were box-office disappointments, though the massive success of *Pirates of the Caribbean* (2003) helped to paper over the difficulties.

In 2003, the same members of Disney's board of directors, Roy Disney and Stanley Gold, who had led the charge to bring in Eisner as CEO now led a charge to get him out. They felt that Disney had lost its way, with too much power concentrated in Eisner's hands and too much emphasis on the bottom line over creativity. This led to a very public, and very ugly, "Save Disney" campaign, in which Roy and Gold resigned from the board and rallied stockholders to vote against Eisner's reappointment as chairman. They succeeded in having him replaced by former U.S. Senator George Mitchell, but Eisner retained his position as CEO. It was clear, however, that his time at Disney was coming to end, and in 2005, he resigned his position and severed all ties with the company. He was replaced by Robert Iger, who had come to Disney via the ABC acquisition.

Today, few Disney fans look back on the Eisner years fondly, and it is certainly true that by the end of his term the theme parks were suffering badly from reduced budgets. But what is often forgotten is that these cuts were the flip side of the massive expansion that took place in Eisner's first decade, a period when Disney conceived and executed a number of theme park projects of dazzling creativity. Perhaps only Tokyo DisneySea fully realized this vision, but Eisner also presided over a massive expansion of Walt Disney World and the transformation of Disneyland into a true resort. On his watch, Disney constructed three entirely new parks in America, two in Paris, one in Tokyo, and one in Hong Kong. Michael Eisner was not Walt Disney: he was not folksy or avuncular, and he sometimes came across as a caricature of a rapacious Hollywood executive. There is no doubt that his overbearing style, his ruthless approach toward negotiation, and his tendency to micromanage alienated many people both within Disney and in Hollywood. Particularly in the second half of his tenure, his effectiveness as a leader diminished sharply. Disney was no princess in the Eisner years: it was neither pretty nor cute, but rather earned a deserved reputation for arrogance in its dealings with not only outsiders but at times its own employees.

Eisner's influence on the Disney theme parks, however, was undeniably massive, and it is unfair to say that it was entirely negative. Before the problems with Euro Disney soured Eisner on the idea that lavish expenditures would produce high profits, the parks saw the greatest injection of resources and attention in their history. Projects like Port Disney and WestCOT were truly exciting, and much of that excitement carried over into Euro Disney, Disney's Animal Kingdom, and Tokyo DisneySea, as well as into the numerous new attractions that were installed in the existing parks. Perhaps the disappointment that so many Disney fans feel about the Eisner years is because of the high hopes that he raised.

ELEVEN
The Present and Future

From the opening of Disneyland in 1955, the Disney theme parks have grown into a massive business. Today, 130,000 of Disney's 180,000 employees work for Walt Disney Parks and Resorts. The theme parks account for roughly a quarter of Disney's annual revenue, or around $14 billion a year, and generate an operating income of around $2.2 billion. In 2014, the eleven parks were visited by 134 million guests, making Disney by far the biggest theme-park operator in the world.[1] Nine of the ten busiest theme parks in the world belong to Disney, with only Universal Studios Japan in Osaka sneaking in at number five on the list. What does the future hold for the Disney theme parks? Disney's propensity for keeping its plans a secret means that it is impossible to know for sure, but there are some things already underway, and we can make educated guesses about others.

In Anaheim in the new millennium, it has been California Adventure that has seen the biggest changes. In October 2007, Disney's CEO Robert Iger announced that the company would spend $1.1 billion—almost twice as much as the park had originally cost—over the next five years to fix its problems. This massive revamp included the creation of a new entrance area called Buena Vista Street, an upgrade of the Paradise Pier area, the addition of a new night-time show called The World of Color, and biggest of all, the creation of a twelve-acre "immersive environment" called Cars Land, based on the 2006 Pixar film *Cars*. Initially, fans were skeptical that anything could fix such a substandard park, and few were excited about the *Cars* theming. But when Cars Land opened in 2012, along with its signature attraction Radiator Springs Racers, it was praised for having the kind of rich detail that had been seen as lacking elsewhere in the park. Although California Adventure would still rarely be named as any Disney fan's favorite park, it is now widely seen as a worthy second gate for the Disneyland Resort.

---

1 That total is more than double the number of guests that visit the attractions owned by Disney's closest rival, the British company Merlin Entertainments, and more than triple the number who visit the parks operated by Universal Studios.

Image 11.1: Radiator Springs Racers, the centerpiece of Cars Land at California Adventure.

In recent years, Disneyland has seen only minor changes, but bigger developments are in the works, many of them derived from Disney's recent acquisitions of Lucasfilm, Pixar, and Marvel. Of these, the acquisition of Lucasfilm in 2012 for $4 billion has generated the most excitement. At Disneyland, it has led to the addition of a fourteen-acre Star Wars Land, construction of which began in early 2016. Though Disney has been characteristically tight-lipped about details, it is believed that Star Wars Land will contain two major attractions. Fans are currently referring to one of these as the "Battle Escape" attraction, which will be set in the time of the new trilogy that began with 2015's *The Force Awakens*. The 150-foot-high show building will be the largest in Disney history. The second attraction is believed to be an advanced flight simulator in which guests will zoom around the *Star Wars* universe on board the *Millenium Falcon*. Both attractions will have elaborately themed queues in order to create an immersive experience. Other components of Star Wars Land include a cantina-themed restaurant, character-greeting areas, and shops. There is no official opening date as yet, but Star Wars Land is expected to be finished in 2019 or 2020.

In the more distant future, a big question facing the Disneyland Resort is the question of a third gate. There have long been rumors that Disney has plans to use seventy-eight acres of land to the south of the current resort for another theme park.[2] In March 2015, Iger stated that no third gate would be in the works for the foreseeable future, but he did confirm that there is room to expand the resort at some point. Speculation continues about a possible theme for a third gate, with the most frequently cited idea being a "heroes" concept that would feature attractions based on the Lucasfilm and Marvel Comics franchises that Disney has recently acquired. Any third gate in Anaheim, however, is at least a decade, and probably much further, in the future.

In Orlando, the Magic Kingdom has recently seen a significant expansion in the form of New Fantasyland, which replaced the lackluster Mickey's Toontown Fair and which was rolled out in phases between 2012 and 2014. This twenty-six acre, $425 million addition to the park includes the Seven Dwarfs Mine Train roller coaster, the Story Book Circus area, the Under the Sea~Journey of the Little Mermaid dark ride, and the Be Our Guest Restaurant, which allows patrons to dine in Beast's castle from the 1991 film *Beauty and the Beast*. It is unlikely that the Magic Kingdom will see more big changes any time soon; future major additions will probably be timed for the fiftieth anniversary celebration that is coming up in 2021.

Image 11.2: The Seven Dwarfs Mine Train, the major attraction of the Magic Kingdom's New Fantasyland, under construction in February 2013, thirteen months before it opened.

Epcot is also not scheduled for any big changes in the near future, but the Norway pavilion in World Showcase has recently been transformed into the kingdom of Arendelle from the 2013 film *Frozen*. The Maelstrom boat ride, formerly themed as a trip through real and mythical Norwegian

---

2   This land was once mostly occupied by the Fujishige family's strawberry farm. For decades the Fujishiges refused to sell, but Disney was finally able to acquire the property in 1998; it is currently occupied by the Toy Story parking lot.

history, became Frozen Ever After in the spring of 2016, while a character meet-and-greet area for Princesses Anna and Queen Elsa was added as well. Also in the works for Epcot is a new night-time show to replace the aging Illuminations: Reflections of Earth. Rumor has it that a new show will debut in 2017. Epcot will probably continue along the path that it has been following toward becoming the most "adult" of the Orlando parks, a path that evolved from World Showcase's role as the most popular drinking destination for Disney guests. Disney has recently added an upscale tequila bar, La Cava del Tequila, to the Mexico pavilion, and a wine bar, Tutto Gusto, to Italy. Epcot has also developed two successful adult-oriented annual events, the springtime Flower and Garden Festival, which began in 1994, and the autumnal Food and Wine Festival, which began in 1995.

The biggest changes in Orlando will be to the other two parks. After Disney-MGM Studios evolved from a working movie studio into a theme park, other changes followed. One involved the park's name. In 1985, Disney signed what it believed was a perpetual agreement to use MGM's name and film library in return for a relatively modest licensing fee of $100,000 for the first three years and $250,000 for the fourth year, with the fee increasing by $50,000 a year after that until it reached $1 million. But when MGM's owner Kirk Kerkorian found out about the deal, he was furious that the studio had sold the rights to its name so cheaply, and he began looking for ways to get out of the contract. In the late 1980s, just as Disney-MGM Studios was getting ready to open, MGM sued Disney, claiming that the park could not be used as a film studio. During the Eisner years, Disney was not likely to take this kind of challenge sitting down, and so the company filed a cross-complaint that MGM was violating the contract by building its own theme parks, since Disney had the exclusive rights to the use of the MGM name for that purpose.[3] Though this legal wrangling was for the most part corporate posturing, it did establish that Disney's contract with MGM was not in fact perpetual, but instead only for twenty years, which meant that it expired in 2005. The Disney-MGM Studios name lingered for two more years after that, but in June of 2007 Disney announced that the park's name would change to Disney's Hollywood Studios the following January.

In recent years, big changes have been announced for the park. After being surpassed in annual attendance by Animal Kingdom in 2010, Hollywood Studios currently draws the lowest number of visitors among the four Orlando parks. Between 2008 and 2013, its attendance increased by only

---

3   Disney's claim was based on the fact that MGM was spending $1 billion to build a theme park next to its MGM Grand Hotel in Las Vegas. MGM Grand Adventures opened in 1993, but it was not successful and closed seven years later.

5.2 percent, as compared to 8.9 percent for the Magic Kingdom and 6.9 percent for Animal Kingdom. To change this situation, Disney announced a $1.2 billion upgrade. To make room for the changes, a number of the park's attractions were closed, including the Backlot Tour, the American Idol Experience, and the Lights! Motors! Action! Stunt Show. They will be replaced by two new lands. First, Hollywood Studios will get a Star Wars Land similar to the one being built in Anaheim. Second, it will add Toy Story Land.

After he became CEO in 2005, Iger worked hard to repair the relationship with Pixar that had been badly damaged in the Eisner years, and Steve Jobs ultimately decided that his best option was to stick with Disney. In January 2006, Disney announced the purchase of Pixar for $7.4 billion. This has led to a growing Pixar presence in the theme parks, as embodied by the popular Toy Story Midway Mania attractions in Orlando, Anaheim, and Tokyo and by the aforementioned Cars Land in Anaheim. Hollywood Studios' Toy Story Land will include a Slinky Dog-themed roller coaster and a spinning attraction featuring the little green aliens. The combined addition of Star Wars Land and Toy Story Land represents such a dramatic makeover of Hollywood Studios that the park may get yet another name change. In March 2015, in response to a question from a six-year-old girl at Disney's annual shareholders' meeting, Iger announced that "we're doing some significant work there right now that I guess will result in a name change," though he would not say what the new name might be. Rumors suggest that it will be Disney's Hollywood Adventure.

If most of the new additions to Hollywood Studios are still in the future, at Disney's Animal Kingdom, some major enhancements are already well underway. First, a new night-time show called Rivers of Light and a night-time version of Kilimanjaro Safaris is expected to debut in 2016, as part of a campaign to convince guests to remain in the park in the evening. Second, Animal Kingdom is getting a new land based on the 2009 blockbuster film *Avatar*. In 2011, after *Avatar* became the most profitable film in history, Disney approached its director, James Cameron, about the possibility of building an attraction based on the film in Disney's Hollywood Studios. The chairman of Disney Parks and Resorts, Tom Staggs, however, suggested that *Avatar* serve as the inspiration for an entirely new land in Animal Kingdom that would emphasize the film's environmental/conservation theme. Built at a cost of $500 million, the new land, called Pandora: The World of Avatar, will take the place of the never-built Beastly Kingdom section of the park, which was previously occupied by Camp Minnie Mickey. The land will contain two major attractions: a 3D flight simulator called Avatar Flight of Passage, in which guests will fly on one of the film's banshees, and Na'Vi River Journey, a tour of Pandora by boat. Ground was broken in January 2014, and Pandora is expected to open in 2017.

The impact of another recent Disney film-franchise acquisition on the theme parks, and on those in Orlando in particular, remains to be seen. In 2009, Disney purchased Marvel Entertainment for $4 billion, which gave it control of over 5000 Marvel characters. The deal was complicated, though, by the fact that Marvel already had contracts with Paramount, Sony, and Fox for future films, and these contracts had to be honored before Disney could release films featuring the characters in question. This resulted in some complex financial arrangements for films that were already in production. For example, Disney paid $115 million for the international distribution rights for *The Avengers* (2012) and *Iron Man 3* (2013), but Paramount retained its 8 percent fee.

The meaning of the Marvel acquisition for the theme parks is even more complicated. In 1994, Marvel signed a deal with Universal's parent company MCA that granted it the use of the Marvel characters in Universal's Islands of Adventure theme park, which opened in Orlando in 1999. Most industry experts believe that the contract gave Islands of Adventure permanent exclusive rights to use the characters in theme parks that were located east of the Mississippi. So Disney has to be very careful in how it uses the characters in Orlando. Themed monorails, for example, have been used to advertise the release of recent films featuring Iron Man and the Avengers, but only on the Magic Kingdom loop, because the line that goes to Epcot actually enters the park before it reaches the station. Marvel's presence is likely to increase, however, in Disneyland, which has begun featuring character meet-and-greets with Iron Man, Thor, and Captain America, and in the international parks. Spider Man currently appears in the Walt Disney Studios Park in Paris, while Hong Kong Disneyland is building a 3D motion-simulator ride called the Iron Man Experience.

Back in Orlando, the biggest recent change at Disney World does not involve new attractions. Instead, it relates to Disney's queuing and ticketing system. In 1999, Disney introduced a ride-reservation system called FastPass, which worked by calculating the maximum number of guests that a ride could handle in a day. A certain percentage of the places in line were then set aside for guests with FastPasses, which were distributed according to time intervals, usually of five minutes; as guests collected more FastPasses, the time intervals were filled up, and their return times moved to later in the day. The system essentially saved a space in line for them by calculating the time when their place would come to the front. If the system worked properly, a FastPass holder did not wait more than five minutes to ride a particular attraction.

The original system, which is still in use everywhere but Orlando, required guests to go to a kiosk and insert their park tickets in order to obtain a paper FastPass that told them what time to return to the attraction. But in late 2013, Disney World began introducing a new system, called FastPass+, in which guests make their attraction reservations as much as sixty days in advance, using the My Disney Experience website. FastPass+ initially allows guests three reservations per day, and after those are used they can get additional FastPasses from kiosks in the parks. It was introduced in conjunction with wristbands called MagicBands, which use radio-frequency identification (RFID) technology to record a guest's park tickets, resort and restaurant reservations, and FastPass+ return times. Guests can also link credit cards and a PIN to their MagicBands and use them to pay for in-park purchases.

The idea for all of this originated in 2008. Disney executives were alarmed by surveys showing that guests' "intent to return" was in decline. Meg Crofton, then the president of the Walt Disney World Resort, assigned a team to a project called the Next Generation Experience, which was charged with eliminating all sources of guest friction and frustration, or what she called pain points. When they tracked guest movements through the parks, the team found that guests often had to fight their way through thousands of people at the turnstiles to enter, and that they were crisscrossing spots like the hub in front of Cinderella Castle dozens of times daily in an effort to avoid long lines. The first idea that the team came up with was for a park entrance at which guests would simply "touch in" rather than passing through traditional turnstiles, and everything else proceeded from there.

But how to make it possible for Disney guests to carry the requisite technology with them? Hats and lanyards were considered, but business development vice-president John Padgett, who became the leading advocate of the project, was flipping through a SkyMall catalog on a plane when he saw a magnetic wristband called the Trion Z that was supposed to help golfers improve their swing. This led Padgett to explore the growing "wearables" market for data, in particular the growing number of wristbands that monitored people's exercise habits. In a lab located in the former Wonders of Life pavilion in Epcot, the team built a prototype wristband, which they called the xBand, out of a strip of Velcro and a piece of plastic and stuck an RFID tag in it. When they gave one to Bob Iger to test, he told them, "This little thing is going to be special. If I gave you more money, could I have it faster?"

Eventually, the designers came up with a wristband in a tear-away configuration that could be adjusted to fit every wrist size. (It took six months just to get the tear-away perforation perfect so that it was easy to tear but did not accidentally separate.) The wristband had to be intuitive to use, which led the designers to the Mickey-to-Mickey concept: guests touch the

Mickey head on the band to the Mickey head on the post, which then lights up green and makes a pleasant chiming sound. Now called MagicBands, the wristbands were tested on a former soundstage in Disney's Hollywood Studios, on which replicas of typical Disney hotel rooms and theme park attractions were built. It took two years to transform the prototype into something that was ready for the parks, and another eighteen months to roll out the new technology completely.

The MagicBands faced plenty of internal opposition, much of it from the Imagineers. According to a former Disney executive, the Imagineers "dream of building these big icons of their creative expression, but when a capital budget shows we're going to invest in changing the established guest experience rather than spend on a big fixed asset, that doesn't get met with love." Much of the work of designing the different parts of the system was undertaken by Frog, a San-Francisco-based industrial design firm. Frog quickly became immersed in a turf battle with Imagineering, which was accustomed to controlling the look of everything in the parks.[4] Internal opponents of the project would try and sneak past the new entrance gates when they were being tested to prove that they did not work, or they would sit on their hands during ride tests to make it harder for the sensors to receive the signal from the wristbands. One of the biggest fights was over the posts that guests would touch their MagicBands to: Frog wanted them to be uniform, so that guests would know what to look for, but the Imagineers protested that this would ruin the unique individual theming of their attractions. The Imagineers won this one: Mickey's head is on every access point, but the design of the posts is themed to each attraction.

Disney spent $1 billion on the new technology, with the idea that it would encourage people to spend more time and money in Walt Disney World by making it easier to negotiate. It also hopes that the preplanning that the system requires will discourage people from spontaneously heading over to rival theme parks like Universal and SeaWorld after they arrive in Orlando. People should spend less time in line, which means they will spend more time shopping, eating, and spending money. The RFID technology also enables Disney to track their guests' every move; when guests order a meal at Be Our Guest, cast members locate them in the cavernous dining rooms by tracking their MagicBands. At present, however, Disney has not installed the sensors that would allow them to do this throughout the park.

How successful has the system been thus far? Certainly, it has reduced

---

4   The name of WED Enterprises was changed to Walt Disney Imagineering in 1986.

the length of time it takes to get into the parks at peak periods, because guests no longer have to insert cumbersome paper or plastic tickets into the turnstiles. The technology also allows thousands of extra guests to be accommodated on days when the park reaches maximum capacity.[5] The FastPass+ system eliminates much of the old need to zig-zag back and forth across the park to collect FastPasses, therefore cutting down on walking and guest exhaustion. It eliminates the need to run to the FastPass kiosk for the most popular attractions as soon as the park opens in order to avoid a return time late in the day or even missing out on the FastPasses altogether. On some attractions, the technology is used to create interactive experiences. In the queue for Epcot's Test Track, guests design simulated cars and save their designs to their MagicBands; their design's performance is then tested on the ride.

Thus far, however, the full potential of the technology has not been utilized. If Disney does install the necessary sensors, it will be possible for characters to greet guests by name, or for Disney to compile a video of the various experiences that a particular guest has in a day. Disney could know if a guest has a negative experience and send them compensation electronically—a coupon for a free meal, for example—before they even have a chance to complain. Future attractions, such as those being built for Pandora: The Land of of Avatar in Animal Kingdom, are likely to take advantage of the new technology to increase interactivity. At the same time, the Imagineers are concerned to limit "switching behavior," in which guests' attention is so distracted by technology that they cannot enjoy the actual experience. At present, Disney believes that it has instituted something that has both made the guest experience more positive and has established a platform for the future that puts it at least a decade ahead of its rivals. What the future of FastPass+ and the MagicBands will bring, though, is not fully clear. Nor does it seem likely that they technology will be brought to other parks beyond Orlando. Only there do most guests plan their trips well in advance, which is necessary for FastPass+ to work properly. In contrast, Disneyland and Tokyo Disneyland are visited predominantly by locals who might not decide until that morning that they are going to the park that day.

What is on the horizon for Disney's international parks? The Tokyo Disneyland Resort continues to be massively successful, with a record

---

5   Park capacity is greater because FastPass+ allows Disney to distribute guests more evenly through the park. Because there are many more FastPass+ attractions than there were FastPass ones under the old system, Disney can divert people into the queues for traditionally less-popular attractions. This means that even without increasing overall attraction capacity, more people can be in the park at one time.

31.4 million guests in 2014, its third consecutive year of breaking its annual attendance mark. The Oriental Land Company has announced that it will spend $4.9 billion on the parks over the next ten years. This investment will fund a major upgrade of Fantasyland in Tokyo Disneyland, which will get Beauty and the Beast and Alice in Wonderland-themed areas. Tokyo DisneySea, meanwhile, will get a Finding Nemo simulator ride and a "Scandinavia" port themed to Arendelle from the film *Frozen*.

What about the most troubled of the international parks? In recent years, Disneyland Paris's problem has not been a lack of attendance: attracting over 15 million visitors annually, it is consistently the most popular tourist attraction in Europe. Instead, its problem is a vicious cycle in which the high level of debt that has burdened it from the beginning prevents it from making investments in new attractions. In 2012, Disney attempted to remedy this problem by assuming and refinancing at a lower rate of interest the $1.7 billion debt that Disney SCA, the company that owns most of the resort, owed to French banks. This has allowed Disneyland Paris to refurbish its most popular attractions and to introduce a few new ones, such as Ratatouille: The Adventure, a trackless 3D dark ride that opened in Walt Disney Studios in 2014. No other new additions are planned for Disneyland Paris until a possible Star Wars Land in 2022, however, and none for Walt Disney Studios until 2023, when a possible Marvel Land might arrive. The future of Disney's European resort thus remains somewhat murky, but the relief from the crushing debt burden should go a long way toward getting it on a sounder financial footing.

Image 11.3: (*Opposite, top*) A trackless 3D dark ride, Ratatouille: L'Aventure Totalement Toquée de Rémy (Remy's Totally Zany Adventure), opened in Walt Disney Studios, the Disneyland Paris resort's second theme park, in 2014. Built at a cost of an estimated $270 million, it reflects a new commitment to adding major attractions in Paris as the resort's finances continue to improve.

After it opened in 2005, Hong Kong Disneyland also got off to a shaky start, as its small size and low number of attractions led to angry guests. As recently as 2011, the resort was still losing $100 million a year, but it has slowly been finding its feet. In 2014, its profits rose 36 percent from the previous year, thanks to increased attendance and higher guest spending. Hong Kong has been adding new attractions at a rapid clip, including Toy Story Land in 2011; Grizzly Gulch, with its Big Grizzly Mountain Runaway Mine Cars roller coaster, in 2012; and Mystic Manor, its updated version of the Haunted Mansion, in 2013.

Image 11.4 Mystic Manor, Hong Kong Disneyland's version of the Haunted Mansion, which opened in 2013. Because ghosts are seen in Chinese culture as malevolent, the storyline of the attraction was altered to focus on an explorer named Lord Henry Mystic, who acquires a magical music box that brings the objects in his house to life.

These new attractions have increased the park's diminutive size by about a quarter. Another major attraction, the previously mentioned Iron Man Experience, which will be part of a new Marvel Super Hero Land, and a new luxury hotel are in the works as well. The biggest question about Hong Kong's future, however, relates to the likelihood of a second theme park, which was part of the original master plan. Now that Hong Kong Disneyland is turning a consistent profit, it seems possible that these plans will finally get off the ground. Guests have reported seeing height-check balloons flying over the potential site, which is directly across from the existing park.

By far the biggest development for the international parks, however, is the construction of a Disney resort in Shanghai, which opened in June 2016. This is slightly delayed from the original late 2015 date, but many observers believe that the opening was deliberately pushed back so that the park would open at a time when the weather was warm. Located across the Huangpu River from Shanghai's historic center, the resort will cover 988 acres, making it about three times the size of Hong Kong Disneyland, slightly larger than Disneyland in Anaheim, and roughly the same size as Paris and Tokyo. Around 330 million people live within a three-hour journey of the resort, and a high-speed rail link will be built to help them get there efficiently. The resort will eventually contain three theme parks, along with two hotels and a shopping and entertainment district called Disneytown, all built at a total cost of $5.5 billion. Like Hong Kong Disneyland, the resort is a joint venture, in thi case between Disney, which owns 43 percent of the project, and a Chinese government body called the Shanghai Shendi Group, which owns 57 percent.

Disney had courted the Chinese government for years. After Shanghai's mayor Zhu Rongji visited Anaheim in 1990, he returned home determined to build a Disneyland in his city. Zhu later rose to become premier of China from 1998 to 2003, and he remained a strong supporter of the project. Rumors that Disney was going to build a resort in Shanghai began as early as 2000, but the official announcement of the project did not come until 2007. Ground was broken four years later. Shanghai Disneyland will contain a number of distinctive features. It will have no Main Street, U.S.A., while its Enchanted Storybook Castle will be Disney's largest and most technologically advanced, containing two attractions, a Snow-White-themed walkthrough called Once upon a Time Adventure and an underground boat ride called Voyage to the Crystal Grotto. The castle will be surrounded by the Garden of the Twelve Friends, a green space filled with cherry trees and containing twelve mosaics depicting the signs of the Chinese Zodiac using Disney characters. Shanghai Disneyland will feature not only a version of Pirates of the Caribbean but an entire pirate-themed land called Treasure Cove, one of six themed lands in the park.

Image 11.5: The Pudong district of Shanghai, where the Shanghai Disney Resort will be located. Established as a Special Economic Zone by the Chinese government in 1993, Pudong has since become home to many of Shanghai's most famous modern landmarks, such as the Oriental Pearl Tower at the left of the image.

In Shanghai, Disney has attempted to a greater degree than in its other international parks to incorporate local tastes and preferences. "We're building something that's authentically Disney and distinctly Chinese," said Bob Iger in 2015. "It definitely will be Disneyland in China, but we'll obviously be respectful of the Chinese culture and relatable to the people of China." Chinese consultants were included in the team that designed the park, and the restaurants will offer mostly Chinese dishes. There were also serious efforts to take into account Chinese patterns of leisure. The government policy that limits families to one child and the fact that Chinese extended families often vacation together means there will be a high ratio of adults to children—perhaps as much as four to one—in the park. Disney has to provide more places for adults can relax while the children enjoy the attractions. Because Chinese companies rarely offer paid vacation time, the park is likely to be very crowded during national holidays. Disney will provide more parades and street performances in these periods, and it has also installed games, videos, and robots to distract guests while they wait in long lines. Another challenge is the Chinese penchant for queue-jumping; Disney has tried to curb this behavior with single-file lines.

Disney's primary objective in building both Hong Kong and Shanghai Disneylands was to tap into the massive market among the rapidly growing Chinese middle class. Disney typically relies on the creation of new Disney television channels to promote its brand overseas, but China's strict limits on foreign media preclude that strategy. The Chinese parks are thus key parts of a broader strategy to double Disney's international presence and profits, which at present account for about half of the company's income. On the Chinese side, many economists interpreted the decision to move ahead with Shanghai Disneyland as an indication that the Chinese government was now willing to tolerate a greater degree of Western investment and cultural influence. But as opening day for Shanghai Disneyland grew closer, the Chinese economy began to falter. Economists suggest that Chinese consumer spending is likely to dip sharply as the growth of China's over-heated investment and industrial sectors slows. Disney insists, however, that its focus is on the long-term, and that China's massive population represents a crucial and reliable market for future theme park projects.

As the Walt Disney Company looks toward the future, one of the biggest questions relates to its leadership. When Bob Iger took over as CEO in 2005, he inherited a company steeped in turmoil, as it emerged from the nasty battle among shareholders and the board of directors over Michael Eisner's performance. There were low expectations for what Iger could achieve, due both to his status as an insider and his low-key management style. But Iger has taken Disney to new heights with the acquisitions of Pixar, Lucasfilm, and Marvel. Disney Feature Animation has enjoyed yet another renaissance, with a string of hits that include *The Princess and the Frog* (2009), *Tangled* (2010), *Wreck-It Ralph* (2012), *Big Hero 6* (2014), and, of course, the billion-dollar juggernaut that is *Frozen*, now the seventh-highest-grossing film of all time. Disney's live-action films have also performed extremely well in the last decade, with a roster of notable successes that includes *Pirates of the Caribbean: At World's End* (2007), *Alice in Wonderland* (2010), *The Avengers* (2012), *Iron Man 3* (2013), *Guardians of the Galaxy* (2014), *The Avengers: Age of Ultron* (2015), and, of course, *Star Wars Episode VII: The Force Awakens* (2015). All of these films are on the list of the twenty most profitable films in Disney history; *The Force Awakens*, which has grossed over $2 billion worldwide, currently ranks as the third-highest-grossing film in history, behind only *Avatar* and *Titanic*. Defying fears that Disney would destroy its creativity, Pixar has continued to flourish, with a roster of post-acquisition box-office hits such as *Cars* (2006), *Ratatouille* (2007), *WALL-E* (2008), *Up* (2009), *Toy Story 3* (2010), *Brave* (2012), *Monsters University* (2014), and *Inside Out* (2015). In 2015, Disney enjoyed revenues of $52.5 billion and net income of $8.4 billion, both significant increases over the previous year. Since Iger took over, Disney shareholders have seen more than a 200 percent increase in the value of their stock, thanks to these high film grosses and record theme park attendance.

Iger also instituted what he termed a "cultural change" that was directed both internally and externally, with the intention of restoring respect and admiration for the company in the wake of the negative feelings of the Eisner era. In this he has largely been successful. The elimination of the top-down style of strategic planning, which many executives viewed as micro-managing, of the Eisner years did much to restore morale, and Disney has returned to the top of the lists of the world's most admired companies. Iger's contract expires in 2018, when he will be sixty-seven, and he is widely expected to step down. Who will succeed him? Many observers thought that the most likely candidate is Tom Staggs, who was promoted to chief operating officer in February 2015 in a move that was widely interpreted as his official anointment as Iger's successor. But in April 2016, Staggs announced that he would be leaving Disney. At present, the question of Disney's future leadership is thus wide open.

Today, there are twelve Disney theme parks on three continents. Disneyland and the Magic Kingdom are the elder statesmen: the former celebrated its first half-century in 2005, and the latter will follow in 2021. As the two parks have aged together, the difference in time between them, in relative if not absolute terms, has shrunk. They are now both old, which means that they share long histories, histories that converge at some points and diverge at others, but which are sufficiently distinct that each park has to be understood on its own terms. One is not better than the other; rather, they represent different, and complementary, parts of the Disney theme park universe. Their four "children"—Tokyo Disneyland, Disneyland Paris, Hong Kong Disneyland, and Shanghai Disneyland—each represent unique evolutions of the original models. They, too, juxtapose old and new in fascinating ways.

And the other six parks, as well, each have their own distinct histories and identities. They are the products of what, at the time they were built, was the latest technology and the cutting edge of theme park design, and in many cases ideas that had floated around Imagineering headquarters for decades. Almost all of these parks divide opinion among Disney fans in some way: Tokyo DisneySea is probably the most praised, and Walt Disney Studios in Paris the most criticized (though Orlando's Hollywood Studios might challenge for that dubious distinction). Like the classic parks, however, they have to be taken on their own terms, and understood as the embodiments of particular moments in Disney theme park history. Most of these parks were products of the period from 1984 to 2005 when Michael Eisner was Disney's CEO, but over those two decades Disney's corporate philosophy regarding the construction of theme parks fluctuated dramatically, from the lavish spending on Euro Disney to the reduced but still highly detailed Animal Kingdom to the built-on-the-cheap Walt Disney Studios.

In all twelve parks, a true Disney theme park fan can find something to love.

Bibliography

Chapter 1

Barrier, Michael, *The Animated Man: A Life of Walt Disney* (University of California Press, 2007).

Fogelson, Robert M., *The Fragmented Metropolis: Los Angeles, 1850-1930* (Harvard University Press, 1967).

Gabler, Neal, *Walt Disney: The Triumph of the American Imagination* (Random House, 2006).

Lesjak, David, *In the Service of the Red Cross: Walt Disney's Early Adventures, 1918-1919* (Theme Park Press, 2015).

Silvester, William, *The Adventures of Young Walt Disney* (Theme Park Press, 2014).

Starr, Kevin, *Americans and the California Dream* (Oxford University Press, 1973).

Starr, Kevin, *Inventing the Dream: California through the Progressive Era* (Oxford University Press, 1985).

Starr, Kevin, *Material Dreams: Southern California through the 1920s* (Oxford University Press, 1990).

Thomas, Bob, *Walt Disney: An American Original* (Disney Editions, 1994).

Chapter 2

Apgar, Gary, *Mickey Mouse: Emblem of the American Spirit* (Walt Disney Family Foundation Press, 2015).

Baxter, John, *Disney during World War II: How the Walt Disney Studio Contributed to Victory in the War* (Disney Editions, 2014).

Broggie, Michael, *Walt Disney's Railroad Story: The Small-Scale Fascination that Led to a Full-Scale Kingdom* (Pentrex, 1997).

Cline, Becky, *The Walt Disney Studios: A Lot to Remember* (Disney Editions, 2016).

Ganz, Cheryl R., *The 1933 Chicago World's Fair: A Century of Progress* (University of Illinois Press, 2012).

Kaufman, J.B., *The Fairest One of All: The Making of Walt Disney's Snow White and the Seven Dwarfs* (Walt Disney Family Foundation Press, 2012).

Kaufman, J.B., *Pinocchio: The Making of a Disney Epic* (Walt Disney Family Foundation Press, 2015).

Kaufman, J.B., *Snow White and the Seven Dwarfs: The Art and Creation of Walt Disney's Classic Animated Film* (Walt Disney Family Foundation Press, 2012).

Kaufman, J.B. and Merritt, Russell, *Disney's Silly Symphonies: A Companion to the Classic Cartoon Series* (Disney Editions, 2016).

Korkis, Jim, *The Book of the Mouse: A Celebration of Walt Disney's Mickey Mouse* (Theme Park Press, 2013).

Lesjak, David, *Service with Character: The Disney Studios and World War II* (Theme Park Press, 2014).

Zim, Larry, Lerner, Mel and Rolfes, Herbert, *The World of Tomorrow: The 1939 New York World's Fair* (Harper Collins, 1988).

Chapter 3

Boulé, David, *The Orange and the Dream of California* (Angel City Press, 2014).

Brigandi, Phil, *Orange County Chronicles* (History Press, 2013).

Eng, John and Biondo, Adriene, *Modern Tract Homes of Los Angeles* (Schiffer Publishing, 2011).

Farmer, Jared, *Trees in Paradise: A California History* (W.W. Norton, 2013).

Hyslop, Stephen G., *Contest for California: From Spanish Colonization to the American Conquest* (Arthur H. Clark, 2012).

Jacobs, James A., *Detached America: Building Houses in Postwar Suburbia* (University of Virginia Press, 2015).

Lane, Barbara Miller, *Houses for a New World: Builders and Buyers in American Suburbs, 1945–1965* (Princeton University Press, 2015).

Lewis, Tom, *Divided Highways: Building the Interstate Highways, Transforming American Life* (Cornell University Press, 2013).

Rayner, Richard, *The Associates: Four Capitalists who Created California* (W.W. Norton, 2009).

Sackman, Douglas Cazaux, *Orange Empire: California and the Fruits of Eden* (University of California Press, 2007).

Starr, Kevin, *Embattled Dreams: California in War and Peace, 1940–1950* (Oxford University Press, 2003).

Starr, Kevin, *Golden Dreams: California in an Age of Abundance, 1950–1963* (Oxford University Press, 2011).

Swift, Earl, *The Big Roads: The Untold Story of the Engineers, Visionaries and Trailblazers who Created the American Superhighways* (Mariner, 2012).

Walker, Jim, *Pacific Electric Red Cars* (Arcadia, 2007).

Westcott, John, *Anaheim: City of Dreams* (Windsor, 1990).

Chapter 4

Anderson, Paul F., *The Davy Crockett Craze: A Look at the 1950s Phenomenon and Davy Crockett Collectibles* (R&G Productions, 1996).

Cotter, Bill, *The Wonderful World of Disney Television: A Complete History* (Disney Editions, 1997).

Gennawey, Sam, *The Disneyland Story: The Unofficial Guide to the Evolution of Walt Disney's Dream* (Unofficial Guides, 2013).

Kurti, Jeff, *The Art of Disneyland* (Disney Editions, 2008).

Kurti, Jeff, *Walt Disney's Imagineering Legends and the Genesis of the Disney Theme Park* (Disney Editions, 2007).

Marling, Karal Anne, *Designing Disney's Theme Parks: The Architecture of Reassurance* (Flammarion, 1998).

Pierce, Todd James, *Three Years in Wonderland: Walt Disney, C.V, Wood and the Making of the Great American Theme Park* (University of Mississippi Press, 2015).

Strodder, Chris, *The Disneyland Encyclopedia: The Unofficial, Unauthorized and Unprecedented History of Every Land, Attraction, Restaurant, Shop and Major Event in the Original Magic Kingdom* (Santa Monica Press, 2012).

Wright Alex, *The Imagineering Field Guide to Disneyland* (*Disney Editions*, 2008).

Chapter 5

Baham, Jeff, *The Unauthorized Story of Disney's Haunted Mansion* (Theme Park Press, 2014).

Ballard, Donald W., *The Disneyland Hotel: The Early Years, 1955–1988* (Ape Pen, 2005).

McLaughlin, Robert, *Freedomland* (Arcadia, 2015).

Merritt, Christopher and Priore, Domenic, *Pacific Ocean Park: The Rise and Fall of Los Angeles' Space-Age Nautical Pleasure Pier* (Process, 2014).

Moran, Christian, *Great Big Beautiful Tomorrow: Walt Disney and Technology* (Theme Park Press, 2015).

Samuel, Lawrence, *The End of the Innocence: The 1964–1965 New York World's Fair* (Syracuse University Press, 2010).

Surrell, Jason, *The Haunted Mansion: Imagineering a Disney Classic* (Disney Editions, 2015).

Surrell, Jason, *Pirates of the Caribbean: From the Magic Kingdom to the Movies* (Disney Editions, 2006).

Tirella, Joseph, *Tomorrow-Land: The 1964 World's Fair and the Transformation of America* (Lyons, 2014).

Chapter 6

Allman, T.D., *Finding Florida: The True History of the Sunshine State* (Globe, 2014).

Clark, James, *Orlando, Florida: A Brief History* (History Press. 2013).

Clark, James C., *A Concise History of Florida* (History Press, 2014).

Drye, Willie, *For Sale American Paradise: How Our Nation Was Sold an Impossible Dream in Florida* (Grove, 2015).

Emerson, Chad Denver, *Project Future: The Inside Story Behind the Creation of Disney World* (Ayefour, 2010).

Folgelsong, Richard E., *Married to the Mouse: Walt Disney World and Orlando* (Yale University Press, 2003).

Kriplen, Nancy, *The Eccentric Billionaire: John D. MacArthur, Empire Builder, Reluctant Philanthropist, Relentless Adversary* (Amacom, 2008).

Revels, Tracy J., *Sunshine Paradise: A History of Florida Tourism* (University Press of Florida, 2011).

Chapter 7

Beevers, Robert, *The Garden City Utopia: A Critical Biography of Ebenezer Howard* (Palgrave Macmillan, 2015).

Frantz, Douglas and Collins, Catherine, *Celebration, U.S.A.: Living in Disney's Brave New Town* (Holt, 2000).

Gennawey, Sam, *Walt Disney and the Promise of Progress City* (Theme Park Press, 2014).

Hall, Peter, *Cities of Tomorrow: An Intellectual History of Urban Planning and Design since 1880* (Wiley-Blackwell, 2014).

Hardwick, M. Jeffrey, Mall Maker: *Victor Gruen, Architect of an American Dream* (University of Pennsylvania Press, 2009).

Mannheim, Steve, *Walt Disney and the Quest for Community* (Routledge, 2002).

Mitchell, Joseph Rocco and Stebenne, David L., *New City upon a Hill: A History of Columbia, Maryland* (History Press, 2007).

Parsons, Kermit C. and Schuyler, David, eds., *From Garden City to Green City: The Legacy of Ebenezer Howard* (Johns Hopkins University Press, 2002).

Ross, Andrew, *The Celebration Chronicles: Life, Liberty and the Pursuit of Property Values in Disney's New Town* (Ballantine, 2000).

Chapter 8

Disney Book Group, *Marc Davis: Walt Disney's Renaissance Man* (Disney Editions, 2014).

Fjellman, Stephen M., *Vinyl Leaves: Walt Disney World and America* (Westview, 1992).

Koenig, David, *Realityland: True-Life Adventures at Walt Disney World* (Bonaventure, 2014).

Krause Knight, Cher, *Power and Paradise in Walt Disney's World* (University Press of Florida, 2014).

Kurti, Jeff, *Since the World Began: Walt Disney World, the First 25 Years* (Disney Editions, 1996).

Surrell, Jason, *The Disney Mountains: Imagineering at Its Peak* (Disney Editions, 2007).

Wright, Alex, *The Imagineering Field Guide to the Magic Kingdom* (Disney Editions, 2009).

Chapter 9

Beard, Richard R., *Walt Disney World's EPCOT Center: Creating the New World of Tomorrow* (Harry N. Abrams, 1982).

Crawford, Michael, *The Progress City Primer: Stories, Secrets and Silliness from the Many Worlds of Walt Disney* (Progress City Press, 2015).

Killingsworth, Rick and Novak, Cassie, *Epcot's World Showcase: A Pavilion-by-Pavilion Guide* (Theme Park Press, 2015).

Raz, Aviad E., *Riding the Black Ship: Japan and Tokyo Disneyland* (Harvard University Asia Center, 1999).

Wright, Alex, *The Imagineering Field Guide to Epcot* (Disney Editions, 2010).

Chapter 10

Flower, Joe, *Prince of the Magic Kingdom: Michael Eisner and the Re-Making of Disney* (Wiley, 1991).

Lainsury, Andrew, *Once upon an American Dream: The Story of Euro Disneyland* (University Press of Kansas, 2000).

Malmberg, Melody, *The Making of Disney's Animal Kingdom Theme Park* (Disney Editions, 1998).

Masters, Kim, *The Keys to the Kingdom: The Rise of Michael Eisner and the Fall of Everybody Else* (William Morrow, 2000).

Pallant, Chris, *Demystifying Disney: A History of Disney Feature Animation* (Bloomsbury, 2011).

Silvester, William, *Saving Disney: The Roy E. Disney Story* (Theme Park Press, 2015).

Stewart, James B., *Disney War* (Simon & Schuster, 2006).

Wallace, Mike, *Mickey Mouse History and Other Essays in American Memory* (Temple University Press, 1996).

Wright, Alex, *The Imagineering Field Guide to Disney's Animal Kingdom* (Disney Editions, 2007).

Wright, Alex, *The Imagineering Field Guide to Disney's California Adventure* (Disney Editions, 2014).

Wright, Alex, *The Imagineering Field Guide to Disney's Hollywood Studios* (Disney Editions, 2010).

Chapter 11

Price, David A., *The Pixar Touch: The Making of a Company* (Vintage, 2009).

Taylor, Chris, *How Star Wars Conquered the Universe: The Past, Present and Future of a Multibillion Dollar Franchise* (Basic Books, 2015).

Image Credits

Chapter 1
Image 1.1: Colin J. Bird
Image 1.2: Kansas City Public Library, Missouri Valley Special Collections
Image 1.3: Mwkruse
Image 1.4: iknowthegoods

Chapter 2
Image 2.1: Bethcourtneysimmons
Image 2.2: Library of Congress
Image 2.3: San Francisco Public Library
Image 2.4: Library of Congress
Image 2.5: Joe+Jeanette Archie

Chapter 3
Image 3.1: Library of Congress
Image 3.2: Library of Congress
Image 3.3: Orange County Archives
Image 3.4: Orange County Archives
Image 3.5: Orange County Archives

Chapter 4
Image 4.1: Ryman Arts
Image 4.2: Ryan Crierie
Image 4.3: Orange County Archives
Image 4.4: UCLA Library Digital Collections
Image 4.5: Todd James Pierce

Image 4.6: Todd James Pierce

Image 4.7: Todd James Pierce

Chapter 5

Image 5.1: Todd James Pierce

Image 5.2: Todd James Pierce

Image 5.3: San Francisco Public Library

Image 5.4: Orange County Archives

Image 5.5: Public domain

Image 5.6: Todd James Pierce

Image 5.7: United States Navy

Image 5.8: Todd James Pierce

Image 5.9: Todd James Pierce

Image 5.10: Ryman Arts

Image 5.11: Todd James Pierce

Image 5.12: Todd James Pierce

Image 5.13: Ryman Arts

Image 5.14: Todd James Pierce

Image 5.15: Gene Spesard

Chapter 6

Image 6.1: Orange County Archives

Image 6.2: EditorASC

Image 6.3: HikingMike

Image 6.4: Jefferson National Expansion Memorial Archives

Image 6.5: Reference Collection, State Library and Archives of Florida

Image 6.6: Library of Congress

Image 6.7: Department of Commerce Collection, State Library and Archives of Florida

Chapter 7

Image 7.1: Public domain

Image 7.2: Department of Commerce Collection, State Library and Archives of Florida

Image 7.3: Department of Commerce Collection, State Library and Archives of Florida

Chapter 8

Image 8.1: Ryman Arts

Image 8.2: Department of Commerce Collection, State Library and Archives of Florida

Image 8.3: Department of Commerce Collection, State Library and Archives of Florida

Image 8.4: Dale M. McDonald Collection, State Library and Archives of Florida

Image 8.5: Postcard Collection, State Library and Archives of Florida

Chapter 9

Image 9.1: Ryman Arts

Image 9.2: Joe Haupt

Image 9.3: Sam Howzitt

Image 9.4: Dale M. McDonald Collection, State Library and Archives of Florida

Image 9.5: Ryman Arts

Image 9.6: Ryman Arts

Chapter 10

Image 10.1: Loren Javier

Image 10.2: Sam Howzitt

Image 10.3: Greg Goebel

Image 10.4: Dave & Margie Hill / Kleerup

Image 10.5: David Lofink

Image 10.6: Ryman Arts

Image 10.7: Loren Javier

Image 10.8: Steve

Image 10.9: Bruce Washburn

Chapter 11

Image 11.1: RyanJWilmot

Image 11.2: Jared

Image 11.3: HumMelissa_Glee

Image 11.4: Katelulu

Image 11.5: Matt Paish

About the Author

Stephanie Barczewski is a life-long fan of the Disney theme parks, beginning with her first visit to the Magic Kingdom at the age of three. She has visited Disney parks on three continents, and looks forward to adding Shanghai to the list. She counts her annual pass to Walt Disney World in Orlando as one of her most prized possessions.

In her day job, Stephanie is a trained academic historian specializing in modern British history. She has a Ph.D. from Yale University, and has taught since 1996 at Clemson University in South Carolina. She has published books on British heroes, country houses, and national identity, as well as a textbook on the history of modern Britain. Dr. Barczewski has won the Gentry Award, Clemson's highest honor for teaching in the humanities. She teaches a class on the history of the Disney theme parks, along with a variety of classes on British history.

More Books from Theme Park Press

Theme Park Press is the largest independent publisher of Disney, Disney-related, and general interest theme park books in the world, with dozens of new releases each year.

Our authors include Disney historians like Jim Korkis and Didier Ghez, Disney animators and artists like Mel Shaw and Eric Larson, and such Disney notables as Van France, Tom Nabbe, and Bill "Sully" Sullivan, as well as many promising first-time authors.

We're always looking for new talent.

In March 2016, we published our 100th title. For a complete catalog, including book descriptions and excerpts, please visit:

ThemeParkPress.com

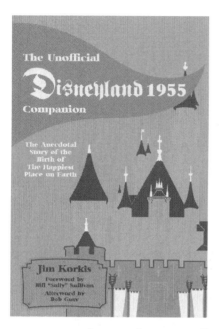

A Year in the Life of Disneyland

And what a year! In 1955, Walt Disney's dream of a theme park, the first of its kind in the world, came true. Disney historian Jim Korkis' entertaining tale of an American pop culture icon is power-packed with details, and the most thorough account of Disneyland's early days ever published.

themeparkpress.com/books/disneyland-1955.htm

Walt Disney and the Pursuit of Progress

Think "Walt Disney" and you come up with animation and theme parks and Mickey Mouse. But Walt's real passion was technology. Documentary filmmaker Christian Moran (along with Rolly Crump, Bob Gurr, and others) provides a fascinating history of how Walt shaped the future while entertaining the masses.

themeparkpress.com/books/great-big-beautiful-tomorrow.htm

Disney History— Written by You

Who writes the Disney history you love to read? A select group, immersed in the history and culture of Disney, from films to theme parks. Now these authors reveal their inspirations, their methods, and their secrets. Why just read Disney history when you can write it yourself!

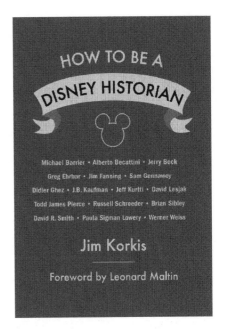

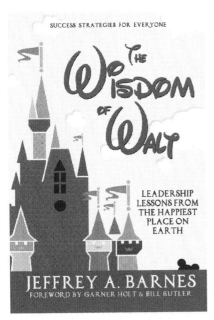

Put Walt to Work for You

How do you go from dreaming of a theme park to building one? Walt Disney laid the blueprint. Learn how he did it, and how his wisdom can guide you toward achieving the things that *you* dream of.

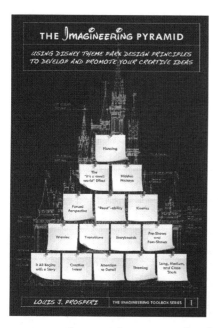

Learn from the Disney Imagineers

Creativity. Innovation. Success. That's Disney Imagineering. It was the Imagineers who brought Walt Disney's dreams to life. Now *you* can tap into the principles of Imagineering to make *your* personal and professional dreams come true.

themeparkpress.com/books/imagineering-pyramid.htm

The Story of Walt's EPCOT

Disney historian and urban planner Sam Gennawey traces the evolution of the EPCOT we didn't get and the Epcot we did, in a tour-de-force analysis of Walt's vision for city-building and how his City of Tomorrow might have turned out had he lived.

themeparkpress.com/books/progress-city.htm

Made in the USA
Columbia, SC
04 June 2024

36625220R00135